D1569966

KNOWING DICKENS

Charles Dickens by Herbert Watkins, 1858. National Portrait Gallery, London.

KNOWING
DICKENS

ROSEMARIE BODENHEIMER

CORNELL UNIVERSITY PRESS
Ithaca and London

First published 2007 by Cornell University Press

Printed in the United States of America

Library of Congress Cataloging-in-Publication Data

Bodenheimer, Rosemarie, 1946–
   Knowing Dickens / Rosemarie Bodenheimer.
       p. cm.
   Includes bibliographical references and index.
   ISBN 978-0-8014-4614-6 (cloth : alk. paper)
   1. Dickens, Charles, 1812-1870—Knowledge and learning. 2. Subjectivity in lieterature. I. Title.

   PR4588.B63   2007
   823'.8—dc22   2007021945

Cornell University Press strives to use environmentally responsible suppliers and materials to the fullest extent possible in the publishing of its books. Such materials include vegetable-based, low-VOC inks and acid-free papers that are recycled, totally chlorine-free, or partly composed of nonwood fibers. For further information, visit our website at www.cornellpress.cornell.edu.

Cloth printing   10 9 8 7 6 5 4 3 2 1

❧ CONTENTS

❧ Acknowledgments

My first tribute belongs to all the scholars and editors who made the Pilgrim Edition of *The Letters of Charles Dickens*, published by Clarendon Press under the general direction of Madeline House, Graham Storey, and Kathleen Tillotson. The twelfth and final volume of this magnificent edition came out in 2002, helping me to complete the groundwork for this study of Dickens's letters and fictions. I am similarly indebted to *The Dent Uniform Edition of Dickens' Journalism*, edited by Michael Slater; both editions are rich with annotations and connections that were invaluable to me.

Janice Carlisle and Andrew Von Hendy, the first readers of these chapters, helped me enormously with editorial suggestions laced with affectionate enthusiasm for the project. Peter J. Potter of Cornell University Press has been a welcoming and efficient editor. My anonymous press reviewers served as excellent guides for the final stages of revision.

I wish there were an adequate way to thank all those friends, students, teachers, and critics, known to me in person or in print, who have helped to shape my thoughts in ways I can no longer retrieve, over the several decades of my fascination with Dickens's work. In recent years, friends and colleagues have directly helped to stimulate parts of this book by offering me opportunities to present or publish my ideas as they were developing; for this I warmly thank Suzy Anger, John Bowen, James Buzard, Janice Carlisle, Margaret Harris, Gerhard Joseph, Richard Kaye, Joss Marsh, Bob Patten, Leah Price, Hilary Schor, and Carolyn Williams. The Dickens Universe, sponsored each summer by the Dickens Project at the University of California, Santa Cruz, played a crucial role by giving me the heart to think of my early biographical-critical forays as the beginnings of a book. I am grateful to all the friends I met or made there for their generous collegiality, with special appreciation for Dickens Project Director John Jordan.

Back at home in the Boston College English department, Judith Wilt shared with me her always inventive Dickens mind, Kevin Ohi inspired me with his uncannily knowing sense of *David Copperfield*, and Mary Crane kept me amused through the toils of chapter-drafting with her interest in what was brewing in the Dickens vat. My brothers Peter and Tom Bodenheimer, unstoppable walkers and writers in their different fields, were often in my mind as I wrote the last chapter. What my husband and colleague Andrew Von Hendy gave to me during the whole process can hardly be measured in words.

Brief sections of chapters 2, 3, and 4 appeared in earlier forms in *Dickens Studies Annual* 30 (2002): 159–74, *Victorian Studies* 48.2 (2006): 268–76, and *Palgrave Advances in Charles Dickens Studies* (2006), ed. John Bowen and Robert L. Patten, 48–68. I thank AMS Press, Indiana University Press, and Palgrave Macmillan for permission to use this material.

❧ FREQUENTLY CITED WORKS

Peter Ackroyd. *Dickens.* New York: HarperCollins, 1991. Cited "Ackroyd."

John Forster. *The Life of Charles Dickens.* Ed. J. W. T. Ley. London: Cecil Palmer, 1928. Cited "Forster."

Madeline House, Graham Storey, Kathleen Tillotson, et al., eds. *The Letters of Charles Dickens.* The Pilgrim Edition. 12 vols. Oxford: Clarendon Press, 1965–2002. Cited by volume and page number.

Michael Slater, ed. *The Dent Uniform Edition of Dickens' Journalism.* 4 vols. Columbus: Ohio State University Press, 1994–2000. Cited "Dent," volume and page number.

Quotations from Dickens novels are taken from the Clarendon Dickens (Oxford, 1966–) for *David Copperfield, Dombey and Son, Great Expectations, Little Dorrit, Martin Chuzzlewit,* and *The Pickwick Papers,* and from Penguin editions (London: Penguin) for all other novels. Text for the *Christmas Books* is taken from the New Oxford Illustrated Dickens (London: Oxford, 1954). I have also quoted from *Christmas Stories,* ed. Ruth Glancy (London: J. M. Dent, 1996), and *American Notes* (Bloomsbury: Nonesuch Press, 1938).

Because there are so many easily available editions of Dickens novels, I have cited them by title initials followed by chapter, or book and chapter, numbers. Page numbers have been used for quotations from *Christmas Books* and *Christmas Stories.*

AN	*American Notes*
BH	*Bleak House*
BR	*Barnaby Rudge*
CB	*Christmas Books*
CS	*Christmas Stories*
DC	*David Copperfield*
DS	*Dombey and Son*
GE	*Great Expectations*
HT	*Hard Times*
LD	*Little Dorrit*

MC   *Martin Chuzzlewit*
NN   *Nicholas Nickleby*
OCS   *The Old Curiosity Shop*
OMF   *Our Mutual Friend*
OT   *Oliver Twist*
PP   *The Pickwick Papers*
TTC   *A Tale of Two Cities*

KNOWING DICKENS

❧ CHAPTER 1

What Dickens Knew

In April 1939 Virginia Woolf began to write an experimental memoir that was to be published posthumously as "A Sketch of the Past." Just a few pages in, Dickens showed up. Woolf had been speculating about what made her a writer: a capacity to receive sudden shocks from life, combined with an ability to make the world whole again by finding the words to explain, and so to blunt "the sledge-hammer force of the blow." Writing is essential to her for this reason, she muses, yet this internal necessity "is one of the obscure elements in life that has never been much discussed. It is left out in almost all biographies and autobiographies, even of artists. Why did Dickens spend his entire life writing stories? What was his conception?" (Woolf 1985, 72–73). Woolf's instinct was to reach for the name of a writer who could hardly be more different from herself, a writer decidedly out of fashion among her Bloomsbury cohort. What, we might wonder, was her conception? Did she sense some kinship that linked the all-too-popular Victorian writer with her own modernist art of interiority?

Our only clue lies in Woolf's most extended meditation on Dickens, a brief review of a new edition of *David Copperfield* published in the *Nation* of 22 August 1925. On first reading, the review appears to be a pungent condensation of critiques that had become familiar ever since the later part of Dickens's career, with an added layer of feminist hostility to Dickens the Victorian man. Like so many others before her, Woolf grants Dickens's genius while bemoaning his inability to treat "the mature emotions." Once she focuses on the novel, however, her tune begins to change:

> As we listen to Micawber pouring himself forth and venturing per-petually some new flight of astonishing imagination, we see, unknown to Mr. Micawber, into the depths of his soul. . . . Why trouble, then, if the scenes where emotion and psychology are to be expected fail us completely? Subtlety and complexity are all there if we know where to look for them, if we can get over the surprise of finding them—as seems to us, who have another convention in these matters—in the wrong places.

The "fecundity and apparent irreflectiveness" in such writing work, Woolf notes, to "make creators of us, and not merely readers and spectators" (1925, 193–94).

Virginia Woolf's reflections raise intriguing questions. If, "unknown to Mr. Micawber," we can see "into the depths of his soul," then who is doing the knowing here? If it is the reader, as Woolf implies, then where does the reader's insight come from? Is Mr. Micawber's unwitting self-revelation comparable to Dickens's own, or is the author in charge of it? And, if psy-chological subtlety and complexity are not to be found in the usual places, then where might they reside?

The astonishing array of critical work that makes up Dickens studies at the beginning of the twenty-first century has become ever more attentive to the revealing and concealing intelligence that lurks somewhere—but where, exactly?—in Dickens's writing. This book is my own attempt to capture something of that knowing Dickens who eludes us. As an interpretive study, it makes its home in the gap between the chronological imperatives of biog-raphy and the literary imperatives of criticism, following some representative clusters of thought and feeling that link Dickens's ways of talking in letters with his concerns in fiction and journalism. When I began this project, the things I wanted to know were similar to those expressed by Virginia Woolf as she meditated on the unsatisfactory nature of biography and autobiogra-phy. What are the internal plots this writer carried around throughout his life, his characteristic patterns of experience, response, and counterresponse? What internal shapes recur in the various forms of writing and acting that make up this life? To what extent is it possible for us to know what and how Dickens knew?

Dickens comes burdened with a long history of critical condescension that arises from just the "apparent irreflectiveness" that Woolf named and questioned. Whether in delight, sorrow, or outrage, it has always been easy for biographers and critics to know Dickens better than he knew himself. During his lifetime he was recognized and loved as the comic genius of the early novels, which retained their nostalgic flavor for many Victorian readers. As his novels grew sadder and his social views more bitter, he retained his popularity but laid himself open to serious critiques that often focused on the "narrowness" of his mind, or on his ignorance of matters he took up as social causes. The word *genius* stuck to him, but many educated reviewers were intent on circumscribing its limits in the strongest terms. For Walter Bagehot, writing in the *National Review* of October 1858, Dickens's genius was "essentially irregular and unsymmetrical" because he was "utterly deficient in the faculty of reasoning." Such a genius was a *"bizarrerie...* rendered more remarkable by the inordinate measure of his special excellences" (Collins 1971, 391–93). Those excellences reside in his capacity for observing and rendering details of city streets and peculiarities of character in isolated scenes and fragments, rather than in the envisioned wholes that Bagehot defines as essential to high art. A regular education would not have helped Dickens's case, Bagehot ventures, because he possessed "an irregular and anomalous genius, whose excellences consist in the *aggravation* of some special faculty" (400).

Bagehot was not alone in depicting Dickens's genius as a kind of nervous disease. The French critic Hippolyte Taine had already published his famous view of Dickens in the *Revue des deux Mondes* of 1 February 1856, cast in hyperbolic sentences that competed with Dickens's own: "The difference between a madman and a man of genius is not very great. ... The imagination of Dickens is like that of monomaniacs. To plunge oneself into an idea, to be absorbed by it, to see nothing else, to repeat it under a hundred forms, to enlarge it, to carry it, thus enlarged, to the eye of the spectator, to dazzle and overwhelm him with it, to stamp it upon him so firmly and deeply that he can never again tear it from his memory—these are the great features of this imagination and this style." Taine captures something here that is missing in the measured rectitude of English reviewers like Bagehot or James Fitzjames Stephen, who held forth regularly on Dickens's ignorance. But Taine is ultimately unforgiving: "These eccentricities are in the style of sickness rather than health" (Taine 124–25).

It is not difficult to see why Dickens, who worked without apology for emotional effect, might stimulate such responses. The Victorian habit of judging writers by comparisons with others also contributed to the negative turn in contemporary reviews of his work. When Thackeray appeared on the scene in 1847, the originality and humor that had amazed Dickens's early readers was set up against Thackeray's more restrained social worldliness;

when George Eliot emerged in the late 1850s, Dickens's treatment of character was measured against her intellectual habits of moral analysis. "The passions are a sealed book to Mr. Dickens," wrote George Stott in 1869; Dickens was "no psychologist; and without psychology, success in the higher walks of idealization is unattainable" (Collins 1971, 496–97). R. H. Hutton, writing just days after Dickens's death, was more generous in his attempt to capture the secret "of a genius so rich to overflowing in the creation of English types of humour." As he put it, "the great intellectual mystery of Dickens's fertile genius was his power of reduplicating a single humourous conception of character into an elaborate structure of strictly analogous conceptions." The power of multiplying a single effect did not mean, of course, that Dickens was "a realist as regards *human* nature" (Collins 1971, 519–22). It is notable that few of the reviewers who created the image of Dickens as the genius of English humor were inclined to consider the kind of intelligence on which humor depends.

The publication of the first volume of John Forster's *Life of Charles Dickens* late in 1871 prompted George Henry Lewes to enter the fray of Dickens criticism. Abandoning the enthusiasm with which he had initially greeted Dickens's arrival on the literary scene, Lewes reacted to Forster's representations of his friend by rolling Taine, Bagehot, and Hutton into a ball of Lewesian argument and hurling it toward posterity in defiance of Forster. "Dickens in Relation to Criticism" begins mildly enough, as though it were intended to defend Dickens against the accumulation of critical contempt that had formed around him in his later years. In language redolent of George Eliot, Lewes writes about the pain of writers whose genius goes unappreciated, noting that Dickens critics "insisted on his defects as if these outweighed all positive qualities; and spoke of him with condescending patronage, or with sneering irritation...How are we to reconcile this immense popularity with this critical contempt?" The very reviewers who scorned Dickens in print cherished him in private, he asserts; for a moment it seems that Dickens and George Eliot have merged as figures of sympathetic identification for Lewes (Ford and Lane 57).

Once at work on his definition of his subject's genius, however, Lewes is ruthless. He adopts Taine's view of Dickens's "imperial" imagination, substituting the term "hallucination" for Taine's "monomania" (59). Arguing in a scientific vein about the mental processes that feed the hallucinations of the insane and their belief in the reality of their visions, he distinguishes Dickens—in whom "I have never observed any trace of the insane temperament"—only to collapse the distinction: "To him also *revived* images have the vividness of sensations; to him also *created* images have the coercive force of realities, excluding all control, all contradiction." Following Taine, Lewes finds the "glorious energy of imagination" a force coercive to its readers: "So definite and insistent was the image, that even while knowing it was false we could not help, for a moment, being affected, as it were, by his hallucination" (60–61). This power, which Lewes purports to celebrate, is also depicted as a delusion for "the mass of men" whose "minds are for the most part occupied with sensations rather than ideas." Like children who cherish a wooden horse and call it real, this public, deaf to the truth-telling critics, loved Dickens for his feelings, but the "world of thought and passion lay beyond his horizon" (62–63).

Having mobilized most of the critical warhorses he had promised to transcend, Lewes charges ahead with a long and predictable attack on Dickens's "incorrect" and "false" depictions of human character, with George Eliot invisibly present as the standard of truth and correctness. Couched in the authoritative language of the mental sciences, Lewes's verdicts on Dickens's mind are nonetheless barely distinguishable from those of his contemporaries: "the writer presents almost a unique example of a mind of singular force in which, so to speak, sensations never passed into ideas. Dickens sees and feels, but the logic of feeling seems the only logic he can manage" (69). Reading such accounts, one begins to wonder how Dickens managed to write at all, let alone to organize a life of considerable complexity. Clearly there was something about the concreteness of his intelligence and his disinclination to move rapidly from the particular to the general that disqualified him from "thought."

Once Freud's ideas had permeated early twentieth-century culture, Dickens's kinds of knowledge became more plausible and interesting to his critics and biographers. Current studies of nineteenth-century physiological psychology bring Dickens into perspective as an early, if idiosyncratic, assimilator of pre-Freudian ideas about the unconscious mind, placing him helpfully within the intellectual context that he shared, after all, with George Henry Lewes. In his own time, however, Dickens's use of the uncanny and his ways of externalizing interior conflict subjected him to a great deal of condescension from critics who saw him as an uneducated popular writer whose genius for humor compensated for his failures to represent the inner lives of his characters. Because they could not be pinned down analytically, or attributed directly to a knowing narrative voice, Dickens's forms of knowledge were often attributed to the vagaries of a nonrational creative process from which educated men and women found it necessary to distance themselves.

A conversation about what Dickens did know might begin with a look at the special kinds of knowledge he cultivated and practiced. Dickens was consistently interested in what his characters know and do not know, what they tell and do not tell. As the Victorian novelist most deeply intrigued by nineteenth-century ideas about the unconscious mind, he found ways to dramatize through his invented figures both subconscious processes and acts of self-projection—the very processes and acts that we so often define as characteristic of Dickens's own modes of creation. We are right to do so, but probably wrong when we assume that his left hand did not know what his right hand was doing. As with all complex human beings, his states of self-knowledge were fluid, inconsistent, and subject to the influence of strong emotions. The same fluidity is evident in his writing: states of "knowing but not knowing" are—knowingly—represented in Dickens's characters, but the reader can often discern a similar hovering on the edge of self-recognition in the projected fantasies of the author himself.

Dickens was a magpie of literary and conversational styles, and parody is central to his apprehension of the world. As a way of knowing, parody sits in the realm between self-conscious knowledge and the distancing verbal play that is so characteristic of Dickens's world. Parody implies a kind of knowingness that never quite speaks its name. Character splitting, in which different characters display extreme versions of qualities that more realistically belong to the mixed nature of one character, is also a well-recognized Dickens strategy. Critics have treated it as melodrama, analyzed it as a child's black-and-white vision, or placed it in the tradition of the Doppelgänger. But character splitting has something more to tell us about how Dickens knew himself through others, and how he thought about the human capacity for self-knowledge. Oddly like parody, splitting manages to know without displaying the connective tissue that would advertise the writer's acknowledgment that he knows.

While he displayed them himself, Dickens was deeply interested in just such in-between states of consciousness. He dramatizes them in fiction when he puts characters in a condition between sleeping and waking. Oliver Twist is in that state when he sees Fagin gloat over his secret box of jewels, as is David Copperfield when he hears Mr. Mell play the flute for his old mother in the almshouse, as is Esther Summerson when she falls into twilight moods, her unknown parentage hovering in ghostly shadow. Such knowledge is problematic, enmeshed with the child's shame of knowing what it shouldn't; the dream state allows that knowledge to be disavowed and put away from the self. Dickens knows that, as he demonstrates in *Little Dorrit* when Jeremiah Flintwinch squelches his wife's knowledge by redefining it as dream, or in *David Copperfield* when David experiences Uriah Heep's expressed designs on Agnes Wickfield as an intrusion of the uncanny in the form of déjà vu.

Freud's idea of the uncanny as a return of repressed but intimately familiar material is something Dickens knew, not in theoretical terms of course, but in experiential ones. He was, as Kate Flint has put it, an explorer of "the incessant interaction between the conscious and the unconscious mind," fascinated "with the blurred ground between the inner and the outer self" (Flint 34, 39). Such descriptions are most often generated by Dickens's middle and later work, and it is true that he grew increasingly capable of writing in a recognizably psychological way. But surely there is something to be said for the understanding of a young novelist who reports that Mr. Pickwick must fall asleep rather than absorb the contents of morbid interpolated tales about intra-familial suffering and violence.

Dickens's minimal formal education complicated his relation with conventionally defined knowledge. As a child he was a voracious reader. For about two years between the ages of ten and twelve he had no schooling, and when he attended the Wellington Academy he got a mediocre training. He left school at fifteen for a position as solicitor's clerk, continuing his education by reading in the British Museum and faithfully attending London theaters. Thereafter he learned from friends and mentors, sometimes developing interests born from contacts with literary and professional associates. When he died, he left a library at Gad's Hill that gives some idea of the range of his curiosity. He had a substantial collection of English and American literature from Chaucer through the mid-nineteenth century (though it included very few works by women; no Austen or Brontë novels, for example). Travels, voyages, and adventure narratives filled many shelves, as did naval tales and naval military histories. His two trips to the United States left him with a large collection of American history and biography. Classical writers and ancient history had a substantial place. There were many books of natural history (including Darwin and Lyell), encyclopedias and literary collections, and anthologies of eccentric characters. There were piles of Blue Books and pamphlets on contemporary social issues, prison memoirs, and books about London and its history.

Many of the books were presentation copies, so we cannot be sure of what Dickens actually read. His range of reference (whether serious or facetious) suggests a man whose head was always full of sentences gathered from a wide variety of sources. Among them, in a category I have not yet named, are over thirty books on the workings of the mind, ranging from contemporary studies in physiological psychology to miscellanies on the spirit world covering ghosts, apparitions, omens, dreams, daemons, "and other Magical Practices," as one early-eighteenth-century title proclaimed. Dickens learned a good deal from his friend and family physician Dr. John Elliotson, who was forced to resign from his position as Professor of Medicine at the University of London when he became too interested in the curative powers of mesmerism. Dickens himself became a mesmerist under Elliotson's direction, and conducted his own experiments on family members and friends. But his library of mental philosophy was not confined to that subject; it included Dugald Stewart's *Elements of the Philosophy of the Human Mind* (1792), Robert Macnish's *Philosophy of Sleep* (1830), and John Abercrombie's *Inquiries Concerning the Intellectual Powers and Investigation of Truth* (1843), along with studies of insanity and essays demonstrating the physiological sources of apparitions. George Henry Lewes's *The Physiology of Common Life* (1859) and E. S. Dallas's *The Gay Science* (1866) were late additions to the collection.

Dickens made use of such influences in a number of ways. His interest in the trance-like state between sleeping and waking, twice described in *Oliver Twist*, predated his acquaintance with Dr. Elliotson, and occasioned a special query from George Henry Lewes, who had enthusiastically reviewed Dickens's early books in December 1837. Still in his pre–George Eliot days, Lewes was rather like Dickens: he too came from an obscure background, virtually educated himself, and made his way as aspiring writer and amusing *raconteur* in London's journalistic milieu. It is not surprising that his praise led Dickens to suggest a meeting; Lewes's review asserts that "'Boz' should be compared to no one since no one has ever written like him—no one has ever combined the nicety of observation, the fineness of tact, the exquisite humour, the wit, heartiness, sympathy with all things good and beautiful in human nature, the perception of character, the pathos, and accuracy of description, with the same force that he has done" (Collins 1971, 65). In a letter of June 1838 we find Dickens responding to a question put by Lewes, who was already interested in the philosophy of mind, about the waking-sleep states in *Oliver Twist*. "I scarcely know what answer I can give you," Dickens returned. "I suppose like most authors I look over what I write with exceeding pleasure and think (to use the words of the elder Mr. Weller) 'in my innocence that it's all wery capital.' I thought that passage a good one *when* I wrote it, certainly, and I felt it strongly (as I do almost every word I put on paper) *while* I wrote it, but how it came I can't tell. It came like all my other ideas, such as they are, ready made to the point of the pen—and down it went. Draw your own conclusion and hug the theory closely" (1.403).

It is a suggestive answer, both for what Dickens insists on and for what he conceals. He backs resolutely away from naming a source or conceding to an intellectual interest in mental phenomena, emphasizing instead the mysterious nature of writing and its emotional sources. In the face of Lewes's philosophical inclinations, he deflects attention from theory to the practice of cultivating a readership: he does not italicize much, he says, because "It is framing and glazing an idea and desiring the ladies and gentlemen to walk up and admire it." With a kind of anti-intellectual truculence, he asserts his policy: "if readers cannot detect the point of a passage without having their attention called to it by the writer, I would much rather they lost it and looked out for something else" (1.404). It's not ideas but effects he's after, Dickens implies, as if—like his characters—he did not want to know what he knew. Awake but paralyzed, Oliver sees Fagin's greed displayed, and later becomes terrified by the faces of Fagin and Monks peering into the window of his safe pastoral retreat. In both scenes he knows something without bearing the responsibility for knowing it, as one might know in a dream. His writing is rather like that, Dickens suggests; it comes to him and then he admires it after it has made its way onto the page. He is not required to discuss the sources or nature of such ideas as may appear in his sentences, although he would, throughout his career, vehemently defend their truth.

The touchy undercurrent in Dickens's reply to Lewes's question was to emerge again fourteen years later, after Dickens described Krook's death by spontaneous combustion in *Bleak House*. By that time both writers were well established. In 1847 Lewes had joined Dickens's acting group in a production of *Every Man in His Humour* arranged to benefit Leigh Hunt. Despite their nominal friendship, Lewes found it necessary to take Dickens to task in his journal *The Leader* for disseminating superstition in the tenth number of *Bleak House*. Lewes argued that that contemporary science had proven that a human body destroyed by spontaneous combustion was an impossibility, and suggested that Dickens had "doubtless picked up the idea among the curiosities of his reading" (qtd. Haight 54). Dickens responded in the next number of *Bleak House* by inventing a passage that cites numerous writers who had verified instances of spontaneous combustion, and staging it as a satirical contest between so-called learned gentlemen and those in the know. In two further open letters in *The Leader*, Lewes ridiculed Dickens's sources, explained the scientific facts, and asked Dickens to set the public right in a preface to the novel.

It was clearly a contest between kinds of knowledge: the scientific versus the anecdotal. Dickens refused to budge from his position, and sought out further support from Dr. Elliotson, to whom he wrote, "It is inconceivable to me how people can reject such evidence, supported by so much familiar knowledge, and such reasonable analogy. But I suppose the long and short of it, is, that they don't know, and don't want to know, anything about it" (7.23). Siding with the officially rejected Elliotson, he claimed the high ground of experiential knowledge that trumped scientific hypothesis and experiment.

In a long letter to Lewes of 25 February 1853, he claimed to know everything about the scientific views, but insisted that the numerous practical accounts of the phenomenon—and he cited many more—took precedence in his opinion. He made it clear that he had resented Lewes's assumption that "I knew nothing at all about the question—had no kind of sense of my responsibility—and had taken no trouble to discriminate between truth and falsehood." Once he had had the idea for Krook's death, he assured Lewes, he had consulted numerous books to verify the truth. While Lewes's arguments were "ingenious," Dickens was right to believe "testimony" rather than "hypothetical explanation of the fact." Two days later he wrote again, trying to undo what he had clearly intended as a rebuke to Lewes for writing "not quite, I think in all good humour, with that consideration which your knowledge of me might have justified" (7.28–31). He had realized that Lewes retained the power to undermine him, and urged him not to publish their correspondence: "I would infinitely rather be unheard in this regard" (7.33). Lewes, for once as stubborn as Dickens himself, did so anyway.

The truth was that spontaneous combustion was just the metaphor Dickens needed to express the quality of his death wish for the Court of Chancery and British institutions in general. Had Lewes not gotten under Dickens's skin with a public questioning of his knowledge and his responsibility to readers, Dickens might simply have appealed to his art as he had done fourteen years earlier. Both Dickens and Lewes had experienced condescension from men who rested secure in their classical educations; in this case they managed to act out their sensitivities by sparring with each other about incomparable forms of knowledge. Dickens was wrong about spontaneous combustion and his sources were long out of date; yet he turned the controversy into a defense of witnessed experience against scientific theory. Someone had believed it; therefore it was worthy of belief, at least in an allegorical sense.

When it came to spiritualism, Dickens's position appeared to be just the reverse: he refused to believe that people could communicate with the dead through séances, or that ghost sightings were plausible. In February 1848 he reviewed Catherine Crowe's *The Night Side of Nature; or, Ghosts and Ghost Seers* in John Forster's paper *The Examiner* (Dent 2.80–91). Putting on his best rational style, Dickens argued that experiences attributed to connections between the human and spiritual worlds could be explained by mental delusions or illnesses in the human frame itself. His favorite state between sleeping and waking now appears as an unreliable condition that encourages ghost fantasies; the belief that the dead return is very sensibly explained as an effect of "the universal mystery surrounding universal death" (84). He makes fun of "the Doppelgänger, or Double, or Fetch" as a fantasy peculiar to

Germans (85), and in general suggests that one need go no further to account for apparitional appearances than the human tendency toward heightened imagination. In the end his review is not so much a rationalist's dismissal of spiritual phenomena as a relocation of such phenomena within the normal operations of the mind-body system. The influence of Dr. Elliotson is once again palpable, especially when Dickens argues for a serious view of "animal magnetism" (or mesmerism) as "a power that can heal the sick, and give the sleepless rest" (87). Thus, while Dickens seems to be a believer on the subject of spontaneous combustion and a skeptic on the subject of spiritualism, his positions share a fascination, stimulated by Elliotson, with what we might now call "alternative" knowledge of the commerce among bodily states, mental illnesses, and sensory apparitions.

Dickens's attraction to haunted minds powered the extensive experiments in mesmerism he performed on Augusta de la Rue for six or seven months during his family's residence in Genoa in 1844–45. The de la Rue couple—a Swiss banker and his English wife—were neighbors of the Dickenses, and quickly became informal friends. Mme de la Rue suffered from an array of nervous symptoms that Dickens thought he could treat by hypnotizing her, as he had seen Dr. Elliotson and others do in similar cases. A strange triangular relationship developed as he became obsessed by his power to meddle in her inner life, all the while making meticulous reports in "scientific" language to Emile de la Rue about what transpired during his wife's mesmeric slumbers.

It was not long before Dickens had discovered the phantom of an evil man who haunted and terrified her (it is deeply tempting to imagine that the phantom was her unconscious projection of Dickens himself). As Dickens saw it, he had broken the first link of her disease by destroying the secrecy of the phantom. "I cannot yet quite make up my mind," he continues, "whether the phantom originates in shattered nerves and a system broken by Pain; or whether it is the representative of some great nerve or set of nerves on which her disease has preyed—and begins to loose its hold now, because the disease of those nerves is itself attacked by the inexplicable agency of the Magnetism." It would be difficult to articulate his distinction between these conditions, but he was clearly determined to sound medical. In either case, he thought, Mme de la Rue's phantom *must not make head again*" (4.254–55). He began to see himself as the force of good, fighting with all his might against "that Devil," who might, he feared, go so far as to threaten his patient "with revenge against herself and upon me" (4.259). His medical fantasies were quickly being transformed into fictions of triangular desire and rivalry.

By the time Dickens left Genoa at the end of June, he had convinced himself that his patient was nearly cured, and that her tormentor was on the retreat: "She tells me that she has seen a Shadow for an instant—the Shadow of the Bad Shadow—passing in a great hurry; escaping observation; hanging its head; and nearly worn away" (4.323). Dickens "knew" somehow that he had intertwined Mme de la Rue's Shadow with his own; he told her husband that he had woken up in "a state of indescribable horror and emotion" one night, that he thought about his patient both in waking and in sleep, and that he had "a sense of her being somehow a part of me" (4.264). The full extent of the mutual transference between the two participants in this bizarre episode can only be imagined.

When, in the autumn of 1848, Dickens wrote a story about a ghost Doppelgänger who holds the power to erase the troubled memory of his double, he recurred to his mesmeric experiments, while registering some doubt about their effects. *The Haunted Man*, like its predecessor *A Christmas Carol*, personifies its hero's submerged fears and resentments in the form of ghostly figures that bring his interior tortures to light, at the cost of spreading moral chaos to everyone he knows. Although such tales mix psychological probing with optimistic moralized plotting, they attest to Dickens's interest in a kind of interior knowledge that flies under the radar for psychological realism. He was quite clear about what he was doing. In a letter of January 1849 to George Howard, the earl of Carlisle, he defended the atmospheric opening of *The Haunted Man*: "the heaping up of that quantity of shadows, I hold to be absolutely necessary, as a preparation to the appearance of the dark shadow of the Chemist. People will take anything for granted, in the Arabian Nights or the Persian Tales, but they won't walk out of Oxford Street, or the Market place of a county town, directly into the presence of a Phantom, albeit an allegorical one" (5.466–67). Realities played second fiddle to fictional effects, but the effects stood for inner realities in allegorical fashion. An often-repeated formula about the construction of ghost stories is built on a similar wish to naturalize the meaning of literary ghosts. One version appears in the review of Catherine Crowe's book; another in an 1859 letter to a fellow writer, William Howitt, who was involved with the spiritualist movement: "I have not yet met with any Ghost Story that was proved to me, or that had not the noticeable peculiarity in it—that the alteration of some slight circumstance would bring it within the range of common natural probabilities" (9.116). Presumably the formula included his own ghost tales: as allegories, his Phantoms were clearly exterior embodiments of common and naturally occurring aspects of the inner life.

The idea of allegory also helped Dickens when it came to thinking about dreams. His ideas about dreams, along with other sensations along the continuum of waking and sleeping states, were certainly stimulated by Robert

Macnish's *The Philosophy of Sleep* (1830), but Dickens was always keen to test theoretical formulations against his personal experience. Recounting dreams and hearing others' dreams never failed to arouse his curiosity. After the death of his young sister-in-law Mary Hogarth he dreamed of her every night until he broke the spell by telling his wife about it, he reported to his mother-in-law in May 1843 (3.483–84). A year and a half later he wrote to Forster from Italy with a sentence-by-sentence account of a dream dialogue he had held with a female figure he "knew" to be Mary's spirit. Working with the theory that dreams are made up of fragments retained from actual recent experience, he attempted to list its immediate sources, only to find them inadequate: "And yet, for all this, put the case of that wish being fulfilled by any agency in which I had no hand; and I wonder whether I should regard it as a dream, or an actual Vision!" The wish he referred to was a desire to know *"what the face was like"* in a religious picture that had been removed from a Roman Catholic altar in his bedroom (4.496–97). In his knowing but unknowing fashion, he had stumbled close upon the idea of dreams as wish fulfillments, by the way attesting to an attraction for the Mariolatry of the very Catholicism he took pains to protest in his waking life. In Dickens's novels, characters' dreams similarly express wishes or feelings that are rigorously suppressed in their conscious self-representations.

By 1851 Dickens had developed a full critique of the standard "scientific" dream theories of his time: that dreams reflect recent impressions or respond to bodily states during sleep and that they reflect the moral character of the dreamer. His ideas were summarized in a remarkable letter of 2 February 1851, written in response to Dr. Thomas Stone's submission of an article on dreams for *Household Words* (6.276–79). His dreams and those of others were more likely to take place in the distant past, Dickens claimed, and "I should say the chances were a thousand to one against anybody's dreaming of the subject closely occupying the waking mind—except—and this I wish particularly to suggest to you—in a sort of allegorical manner." Here he gave an example: if he has been perplexed in his writing during the day he might dream of other frustrating situations like trying to shut a door that will not close, or driving a horse that turns into a dog and can't be driven. "I sometimes think," he concludes, "that the origin of all fable and Allegory—the very first conception of such fictions—may be referable to this class of dreams."

If, as some critics have suggested, Dickens's narratives bear some relation to the action of dreams, they did not arise in a mind unconscious of what it was doing. On the contrary, it would seem that Dickens had learned a great deal from watching his own dreams: he recognized, for example, that dreams are closely linked to memories, that fragments of experience we have not consciously noticed during the day would be likely to appear in dreams, that certain types of dreams are common to everyone regardless of class, gender, moral status, or experience, and that we are often conscious of being in critical dialogue with dreams as they are occurring. "We all confound the living with the dead, and all frequently have a knowledge or suspicion that we are doing it," he writes to Stone; "we all astonish ourselves by telling ourselves, in a dialogue with ourselves, the most astonishing and terrific secrets" (6.279). Dickens's interest in ways of knowing what we don't know, and not knowing what we do know, is fully in evidence. His attention to the workings of his own mind, no less than his observation of London streets, was a form of research that contributed directly to his creative representations.

The chapters of this book are built around certain recurrent clusters of thought and feeling in Dickens's writing, in order to illuminate some of the ways of knowing that drove his creative life. With some important exceptions, critical studies of Dickens tend to ascribe significance to parts of novels as they contribute to a reading of the novel as a whole; the assumption that novels can be read as self-contained systems of meaning is still with us, surviving all the recent shifts in theoretical approach. In the course of writing these pages, I was amused to find myself reviving the nineteenth-century notion that Dickens wrote in pieces rather than wholes. Familiar passages light up differently when they are momentarily lifted out of their novels and set in the alternative contexts provided by letters and journalism. Those contexts have allowed me to understand the depth and strangeness of certain intensely charged scenes, and to focus on odd moments when Dickens's evocative language suggests layers of knowledge that remain otherwise unarticulated. The process has also convinced me that Dickens's ways of knowing were often more fully invested in the dialogue of his characters and the shape of his plots than in his omniscient narrative voice.

Each of the following chapters juxtaposes letters, stories, articles, and sections of novels that bear on its subject area, discovering patterns that are common to the life and the writing. If the topics themselves appear to make an idiosyncratic collection, the stories told in each chapter are intended to illuminate different facets of a complex but recognizable inner dynamic, in which projection outward functions as a primary mode of self-recognition. I have also organized the chapters in ways that cut across familiar story lines in Dickens biography and criticism, in the hope of shedding new perspectives on old ground.

"Language on the Loose" makes connections between the keen sense of injury expressed in Dickens's angry or self-defensive letters and his portraits of hyperbolic talkers, examining the interplay of hyperbole, parody, and self-parody in Dickens's work. "Memory" proposes a split between valorized and fearful models of memory in Dickens, and follows his many peculiar ways of setting up negotiations between past and present, particularly during the autobiographical decade of the 1840s. "Another Man" is a study of triangular desire, centering on the erotic fascination of identification and rivalry between men in Dickens's male friendships and in his fiction. "Manager of the House" focuses on Dickens through the lens of his intense involvement with houses: his ordering of family homes, his management of the Home for Homeless Women, and the fictional houses that became prominent from the late 1840s to the late 1850s, when Dickens's managerial activities reached a peak. "Streets" is concerned with the relationship between Dickens's writing and the long-distance walking he found essential, both to his creative process and as an antidote to his fears of solitude and solitary confinement. Working between public and private writing, between biography and criticism, I have hoped to develop a picture of Dickens's mind and art that emerges from his own connections between the inner world and its exterior manifestations.

While chronological sequences appear within each chapter, the chapters themselves do not trace out the course of Dickens's career from beginning to end. It has long seemed to me that chronology is the great limitation of biography, at once the spinal column that holds the story together and the straitjacket that prevents its freedom of motion. No matter how well it is concealed by the biographer's art and analysis, the plot is the same: the movement from birth to death. Biographer and reader alike are enchanted and enchained by the necessity of proceeding to the next day, week, or year. There must be a childhood, a youth, an early and a later adulthood. But the evidence available differs considerably from one period to another. Particularly when it comes to the years of childhood, there are many things we cannot know; stories must nevertheless be told about them. Such necessities create some of the problems that beset literary biography, along with its first cousin biographical criticism. The biographer relies on a writer's retrospective life writings—letters, diaries, or memory pieces—as if their recollections were true, when they may have more to reveal about the moment of writing than about the past to which they refer. The psychodynamics of the writer's early family life may be extrapolated from the fictions and built into explanatory narratives of formation. Characters may be identified as people the writer knew, or people identified as models for characters.

The problematic nature of such interpretive practices helps to explain why biographical criticism went out of fashion for much of the twentieth century, during the successive reigns of formalism and New Historicism. Its gradual revival at the turn of the twenty-first depends on the recognition that an individual career can be a significant window into a cultural history, and on the loosening of the boundaries between psychoanalytic and historical approaches to interpretation. The practice of literary biography or biographical criticism at this juncture calls on us to discover plausible ways of negotiating between "the life" and "the work," or what we might now call the lost "real" and the textual imaginary. In effect, the distinction itself cannot hold. We cannot go back and forth between life and work because we do not have a life; everything we know is on a written page. To juxtapose letters and fiction, as I am doing, is to read one kind of text alongside another. Neither has explanatory power over the other; all we can do is observe, make connections and interpretive suggestions.

My story begins, then, with a twenty-one-year-old Dickens in 1833, the year of the first significant group of surviving letters. I discuss his ways of negotiating with memory, but not his childhood as such. The most famous piece of evidence about his youth, the autobiographical fragment in which Dickens told John Forster the story of his work at Warren's Blacking warehouse as a child of twelve, is treated in "Memory" as a piece of writing performed in 1848, when Dickens was thirty-six years old. I do not know or pretend to know what really happened at Warren's in 1824, what Dickens's relationships with his father or mother were like, or what transpired in the privacies of his marriage with Catherine Hogarth or in his long relationship with the young actress Ellen Ternan. When I do take guesses about matters I cannot be sure about, I have tried to draw attention to the speculative nature of my comments. But no one invents a project like this without desiring the strange kind of intimacy that arises in the relation between a biographer-critic and her subject, and that gives any such work its own tinge of projection—or, as Virginia Woolf would have it, that makes us creators, not just readers and spectators. For various reasons I have been compelled to attempt once more, after all the other attempts, to bring certain aspects of Dickens to life. The fascinating complexity of this figure does not diminish even after almost everything we can imagine has been said and written about him.

Dickens is, of course, a bit of a Tough Subject. Were he among us now, many would call him a narcissist and a control freak. Some of the most dramatically neurotic episodes in his life include the extravagant mourning after the death of his seventeen-year-old sister-in-law Mary Hogarth in 1837, the contemptuous silence he maintained about his mother during his adult life, the willful casting away of his wife Catherine in 1858, and the secret affair with Ellen Ternan that occupied his last twelve years. While these and other episodes with women make regular appearances in this book, I have not chosen them as organizing topics both because they are quite familiar and because we have relatively little evidence about their inner workings. In "Another Man," the chapter that centers on Dickens and gender, I have suggested that Dickens's ways of imagining women are inextricable from a structure of rivalry and fascination among men. In "Manager of the House," I have treated the separation from Catherine in the context of Dickens's extreme propensity for managerial control.

The long shadow of the blacking warehouse offers a different challenge to any sort of biographical study. All roads, it sometimes seems, lead back to Warren's Blacking. The episode provides the essential material for the second or third chapter of any conventional biography, as well as the cornerstone of many interpretive approaches to Dickens's art. Ever since Dickens's closest friend and biographer John Forster published Dickens's autobiographical fragment in the first volume of *The Life of Charles Dickens*, it has been impossible to separate Dickens from the memory of his employment at Warren's. Unlike other major "stories" in Dickens biography, such as the mourning for Mary Hogarth, the fights with publishers, or the separation from Catherine, this experience is documented only retrospectively, and through a single source alone. Yet its traces appear in Dickens's writing in the very first sketches, and reappear regularly through the end of his career. In giving at the outset a brief summary of the events as we know them from Dickens's account, I want only to remind my readers of the experiences that Dickens found it necessary to conceal from his readers and acquaintances so long as he lived.

In 1822 Dickens's father John was transferred to London from his clerical job in the Chatham branch of the navy payroll office. Ten-year-old Charles remained at school in Chatham for three months, and then traveled alone to join his struggling family in depressing lodgings in Camden Town. No provision had been made for him; he was not sent back to school, while his sister Fanny, just eighteen months older, was sent on scholarship to study at the Royal Academy of Music. In the hands of the improvident John Dickens, the family finances deteriorated until his wife, Elizabeth Dickens, decided to open a school, taking a more expensive house on Gower Street for the purpose. This enterprise failed to produce a single student, and the family resorted to urgent measures, such as pawning their household goods. A relative found a way that Charles could contribute a few shillings a week, and on 9 February 1824, two days after his twelfth birthday, he was sent to work at Warren's Blacking warehouse at Hungerford Stairs off the Strand. His job was to paste labels on jars of boot blacking; his cohorts were working-class boys.

On 20 February John Dickens was arrested for debt and confined in the Marshalsea Prison in the Borough of Southwark. Charles continued to live with his mother and siblings at Gower Street until the end of March, when the rest of the family moved into the Marshalsea, placing Charles in lodgings with a family friend in Camden Town. Finding the separation unbearable, he ventured to complain, and after three weeks a new lodging was found for him on Lant Street next to the prison. Now he could have breakfast and supper with his family before and after his workday across the river at Warren's. By May John Dickens had inherited a legacy from his mother that allowed him to pay his debt; he was released on May 29 after three months in the Marshalsea.

This may have been a crucial juncture, for Charles was not released from work when he rejoined his liberated family in new Camden Town lodgings. At some point Warren's itself moved from Hungerford Stairs to Chandos Street in Covent Garden. In the new warehouse Charles and his co-worker Bob Fagin sometimes worked in the window for light, their dexterity attracting the attention of passers-by. In June of 1824, Charles attended Fanny's prize concert at the Royal Academy and wept at the difference in their positions. His parents did not get around to removing him from the warehouse for some time; there is no established date for his release, nor is there a clear story about why John Dickens decided to take his son out of the warehouse when he did. Biographical guesses about the full length of Dickens's service at Warren's range from five or six months to twelve or thirteen months. Once released, he was sent to school at the nearby Wellington Academy, where he resumed the trappings of a marginally middle-class boyhood. When he wrote about the experience later, Dickens claimed he was unable to express the depth of the shame, humiliation, disappointment, and isolation he had suffered during his time at Warren's.

In *From Copyright to Copperfield*, Alexander Welsh protested against the long biographical and critical tradition of representing Warren's as an originary trauma, proposing in its place an Eriksonian model of development in stages and giving a leading role to a period of internal readjustment triggered by Dickens's first trip to America in 1842. Though Welsh's challenge is a salutary one, I have come to believe that Dickens's memories of Warren's were of a piece with his responses to his American critics: in both cases a blow to his idea of himself occasioned lifelong waves of resentment and pages of brilliantly accusatory rhetoric. "Memory" includes my treatment of the autobiographical fragment in the context of Dickens's increasing attention to memory during the 1840s; I suggest there that Warren's was traumatic for Dickens in the sense that trauma can be recognized through its afterlife in consciousness. When he came to record the memories of his blacking days in 1848, Dickens created a multifaceted metaphor of his being. Each part of the autobiographical fragment had already been and would again be elaborated, in life and in writing, in one variation after another. That is why it is impossible to read Dickens without hearing echoes of the autobiographical memory in many different situations.

One such moment in *David Copperfield* stands out because it makes a direct link between Warren's and the problem of knowledge. After he runs away from his warehouse work and lands safely at Dr. Strong's genteel school, David reports on the lingering anxieties of his early days there. He worries about what his middle-class schoolmates might think of him if they knew of his experiences in the lower-class worlds of prisons and pawning; was there anything about him that would cause them to "find me out"? Even more troublesome, however, is the fear that they might learn what he knows: "How would it affect them, who were so innocent of London life, and London streets, to discover how knowing I was (and was ashamed to be) in some of the meanest phases of both?" (*DC* 16). Having the wrong kind of knowledge is (at least partly) associated with shame; gentility and social acceptance depend upon hiding both the knowledge and the shame from the observation of others. Telling without telling that he's telling, the game Dickens played with his readers throughout his career, rehearses the simultaneous pride and shame in a knowingness that does not want to speak its name.

To ask the question "What did Dickens know?" is, then, to embark on the study of an always open, always compelling question, not because Dickens displayed so uncommon a set of behaviors and defenses, but because of his extraordinary ability to transform them into writing. Just as he made superb comedy from the most ordinary situations, he could, pen in hand, make uncanny representations of the most ordinary feelings. Whether such transformations occur in letters and essays, or in the extended phantasmagoria of novels, the conscious and unconscious artfulness of Dickens's self-creation remains one of the most fascinating aspects of his writing.

✍ CHAPTER 2

Language on the Loose

Dickens wrote little about his own art. Even his letters to John Forster—who claimed to have read everything Dickens wrote before it was published (Forster 89)—are more likely to express his difficulties with deadlines or the agonies of beginning a new book than to throw any light on the private process of composition. The few comments he did make tell a consistent story: Dickens saw himself as inhabiting his characters from the inside, and he believed that characters should reveal themselves in dialogue without a narrator's analysis or explanation. To the generations of readers and critics who have either attacked or justified Dickens's failure to give his characters credible or complex interior lives, he might easily have objected, "I write my characters inside out."

Out from *his* inside, to begin with. As he was writing the early chapters of *Martin Chuzzlewit*, Dickens wrote to Forster, "As to the way in which these characters have opened out, that is, to me, one of the most surprising processes of the mind in this sort of invention. Given what one knows, what one does not know springs up; and I am as absolutely certain of its being true, as I am of the law of gravitation—if such a thing be possible, more so" (3.441). Dickens is hardly the first or last writer to speak of the way characters develop themselves during the fiction-writing process, but the emphases are peculiar to him. Conscious knowing sets off unconscious knowing, which "springs up" into language on the page as though it were suddenly released from the mind's suppressions. For Dickens what results is true—possibly more true than the provable law of gravity—precisely because it arrives from the unknown within. His "absolute" certainty on this point marks the habit of exaggeration that comes into play when doubt lies in his vicinity, but it underlines Dickens's belief that his characters are true and real because they emerge from a partly unconscious psychological process.

Forster's biography follows Dickens in attributing verisimilitude to his characters, and defends Dickens against the condescension of critics who see only exteriority in his work. "There are plenty to tell us that it is by vividness of external observation rather than by depth of imaginative insight, by tricks of manner and phrase rather than by truth of character, by manifestation outwardly rather than what lies behind," he writes. With some acerbity about the George Henry Lewes–George Eliot school of realism, he asserts that it was not Dickens's way "to expound or discuss his creations, to lay them psychologically bare, to analyse their organisms, to subject to minute demonstration their fibrous and other tissues." Instead, he implies, Dickens had genuine fellow feeling: "no man had ever so surprising a faculty as Dickens of becoming himself what he was representing" (Forster 561–62). As Dickens once put it himself, criticizing another writer's work, "It seems to me as if it were written by somebody who lived next door to the people, rather than inside of 'em" (6.453).

In his journalism, as well as in the notes for novels that have been preserved in his *Book of Memoranda*, Dickens sometimes slides from the third to the first person as he becomes invested in the mind of a character he is inventing or parodying. He can "become" any sort of character: Flora Finching, for example: "The lady, *un peu passé*, who is determined to be interesting. No matter how much I love that person—nay, the more so for that very reason—I MUST flutter and bother, and be weak and apprehensive and nervous and what not. If I were well and strong, agreeable and self-denying, my friend might forget me" (*Memoranda* 5). Or, Mr. Dorrit: "I affect to believe that I would do anything myself for a Ten Pound note, and that anybody else would.... While I affect to be finding good in most men, I am in reality decrying it where it really is, and setting it up where it is not" (9). Or, a prostitute: "I am a common woman, fallen. Is it deviltry in me—is it a wicked comfort—what is it—that induces me to be always tempting other women down, while I hate myself!" (11). These notes reveal that moving into the first person is a mode of analysis as well as a form of identification with potential characters: the "I" speaks itself by giving or searching for reasons for its behavior. The narrative of *Little Dorrit* includes a moment in which Arthur Clennam's mind moves from free indirect discourse into his mother's "I." As he attempts to link his mother with Dorrit's imprisonment, he imagines her reasoning: "I admit that I was accessory to that man's captivity. I have suffered for it in kind. He has decayed in his prison; I in mine. I have paid the penalty" (*LD* 1.8). In the published satirical essays, brief slides into the "I" are generally a way to undermine the speaking voice through its blatant lack of logic or sensibility, but the identification is equally compelling. Such passages present an odd variation of the technique of free indirect discourse, which normally retains the third-person past tense, but allows the reader a critical perspective on a character's train of thought. They are especially intriguing because they suggest an inward habit of moral and psychological analysis that is normally submerged in Dickens's fictional world.

Dickens insisted that characters must display and reveal themselves on the page, unassisted by a narrator's interpretation. Soon after he opened shop as the editor of *Household Words*, Dickens rejected one submission in no uncertain terms: "It is not enough to say that they were this, or that. They must shew it for themselves, and have it in their grain. Then, they would act on one another, and would act for themselves whether the author liked it or no. As it is, there is not enough reason for your writing about them, because they do nothing and work out nothing" (6.87). The "Show, don't tell" dictum included the relationship offered to the reader as well as the relation between writer and character. Dickens had little but praise for Wilkie Collins when he read *The Woman in White*, but he felt compelled to worry about the "DISSECTIVE property" of Collins's internal narrators, "which is essentially not theirs but yours." He would prefer to get more out of them "by collision with one another, and by the working of the story." To tell too much, Dickens thinks, is "to give an audience credit for nothing—which necessarily involves the forcing of points upon their attention—and which I have always observed them to resent when they find it out—as they always will and do" (9.194–95). Forster also attests to Dickens's success in this art: "There never was any one who had less need to talk about his characters, because never were characters so surely revealed by themselves; and it was thus their reality made itself felt at once" (Forster 121).

Dickens, of course, did and did not abide by these precepts in his own writing. It would be difficult to find a reader who did not feel that points had been forced—and repeatedly forced—by many of his narratives. But it is worth taking his assertions seriously, because they gesture toward aspects of his art that are particularly difficult to talk about. The image of characters acting upon or colliding with each other gives a central importance to the impact of dialogue. Dickens, everyone agrees, is theatrical, but it has always proved tricky to describe the dynamics of his characters' utterance and the response they provoke. In particular, there are characters whose production of language is an event in itself, characters that tend to render critics speechless, either murmuring phrases like "comic genius" or quoting a particular passage as if it were a joke that can't possibly be explained. What are such characters actually doing with language, and what impact does their speech have on other characters, and on the narrator? Are such classically Dickensian figures—often described as obsessive or mechanical or static—readable from the inside out?

Dickens projects different parts of himself upon every character in a novel, and his letters corroborate that notion when he speaks of living inside his creations and coming to knowledge of them. Does this mean that Dickens "knows himself" in his characters? Since both characters and narrators parody a range of languages, and since Dickens parodies on one page a kind of language we are asked to feel seriously about on another, what is the connection between parody and self-knowledge? It is with such questions in mind that I set Dickens the indignant letter-writer and journalist next to a line of his fictional talkers talking variants of what I like to call "language on the loose."

The Great Protester

Dickens the letter-writer commanded as broad a range of languages and voices as did Dickens the novelist. He could be affectionate, playful, frustrated, or monitory. If he writes angrily and willfully on one page, he is generous and psychologically skillful on another. Sometimes he is the wildly exaggerating storyteller making comic episodes from his own life, sometimes the earnest consoler who feels the closeness of life to death, sometimes the brilliant observer of a new place. Every correspondent has his or her own mode of address; every relationship its own special language. Among these many voices, there is one that calls a special kind of attention to itself through the discomfort it raises. It greets the reader of Dickens's early letters in particular, but it never goes away entirely. This is the voice of indignation and self-justification set off, apparently uncontrollably, by incidents in which Dickens feels slighted, misread, taken advantage of, or unjustly criticized. More explicitly than any other mode of letter writing, it raises questions about feeling and language in Dickens's art.

A few weeks after his twenty-first birthday, Dickens wrote a letter breaking off his flirtation with Maria Beadnell, the young lady who has long figured in Dickens biography as the first love who broke his heart (1.16–17). It is impossible to gauge the actual nature and extent of the relationship, which may have been partially fabricated from the tissue of Dickens's own writing; in his letter he refers to "the feeling of utter desolation and wretchedness which has succeeded our former correspondence." It is clear, however, that Dickens felt himself to be passionately in love, and that he was hurt and humiliated by Maria's indifference to his feeling. The letter begins with two formal and ludicrously extended sentences which show Dickens riding a high horse with minimal control of the reins—a very different kind of writing from the easy, informal, verbally playful addresses to his male friends of the time. The letter professes only generosity to Maria's feelings, pretending that "Your own feelings will enable you to imagine far better than any attempt of mine to describe the painful struggle it has cost me to make up my mind to adopt the course which I now take"; insisting that he has not "the most remote idea of hurting your feelings" by writing these lines; and declaring a sincere and heartfelt wish for her happiness.

What the language performs, however, is quite thoroughly punitive. Declaring that he has always "acted fairly, intelligibly and honorably," Dickens goes on to list all the mean things he has not done—and that she, by implication, has: "I have ever acted without reserve. I have never held out encouragement which I knew I never meant: I have never indirectly sanctioned hopes which I well knew I did not intend to fulfill." As he goes along, Maria becomes a deliberate and calculating hypocrite, one who would "encourage one dangler as a useful shield for—an excellent set-off against—others more fortunate and doubtless more deserving." The young man is not just suffering from unrequited love; he feels he has been rooked.

The correspondence did not end here; Dickens became caught up in a series of letters defending himself against the accusation that he made a confidant of a certain Mary Ann Leigh who had somehow insinuated herself into his relationship with Maria. The notion that he would have desecrated the purity of his love by confiding it in this unworthy vessel arouses immense indignation, perhaps because it was partially true: again Dickens's feelings had been toyed with by others, and he found it necessary to protest in force. This rather absurd coda allows us a glimpse of Maria's response to his initial letter, which she had returned to Dickens with some comment about his anger. "Even now," he responded, "I do think it was written 'more in sorrow than in anger', and to my mind—I had almost said to your better judgment—it must appear to breathe anything but an unkind or bitter feeling" (1.25). Unable to recognize or admit to his attack on Maria, Dickens writes three days later with a final offer to forget the past and to reconcile: "the Love I now tender you is as pure, and as lasting as at any period of our former correspondence" (1.29). Having deflected his rage onto Mary Ann Leigh, he could assure himself that his feeling was beyond censure. Luckily for both of them, Maria did not take up his offer.

Much of this episode belongs to the annals of young love, and Dickens made several charming parodies of the obsessive and hopeless young lover when he created characters like Augustus Moddle in *Martin Chuzzlewit* and Toots in *Dombey and Son*. But the essential pattern of response shows up in very different circumstances throughout Dickens's correspondence. His own intentions and behavior are always exemplary, while others accuse him unjustly or take advantage of him without crediting his excellence. He is not angry or aggressive, only sometimes "hurt." Underlying it all, there is a sense of perpetual disappointment that takes the form of feeling conned.

The turbulent history of Dickens's relations with his publishers is a complicated labyrinth that I will not enter, except to look at some examples of the writing it set off. In November 1836, the twenty-four-year-old Dickens resigned from his job as a reporter for the *Morning Chronicle*. *Pickwick* was in train with Chapman and Hall, and he had just signed a new contract with another publisher, Richard Bentley, to edit *Bentley's Miscellany*. Dickens's career in fiction was taking off, and he could afford to leave reporting behind, with a polite letter of resignation to John Easthope, a proprietor of the *Chronicle*. A week later, having accepted Dickens's resignation, Easthope was treated to one of Dickens's blasts of indignation. Apparently he had failed to show enough appreciation for Dickens's extraordinary service. In his anger, Dickens supplied the missing acknowledgment himself:

> on many occasions at a sacrifice of health, rest, and personal comfort, I have again and again, on important expresses in my zeal for the interests of the paper, done what was always before considered impossible, and what in all probability will never be accomplished again. During the whole period of my engagement wherever there was a difficult and harassing duty to be performed—traveling at a few hours' notice hundreds of miles in the depth of winter—leaving hot and crowded rooms to write, the night through, in a close damp chaise—tearing along, and writing the most important speeches, under every possible circumstance of disadvantage and difficulty—for that duty I have been selected. (1.196–97)

No matter that Dickens expresses his zest for just that kind of competitive activity in other letters; here the breathless rhetoric is used to beat Easthope for his inattention to the prodigy who had just left his service. Easthope himself was rather confounded, and wondered whether Dickens's current illness was making him irritable (1.195n.). He did not know his man: Dickens refused "to retract one syllable of the letter" even some weeks later, after Easthope published a strongly favorable review of the first number of *Bentley's Miscellany* (1.220).

The road to Dickens's resignation from the *Miscellany* in January 1839 was also paved with an acute sense of ill treatment. Understandably exhausted after producing three overlapping novels, and pressed under his contract to begin installments of *Barnaby Rudge*, Dickens asked for a six-month's postponement. When Bentley agreed to it in a note couched in legal and contractual terms, Dickens was infuriated, and set himself on course for resignation: "as one who is enriching you at the expense of his own brain, and for a most paltry and miserable pittance, I have a right to some regard and consideration at your hands; and secondly, because such postponements are matters of common literary custom, taking place as you well know every day, and in three-fourths of the arrangements in which you are concerned." In closing, he threatens to break his contact altogether "if you presume to address me again in the style of offensive impertinence which marks your last communication" (1.495). He had pushed himself through an extraordinary amount of work, and he wanted an extraordinary kind of recognition—not the nagging feeling that Bentley begrudged him terms that he would readily make with any other author.

Not long after he resigned from his brief and ill-conceived editorship of *The Daily News* in February 1846, he wrote to one of the newspaper's publishers, Frederick Evans, to complain about Evans's partner William Bradbury; both were men he had worked with for years. Bradbury, Dickens argued, had been disrespectful, contributing to the failure of his editorship: "he seems to me to have become possessed of the idea that everybody receiving a salary in return for his services, is his natural enemy, and should be suspected and mistrusted accordingly" (4.506). Attempting to insert his own distrust into the bond between the partners, Dickens succeeded only in displaying his own suspicion that anyone who paid him for services rendered "at the expense of his own brain" was bound to be "his natural enemy." It is not difficult to hear echoes of the bright child whose brain was considered expendable so long as he could earn a few shillings a week in the blacking warehouse. Even his way of accusing one partner while confiding in the other sounds like a repetition of the old distinction between his parents: the father who finally took him out of the warehouse; the mother who wanted him to go back. The paranoia he projects in his accusations is the public face of his sensitivity to shame and his—always belated—means of protecting himself against it.

In all of these situations, Dickens himself was the one on his way out the door, yet his rage is the rage of the one cheated or abandoned. His need to blacken retrospectively a relationship that had brought him pleasure or profit for a while is hardly an unusual human impulse, but in Dickens's case it suggests a high susceptibility to feeling imposed on or taken in. If a relationship had gone wrong for him, he suspected that the other person had been cheating him all along, and that he had finally seen through the imposture. The anger aimed at the other was in part the reflex of an anxiety about his own innocence, his youthful appearance, or his unworldliness. In two early letters that anxiety appears straightforwardly: once when he asks a friend to hire the horses for an outing with the Beadnells because "*I* never did anything in the money way without being imposed upon" (1.13–14) and again, six years later, when he reports to Catherine that he has successfully taken a cottage for his parents in Exeter. He has invited his mother down to help put the place to rights, "and I shall be saved—not only a world of uneasiness but a good deal of money, for the people will take me in and I can't help it" (1.518). The expression of that fear disappeared from the later letters as Dickens grew in experience and lost his very youthful looks. But his books never grew out of their obsession with innocents in the hands of con men, nor did his partings—the abandonment of his wife being the extreme case—become less accusatory.

Displays of unacknowledged feeling in reckless accusations are particularly interesting in a correspondent who seems otherwise to command the many voices he inhabits, even when they speak—as they so often do—in exaggerations. The episodes that carried such displays into the public domain are particularly telling, because they worked against Dickens's own best interests. When he toured the United States in 1842, Dickens's propensity to embrace the new with unabated enthusiasm and turn savage at the first sign of disappointment was played out on an international stage. The turn came about a month after he had landed, when he read the American press attacks on a speech in which he had argued for an International Copyright agreement that would prevent the works of British authors from being pirated in America. A budding friendship with the mayor of Boston, Jonathan Chapman, was shaken after Dickens chose him as a confidant:

> I have never in my life been so shocked and disgusted, or made so sick and sore at heart, as I have been by the treatment I have received here (in America I mean), in reference to the International Copyright question. I—the greatest loser by the existing Law alive—say in perfect good humour and disinterestedness (for God knows I have little hope of its ever being changed in my time) that I hope the day will come when Writers will be justly treated; and straightway there fall on me scores

of your newspapers; imputing motives to me, the very suggestion of which turns my blood to gall; and attacking me in such terms of vagabond scurrility as they would denounce no murderer with.

This treatment, he continued, "has been to me an amount of agony such as I have never experienced since my birth" (3.76–77).

The notion that he could be seen to have "motives" at all—and motives that he could not acknowledge—seems to have been especially galling to Dickens; he could render himself only as a person of utterly pure feelings set upon by a lynch mob. Later that year, when Chapman learned that Dickens was planning to publish *American Notes*, he finally replied, expressing anxiety about how the book would fare in the United States. Dickens's response was of course defiant: he swore that "I have never, for an instant, suffered myself to be betrayed into a hasty or unfair expression, or one I shall, at any time, regret" (3.346). His response and his general attitude toward the democracy he had idealized were deeply colored by the notion that in America, opinions could not be freely expressed on any controversial subject (3.81). "Democracy" became a national fraud. Only Boston, the city he had visited before the fatal turn, was exempted.

I am interested here not in the rights and wrongs of Dickens versus the United States, but in the nature of his immediate response. (*American Notes* is a more acute and mixed account than its general reputation would suggest.) He had been welcomed with open arms and then betrayed where he presumed· to trust—that was the shock he was destined by nature and circumstance to feel, even to invent if necessary. The betrayal was to see his motives and feelings differently than he saw them himself—in this case, to accuse him of self-interest when he understood himself to champion the cause of literature. To be read behind his back, so to speak, was an intolerable kind of humiliation.

His own way of putting it was quite different: "I have a strong spice of the Devil in me; and when I am assailed, as I think falsely or unjustly, my red hot anger carries me through it bravely, until I have forgotten all about it," he wrote of the American episode in 1843 (3.493). This little fiction—for Dickens did not forget—stars anger playing the role of a protective hero, with forgetting coming in at the end to erase the evidence on both sides. In the following year, he claimed to have lost interest in the copyright question altogether; the subject "only dwelt [in my mind] when I viewed the influences that make up an American government, through the mist of my hopes and fancies. When that cleared away, I ceased to have any interest in the question" (4.60). What offers itself as self-knowledge—he has effected a classic return to reality—acts as yet another bit of dismissive aggression, addressed in this case to an American who had sent him a pamphlet supporting the international copyright. Many years later, at the end of 1859, Dickens wrote a wonderful satire on the two-bit gossip of journalists who appear to "know" the inner intentions of their highly placed subjects through private and confidential interviews granted only to them; he called it "The Tattlesnivel Bleater" (Dent 4.19–26). By that time he had had the experience of a celebrity author pushed by gossip into making a public defense of his separation from his wife. His continued sensitivity to pretensions of inside knowledge gave the article its especially biting edge.

Dickens simply could not be, would not be, at fault; any suggestion of it generated an overflow of defensive language. When, at twenty-nine, he answered a note from a former colleague of his reporting days, he spent virtually the whole letter disputing the possibility that anyone could think he could forget old friends in his days of fame. As usual, he writes himself into extravagant claims: "I have never in my life—and especially in my later life—no, not once, treated any single human being with coldness or hauteur" (2.241–42). For the reader of Dickens's letters, such claims become familiar parts of his character, signs of an inner imperative that would not be altered. Peter Ackroyd comments, "the truth was always a very fluid concept for Dickens; he did not so much lie as believe in whatever he said at the time" (1002). This sounds right, especially in conjunction with Dickens's belief that what he discovered about his characters was true because he "knew" it to be true. Of course, it leaves many questions unanswered. The question of origins—what made Dickens this kind of man?—cannot, I think, be adequately answered by successive generations. A deep-seated expectation that trust or belief will be rewarded with indifference or betrayal is likely to have originated in a period of childhood earlier than the blacking factory episode, though that experience would of course have deepened the expectation and given it a full-fledged story.

It is also tempting to think that the talkative Dickens was his father's son, and that he reproduced his father's highly elaborated patterns of denial exactly because he was so horrified by them. His acute sensitivity to delusive speech patterns and his power of parody may well have been nourished on John Dickens's circumlocutions, and from the gradual and painful recognition that the father was not as good as his word. Forster quotes a fragment of an 1844 letter in which Dickens juxtaposes his own direct language with a parody of his father's: of a departing physician, he writes, "We are very sorry to lose the benefit of his advice—or, as my father would say, to be deprived, to a certain extent, of the concomitant advantages, whatever they may be, resulting from his medical skill, such as it is, and his professional attendance, in so far as it may be so considered" (4.243–44). Earlier that year Forster had heard the same voice when Dickens worried about a dinner party in a rented house: "Investigation below stairs renders it, as my father would say, 'manifest to any person of ordinary intelligence, if the term may be considered allowable,' that the Saturday's dinner cannot come off here with safety" (4.133). So far as I know these sentences are Dickens's only parodies of John Dickens in his own person. Their back-and-forth rhythm suggests a great self-consciousness—on someone's part—about each pompous phrase as soon as it is uttered. Someone, presumably the father himself, is listening to the language phrase by phrase, and calling it into question. The intimate connection between speech and skeptical hearing resides, then, within the sentence itself.

The scope of Dickens's sensitivity to language as a kind of con game becomes especially evident in certain familiar topics to which he returned again and again with a vehemence that brooks no subtlety or opposition. These topics are highlighted in his journalism for *Household Words* and *All the Year Round*, though they show up in the fictions as well. The rottenness of Parliament belongs at the top of the hit list, which also includes elaborate funerals, savages, Temperance Societies and other fashionable social movements, murderers who go unpunished, schools that do not teach, and middle-class condescension to the poor. Politically, the positions are inconsistent and at times incoherent; Dickens was not a political thinker but a critic and satirist of language. What unites these disparate targets is his animus against fraudulent, pretentious, or manipulative speech, fueled by his readiness to feel himself deceived and betrayed.

At the age of nineteen or twenty, Dickens became a Parliamentary re-porter, doing shorthand transcription from the galleries of the old Houses of Parliament during the stimulating years of the 1832 Reform Bill. Despite his admiration for certain speakers, Dickens left that job with a fund of hostility to government institutions that lasted a lifetime. Every Dickens reader learns to expect nothing but satire on the "circumlocution" subject; as Forster so tactfully puts it, "of the Pickwickian sense which so often takes the place of common sense in our legislature, he omitted no opportunity of declaring his contempt at every part of his life" (Forster 64). The contempt may have sprung in part from what Forster calls his intolerance for "suspense of any kind... The interval between the accomplishment of anything, and 'its first motion,' Dickens never could endure, and he was too ready to make any sac-rifice to abridge or end it" (87). The conviction that Parliament generated nothing but obfuscating oratory may also have arisen from Dickens's actual task of translating speeches, as fast as they were made, into the shorthand language of squiggles and dashes—a kind of parodic enterprise in itself. Whatever its sources, Dickens's sense of outrage was consistently fed by any discernible gap between language and feeling or intention, the more so, perhaps, because he sensed that gap in himself.

Even his blatant and unashamed racism is inflected by this special concern with the misuse of language. In "The Noble Savage," which appeared in a June 1853 issue of *Household Words*, Dickens gets right to the point, describing the savage as "cruel, false, thievish, murderous; addicted more or less to grease, entrails, and beastly customs; a wild animal with the questionable gift of boasting; a conceited, tiresome, bloodthirsty, monotonous humbug" (Dent 3.143). "Boastful" savages and whites who believe them, or who invoke the romantic ideal of the Noble Savage, are called to account for false verbal representations; both the con artists and the conned figure in Dickens's no-holds-barred prose as humbugs who must be found out.

In "The Lost Arctic Voyagers" of December 1854, Dickens was deeply exercised by a report written by Dr. Rae suggesting that the lost crew of Sir John Franklin's 1845 polar exploration had resorted to cannibalism in their last throes of starvation. His arguments against this possibility include a good deal of attention to distorted interpretations of the hearsay evidence offered by the "Esquimaux" who had talked to Dr. Rae. He reaches finally for the suggestion that the Inuit were themselves the killers of the expedition crew: "It is impossible to form an estimate of the character of any race of savages, from their deferential behaviour to the white man when he is strong. The mistake has been made again and again; and the moment the white man has appeared in the new aspect of being weaker than the savage, the savage has changed and sprung upon him" (Dent 3.260). The familiar pattern reappears, now projected onto a racialized landscape: if you allow yourself to trust another's self-representation, you will be ambushed and betrayed.

Officials guilty of what Dickens calls "a preposterous encouraging and rewarding of prison hypocrisy" (Dent 3.403) repeatedly receive the same treatment for believing falsely penitent speech or writing designed by the criminal to fit the specifications of prison reformers. Against all perpetrators and dupes of deceptive language, Dickens brings on his homeopathic weaponry: rhetoric vs. rhetoric, his credibility against the credibility—or credulity—of his targets. The linguistic world he creates is a world of rhetorical performances on high horses vying to claim the high ground of credibility. Although we are tossed from one language zone to another, Dickens does not run a postmodern language circus that exposes the disconnection of all language from the identity of its speaker. The competition for credibility matters intensely. If it did not, the language would not be generated at all.

🐿 Parody and Knowingness

Pompous, hypocritical, and delusional language flourishes in a line of Dickens's comic and not-so-comic figures, stretching from Mr. Pickwick to Mr. Dorrit. Such characters encase themselves in language as if their lives depended on it—and their lives do depend on it. As Dickens unfolds their rhetoric, he emphasizes both its parodic nature and its social and psychological power to silence its audiences. Through these exaggerated fictional talkers, Dickens suggests his capacity to know with one part of his mind the rhetorical defenses he mounts in his own dealings with others.

In the first action of *The Pickwick Papers*, rhetoric is punctured. Mr. Pickwick, holding forth to his club in the pride (and conventional humility) of his authorship, begins to wax hyperbolic, imagining the heroism of travel when coaches are upset, boats overturn, and boilers burst everywhere. A single "No" from his audience turns Pickwick suddenly hostile; he accuses the speaker of jealous rivalry. The naysayer calls Pickwick a humbug. The rest of the scene is a hasty cover-up operation, in which the insult is defanged by the absurd concession that "he had merely considered him a humbug in a Pickwickian point of view" (*PP* 1). But the speech is waylaid forever. Dickens's debut as a fictionist stages a kind of primal scene: language takes off on its own course; it is seen through and deflated; the speaker attacks the deflator, revealing his sensitivity to opposition; harmony is declared with no admissions on either side.

After establishing self-protective rhetoric at the center of his fictional world, Dickens introduces the con artist Jingle, whose fractured sentences call special attention to the phenomenon of language on the loose. Like his creator, Jingle can produce shorthand comic parody in any genre: he bounces from strings of old saws to lower-class slang to a heartless tale about a mother who loses her head going through an archway: "children look round— mother's head off—sandwich in her hand—no mouth to put it in—head of a family off—shocking, shocking." Hearing of Mr. Snodgrass's love of poetry, Jingle invents a turn as a warrior poet: "Epic poem—ten thousand lines—revolution of July—composed it on the spot—Mars by day, Apollo by night—bang the field-piece, twang the lyre." By the time he reaches his soliloquy on Gothic ruins, he is running to seamy anti-Catholicism: "Old cathedral too—earthy smell—pilgrims feet worn away the old steps—little

Saxon doors—confessionals like money-takers' boxes at theatres—queer customers those monks"—and so forth (*PP* 2). After five pages of this, each Pickwickian has found an image of his own obsession in one part of Jingle's repertoire, and his credibility is established—for a few chapters, until the imposter is unmasked, banished, and replaced by his worthy and benevolently knowing double, Sam Weller.

The comedy depends not only on the reader's recognition of Jingle's parodic shorthand, but also on the spectacle of a con man who goes unrecognized by his fictional audience. Jingle brings onstage the other side of Pickwick's self-protective rhetoric: language as inventive aggression. Pickwick seals himself off from the world's horror and insult through his polite abstractions (and through his capacity to fall asleep in the face of unpleasantness); Jingle slides into languages with the virtuosity of the bit-part actor who sings for his supper. Both figures recognize aspects of Dickens himself: the aggressive potential of his freewheeling parodic gift as well as his vulnerable dependence on his audience's willingness to suspend their disbelief. As Dickens developed his line of talkers, the two aspects gradually merged into a single syndrome, retaining and deepening the focus on the necessary collusion between duper and duped that troubles Dickens's letters and journalism.

Entering the Dickens world as a reader entails becoming witness to innumerable con games—a fact so obvious that it goes unmentioned in a good deal of commentary. Characters "work" other characters through parodies of sentiment that extract information or collusion; characters who represent themselves as knowing or possessing information pull in innocent characters who believe in their knowingness and yearn to participate in it; characters with designs appeal to the pretensions of characters who are desperate to be seen as upwardly mobile and in the know. Dickens takes immense pleasure in detailing the strategies of these miniature plots, and for the most part he allows readers to participate in that pleasure by showing us exactly how it's done, or at least by allowing us to be more knowing than the characters who are being duped before our eyes.

Criticism focused on plot tends to emphasize the melodramatic morality of such transactions, but Dickens is clear from the beginning that it's not just a matter of good (and boring) innocents versus bad (and interesting) schemers. The innocent are curiously deaf to the linguistic strategies of the schemers, and their lack—or suppression—of suspicion is often self-serving. For Dickens knowingness is at once corrupt and essential to survival; the tension between the two is rarely resolved in his art. He gets his readers to participate in the tension by allowing us to smile at the dupers at work while our hearts beat—and our impatience rises—for the duped and the entrapped. Readers are occasionally duped, of course, by the big secrets and withholdings of the overarching plot. But it's the little plots, the ones created by the characters, that display the everyday fabric of Dickens's imagination. He demands of virtue a kind of innocence, yet he dramatizes a world in which one can't be suspicious enough; his most virtuous characters often manage to appear innocent while disguising their knowingness as something else. In the last 200 pages of many a Dickens novel the innocents are finally clued in, connected, and ready to do battle fueled by the force of their indignation. How do the virtuous take charge? They become pretenders and schemers.

The coinage of this realm is parodic language. Theorists of parody tend to focus on literary parody, the way that one text incorporates the structure or language of an earlier text so as to mock or ridicule it, or to mock itself by displaying the difference between an earlier ethos and a contemporary decline. Dickens drew heavily on plots and conventions of melodrama and sentiment from the Elizabethan stage through the eighteenth-century novels that he loved, sometimes apparently straight and sometimes in parodic forms. His linguistic parody reaches, however, for every kind of language, not just the literary but every domestic and political piety, every dialect, of his pre-Victorian and Victorian worlds. His point is not a literary one; it is always the way high language conceals low feeling. The lowness may be calculating manipulation or merely an absurd application of inflated language to mundane circumstances. Both Dickens's narrators and his language villains exercise this art of parody. Is there a difference between them?

It is a difficult question. Bakhtin's "Discourse in the Novel" offers the most fluid description of this "comic-parodic re-processing" of language in the comic novel, whose English practitioners Bakhtin identifies as Fielding, Smollett, Sterne, Dickens, and Thackeray. The style of such novels, in Bakhtin's view, is the "usually parodic stylization of generic, professional and other strata of language," along with a more-or-less distanced use of what he calls the "common language," or the "*going point of view*" in the society depicted. The constant, sentence-by-sentence variations in the narrative perspective represent the author's movement in relation to the common language: sometimes he exaggerates one or another aspect of it to expose its inadequacy; sometimes he merges with it, "sometimes even directly forcing it to reverberate with his own 'truth'. . . The comic style demands of the author a lively to-and-fro movement in his relation to language, it demands a continual shifting of the distance between the author and language, so that first some, then other aspects of the language are thrown into relief." Along with the comic-parodic style, Bakhtin notices as well sections of "direct authorial discourse—pathos-filled, moral-didactic, sentimental-elegiac or idyllic"

(Bakhtin 301–2). These descriptions name recognizable sentimental interludes that Dickens apparently wants his readers to believe, while the model of linguistic flux, moving among parody, representations of the common language, and direct authorial discourse, captures something essential about what reading Dickens is like. But Bakhtin does not address the question of what motivates this kind of narrative, nor does he in this context consider the relation between narrative discourse and characters' speech.

When it comes to the motives for parody, Freud's brief remarks in *Jokes and Their Relation to the Unconscious* can be useful. As he puts it, "Caricature, parody and travesty (as well as their practical counterpart, unmasking) are directed against people and objects which lay claim to authority and respect, which are in some sense '*sublime*' [exalted] . . . *Parody* and *travesty* achieve the degradation of something exalted . . . by destroying the unity that exists between people's characters as we know them and their speeches and actions." As for *unmasking*, Freud's definition is particularly suggestive: it "only applies where someone has seized dignity and authority by a deception and these have to be taken from him in reality" (Freud 200–201). Although Freud's emphasis on the degradation of the apparently exalted fails to encompass the range of affects—including sheer fun or affection—that can reside in parody, his notion that parody drives a wedge between a "known" person and his speech or actions is quite resonant in Dickens's case. Dickens's invariable targets are characters that demand respect or homage by insisting that others know their virtues through their self-representations. Freud's definition also suggests a kind of Oedipal struggle in the impulse to parody, which speaks directly to the link between Dickens's parody and the rhetorical excesses of John Dickens.

Dickens's own authorial earnestness (an attitude toward experience that he claimed to prize) veers dangerously close to the borders of parody, because we are always aware that some form of rhetoric is being exercised on our behalf. His tendency to parody at one moment what he asks us to take seriously a few pages later has been repeatedly noticed, but no one has been able to decide exactly what it means. Is it unintentional self-parody? Conscious ambiguity? Self-knowledge, or self-critique? Is it a defensive flight from emotional investment, or a self-protective ironic shield against critical attack? Is it Dickens's comedic instinct revenging itself on his Victorian piety? Is it simply that Dickens believed in whatever he wrote at the moment? The way a critic formulates the issue generally reveals some unacknowledged attitude toward the unconscious and its manifestations in art: perhaps a desire to assume that a writer controls all the colors in his palette; perhaps a slightly hostile embarrassment in the face of the unintentional; perhaps a glee in unmasking the dynamics of self-deception. No doubt on the face of it most people concede that art cannot be made without a mysterious interplay between conscious and unconscious energies—and Dickens, always fascinated by the unconscious mind, would have been the first to agree. What to make of the specifics is another, more difficult matter.

Consider two early examples. In *Oliver Twist*, Fagin parodies middle-class pieties of affection and domesticity, the prostitute Nancy dresses up as a frantic housewife and parodies sentimental distress to get Oliver back, while the Dodger and Charley Bates parody the ideology of work in their attempt to convince Oliver to get with the thieves' program. Meanwhile Dickens lays on the sentimental and the praise of domestic discipline in the portion of the novel where the good middle-class characters reside. In *Nicholas Nickleby* the narrator makes fun of a Parliamentary petition proposed by the United Metropolitan Improved Hot Muffin and Crumpet Baking and Punctual Delivery Company. The petition calls for eliminating the company's competition by outlawing all muffin and crumpet sellers; "a grievous gentleman" supports this motion by waxing eloquent about "the cruelties inflicted on muffin boys by their masters," which he evokes in pathetic detail (*NN* 2). A few chapters on, the barbarous treatment of boys at Dotheboys Hall becomes the serious (though still comically inflected) preoccupation of the text. In both novels, of course, the "bad" characters parody sentiment or moral cant in order to work on the susceptibilities of their dupes and gain their self-serving ends, while the narrator relies on the same kind of language in order to move his audience toward moral indignation or approval. The intention is all; the method is the same.

What do such unacknowledged juxtapositions tell us? Dickens's central subject was the use and misuse of language; he demonstrates everywhere the problematic clash between the two. The knowingness inherent in parody and self-parody is, however, a special kind of knowledge. Parody says, "I simultaneously rely on and ridicule this language"; it represents a bearable self-knowledge, an acknowledgment that is also a disavowal, distanced and controlled by comedy. It is self-recognition projected outwards, a way of knowing and not knowing at the same time. Dickens's narrators and his language villains are alike in that they both ride on other peoples' languages in order both to achieve and to disavow their ambition to persuade others of their good intentions. Dickens recognizes and celebrates an aspect of himself in writing Fagin, as he knowingly calculates the effect on his readers of his own sentimental appeals.

Dickens's interest in the relation between parodic imitation and self-knowledge was evident as he prepared to publish his great book of hypocrites and self-deluders, *Martin Chuzzlewit*. In his preface to the 1844 edition, he cleverly attacked readers who resisted the portrait of Pecksniff: "as no man ever yet recognized an imitation of himself, no man will admit the correctness of a sketch in which his own character is delineated, however faithfully." "But," he continues, "although Mr Pecksniff will by no means concede to me, that Mr Pecksniff is natural; I am consoled by finding him keenly susceptible of the truthfulness of Mrs Gamp." Humankind cannot bear very much self-knowledge, he suggests, but we might delight in a displaced version of follies we are not likely to see in ourselves. Dickens is pointedly addressing himself to his readers here, daring and defying them to criticize his portraiture as exaggeration. Nevertheless the question of self-knowledge is at the center of his concern, as it is throughout the novel. Does Dickens know himself in Pecksniff? Yes, the way he imagines that "the real" Pecksniff recognizes the truth in Mrs. Gamp's flights of delusory but self-revealing language. What Dickens certainly knows is that people project their weaknesses onto their pictures of others, and that they disavow the parts of themselves they do not want to acknowledge.

Dickens is less concerned to unmask the hypocrite Pecksniff than to dramatize his power to endure. With the exception of Tom Pinch, most of the other characters can see through him from the beginning, and the narrator makes very sure that the reader is not taken in by inserting character critiques reported as the opinions of Pecksniff's enemies. The so-called unmasking performed by Old Martin Chuzzlewit at the end of the novel reveals nothing except that Old Martin has had to disguise his motives and play the hypocrite himself in order to get enough hard evidence to humiliate Pecksniff in public. The time and energy Martin expends on this project is itself a testimony to the power of language on the loose.

In an early scene old Anthony Chuzzlewit deflates Pecksniff's pieties in public, calling Pecksniff a hypocrite. Pecksniff has his forgiveness charade at the ready; he piously asks his daughter Charity to "remind me to be more than usually particular in praying for Mr Anthony Chuzzlewit; who has done me an injustice" (*MC* 4). When the two meet again, Anthony analyzes the difference between Pecksniff and other hypocrites, including himself: "you would deceive everybody, even those who practice the same art; and have a way with you, as if you—he, he, he!—as if you really believed yourself" (*MC* 8). The repetition of the "as if," punctuated by Anthony's laughter, points to the question Dickens raises about Pecksniff: does he believe himself? If so, is he a hypocrite or someone who takes himself in through his own powers of rhetoric and impersonation?

Dickens's most direct treatment of this question resides in his paragraph on Dick Swiveller's bed, in *The Old Curiosity Shop*. Dick's bedstead (one of many turn-up bedsteads in Dickens) looks like a bookcase by day, when it "seemed to defy suspicion and challenge inquiry. There is no doubt that by day Mr Swiveller firmly believed this secret convenience to be a bookcase and nothing more; that he closed his eyes to the bed, resolutely denied the existence of the blankets, and spurned the bolster from his thoughts." No one is allowed to allude to the real purpose of this piece of furniture: "To be the friend of Swiveller you must reject all circumstantial evidence, all reason, observation, and experience, and repose a blind belief in the bookcase. It was his pet weakness and he cherished it" (OCS 7). Swiveller both knows and refuses to know that the bookcase is a bed. The fact cannot be mentioned in his presence; his "pet weakness"—Dickens does know how people cherish their delusions—demands a colluding silence from his friends. If we take the bed out of Swiveller's room and put in into Pecksniff's head, the situation is similar, though the analysis is more probing and far less benign.

Pecksniff does not want to know that he is a designing character who entraps young men to pay fees for an architect's apprenticeship that will benefit only himself, so he drapes himself in the language of moral contemplation and sentiment. He arranges himself and his daughters in apparently artless, unconscious displays of innocent work when visitors are expected. He enforces on his daughters a collusion of silence which teaches them to read his meaning through his rhetoric: when he makes statements like "We are not all arrayed in two opposite ranks: the *offensive* and the *defensive*" or "let us not be for ever calculating, devising, and plotting for the future" the daughters take heart, knowing that he has been active in what he disavows (MC 2). When he is angry and vengeful, he professes—like young Dickens in his letters to Maria Beadnell—to be wounded but forgiving. When he wants to arrange a match between Charity and Jonas Chuzzlewit, he pretends to be innocent of Jonas's desires, until Anthony foils him "in the exercise of his familiar weapons" by appropriating and parodying his sentimental rhetoric: "You have never thought of this for a moment; and in a point so nearly affecting the happiness of your dear child, you couldn't, as a tender father, express an opinion; and so forth." Anthony disarms Pecksniff by stating the fact and insisting "that we do see it, and do know it" (MC 11). Less cynical characters learn that their only defense against Pecksniff's arsenal is to get as far away from him as possible. Even the narrator pretends to collude in the conspiracy of silence by never quite mentioning outright that Pecksniff is a drunk and a lecher. The problem does not lie in knowing what Pecksniff is up to, but in the difficulty others have in negotiating with a figure who systematically refuses to recognize or admit anything about himself. Such characters are common in Dickens, and they go on being themselves no matter what humiliations come their way.

Pecksniff's investment in denying that his view of the world is "offensive and defensive" also raises a question of motive. Unlike his fellow imposter Montague Tigg, he does not have to scrounge for shillings; unlike Mrs. Gamp he is not a working-class woman who recommends her imaginary respectability through an imaginary friend. Except for the architect's fees and his scramble for old Martin Chuzzlewit's money, Pecksniff's verbal machinations are gratuitous, rather like Bounderby's in *Hard Times*. Why is it necessary for Bounderby to declare repeatedly that he was born in a ditch and kept in an eggbox? He could be an equally rich and nasty employer without that myth of origin. Such portraits attest to Dickens's interest in the very fine line between the old vice, hypocrisy, and what we might now call narcissistic strategies of self-defense—strategies intimately known to Dickens, that emerged from his creative mind in the form of self-parodic exaggeration. Pecksniff parodies the language of sentiment and Bounderby attempts to literalize the story of the self-made man; both roles are familiar parts of Dickens's repertoire. More important, he knows that his characters need their offensive and defensive delusions in order to exist. Though their stories are exposed, they are incapable of change; once punctured, their balloons of hot air just fill up again.

❧ Talking Fathers

Dickens invented plenty of other figures who solicit power through exaggerated linguistic parody: for example, the hilarious romantic sentimentality of Mr. Mantalini in *Nicholas Nickleby* keeps his wife on the string despite his caddish behavior, while the absurdly unctuous religiosity of Mr. Chadband in *Bleak House* paralyzes everyone who is forced to listen. The more excoriating line of talkers can be traced from Mr. Micawber in *David Copperfield* through Harold Skimpole in *Bleak House*, and finally to Mr. Dorrit in *Little Dorrit*. These major studies are especially personal for Dickens because they raise questions of knowledge and self-knowledge that arise from the blurring of lines between himself and John Dickens. In revealing the fraudulence of the parental rhetoric, the son exposes the father, but he is able to do so only because he inherits precisely the gift for language he wants to expose. With the entrance of Mr. Micawber, long recognized as a partial portrait of John Dickens, the link between rhetorical excess and the extortion of money from others also comes into focus as a prominent aspect of the talker's power to control his audience.

Micawber himself is guilty of nothing more than getting his friends' signatures on Bills of Exchange (promises to pay) that he then sells to bill discounters in the money market. (Dickens was all too familiar with his father's propensity to use or forge his famous son's name as a security on bills without informing him.) This character does not lie about himself; on the contrary he is all too willing to launch into elaborate circumlocutions about his "pecuniary difficulties" at any opportunity. For Micawber, language is a substitute for action as well as a defense against it; if he talks, he imagines he's doing something about his family's poverty. His grandiose Latinate diction and his many literary allusions are meant to guarantee his gentility, much like the "imposing shirt-collar" that adorns his shabby dress (*DC* 11). The language allows him to feel he is conferring hospitality on those whose money he takes; like the IOUs he writes up for creditors as small as the ten-year-old David, the word is in effect the deed. Yet from the beginning he is given the endearing quality of puncturing his own rhetoric—"in short," of saying exactly what he means.

In the early childhood scenes the Micawbers are entwined with Dickens's autobiographical memories of his father's weeks in the Marshalsea. They are part portraits and part wishful versions of his parents, washed clean of responsibility for putting the child into the blacking warehouse. When they leave the child they have confided in as a fellow-adult, Dickens gives himself what he thought his parents did not, a scene in which the Micawbers pay full attention to David's talents and virtues, and—David fancies—Mrs. Micawber realizes "what a little creature I really was" (*DC* 12). Once the Micawbers turn up again—and again—in the text, Dickens deepens his analysis of the *folie à deux* of their marriage and shows how each partner produces delusional rhetoric in their shared anxiety about Mr. Micawber's employment prospects. Mrs. Micawber is hardly reducible to the mantra—"I will never desert Mr Micawber"—with which she has been fixed. She stokes the fantastical fires by extolling her mate's talents, blaming her family and the world for ignoring them, and envisioning him famous and exalted the moment there is the whiff of a job in the air. If her husband knows better, as Dickens sometimes hints, he is too caught up in his own forms of rhetorical excess to do anything but play the marital game.

His part is to veer wildly between melodramatic assertions of failure and the garrulous good cheer that turns up with the appearance of good food or drink. The great comedy of Micawber lies in these instant mood shifts, especially in Dickens's renditions of Micawber in rhetorical despair. He is always on the verge of the grave, whether it's death by shaving razor or other means. "The die is cast—all is over. Hiding the ravages of care with a sickly mask of mirth, I have not informed you, this evening, that there is no hope of the remittance! Under these circumstances, alike humiliating to endure, humiliating to contemplate, and humiliating to relate...": so begins a letter which envisions destruction and death as the only solution to an unpaid hotel bill (*DC* 17). Having the water shut off because of another unpaid bill is "the momentary laceration of a wounded spirit, made sensitive by a recent collision with the Minion of Power" (*DC* 28). A new baby, looked on with favor on one page, soon becomes "one more helpless victim; whose miserable appearance may be looked for—in round numbers—at the expiration of a period not exceeding six lunar months from the present date" (*DC* 28). When he is genuinely upset by the machinations of Uriah Heep, Micawber entreats his friends to leave him "to walk the earth as a vagabond. The worms will settle *my* business in double-quick time" (*DC* 49). Nothing cheers Micawber more than indulging in the direst formulations of distress; humiliation disappears in the power of the exaggerated word.

The guarantee of Micawber's essential decency is the moment when his smooth command of syntax breaks down. After much mysterious ranting to his friends, he finally blurts out his knowledge of his employer Uriah Heep's lies, cheats, and forgeries. The phrases come in little unconnected bursts, punctuated by the explosive syllable of Heep's name: "'I'll put my hand in no man's hand,' said Mr Micawber, gasping, puffing, and sobbing, to that degree that he was like a man fighting with cold water, 'until I have—blown to fragments—the—a—detestable—serpent—HEEP! I'll partake of no one's hospitality, until I have—a—moved Mount Vesuvius—to eruption—on—a—the abandoned rascal—HEEP!'"(*DC* 49). The moment signals that Micawber is on the side of the angels—that is, he has become a secret investigator who will unmask the villain in public when he next comes onstage. It is a measure of the book's generosity that Micawber is allowed to be the unmasker rather than the unmasked, and that his momentarily disrupted syntax is caused by long-repressed feelings of outraged honesty. No sooner has this occurred than a letter arrives, with syntactical powers fully restored. Once again, Micawber is headed directly for the grave.

In a novel packed with different forms of autobiographical writing, the alternation between Micawber's speech making and his letter writing displays his self-representation in a constant process of oscillation between its two extremes, as if speech and writing were engaged in separate kinds of rhetorical appeal and did not know each other. The comedic disconnect seems to "know" about Dickens's own methods of relying in one moment on language he parodies in another. Interestingly, the narrative relation to Micawber falters just when Micawber's speech and writing come together, in his triumphant performance of the letter denouncing Uriah Heep. Suddenly the narrative positions itself at a distance; David comments, "Mr Micawber's enjoyment of his epistolary powers, in describing this unfortunate state of things, really seemed to outweigh any pain or anxiety that the reality could have caused him." Just when he is vindicating Micawber's character, the narrator feels it necessary to spell out what he has dramatized without comment throughout the novel. Micawber is soon associated with one of Dickens's pet peeves: "He read this passage, as if it were from an Act of Parliament, and appeared majestically refreshed by the sound of the words." Then the monitory tone extends itself out of the novel altogether; suddenly Dickens is lecturing the whole nation on its "relish in this formal piling up of words" valued more for the sense of grandeur they impart than for their meaning (*DC* 52). What has happened?

The glitch in the novel's tone suggests Dickens's sudden discomfort with his own pleasure in writing Micawber's linguistic extravaganzas. Reinventing the father meant becoming the father, and Dickens had done so with enormous relish. When he turns to vaguely disapproving generalizations about wordiness and pretense he covers over his more intimate analysis of Micawber, and of himself: the way language stands in for action; the way melodramatic fantasies serve to derail the self and others from focusing on the mundane facts at hand; the way language functions as a pain-reducing drug. Probably such insights fell too close to home; some disavowal of his investment in the figure was necessary. Although Micawber is finally allowed to flourish as a journalist in Australia, Dickens had first to send him to the ends of the earth, exporting him as if he were a convict or a fallen woman.

After the death of John Dickens in 1851, Dickens returned to the fray with a more punitive rendition of the feckless talker. The case of Harold Skimpole in *Bleak House* was complicated by the character's resemblance to Dickens's literary colleague, the poet and essayist Leigh Hunt. Just as Dickens had predicted in the preface to *Martin Chuzzlewit*, the portrait was quickly recognized by everyone except Hunt himself. Once Hunt's friends had clued him in, Dickens was forced to squirm through several embarrassing attempts to convince Hunt that he had borrowed only the delightful aspects of his character and invented the rest. He knew that was not the case; in September 1853 he had boasted in confidence to Lavinia Watson that Skimpole "is the most exact portrait that was ever painted in words!... the likeness is astonishing... It is an absolute reproduction of a real man." His guilt came through as well: "It is so awfully true, that I make a bargain with myself 'never to do so, any more'" (7.154).

Even as he was writing Skimpole, Dickens knew he was doing harm. He was pleased that his illustrator Hablot Browne had drawn Skimpole as a rounded figure, "and helped to make him singularly unlike the great original" (6.623). (Hunt was tall, slender and striking, as the name Skimpole might suggest). He also asked Forster to oversee changes that would make the character "much less like . . . I have no right to give Hunt pain, and I am so bent on not doing it that I wish you would look at all the proof once more, and indicate any particular place in which you feel it particularly like. Whereupon I will alter that place" (6.628). Although Forster did so, the essentials remained; Dickens's unconscious was bent more powerfully than his will on the need to pillory Leigh Hunt. Why?

The answer lies in the course of Dickens's relationship with Hunt, which echoed the relation with his father. Dickens met Hunt through John Forster in 1838, when he was twenty-six and Hunt fifty-four—probably just a year or two older than John Dickens. The original attraction was a sentimental one: Dickens was moved by hearing of a comment Hunt made about the inscription Dickens had placed on the grave of his beloved sister-in-law Mary Hogarth, and asked Forster to relay his deep gratitude (1.340–41). For a few years Dickens seems to have been one among the young literary men that Hunt collected around him. In at least one surviving letter to Hunt we see Dickens busily sucking up, waxing eloquent in a lively Hunt manner about a poem the older man had sent him (2.66–67). In another 1840 note Dickens feels intimate enough to tease Hunt about "the faintest smack of wine running through" his oral delivery at a party the previous night (2.99). In June 1847, when Hunt was ill and in financial need, Dickens proposed a series of dramatic performances to benefit him, writing that "Leigh Hunt has done more to instruct the young men of England, and to lend a helping hand to those who educated themselves, than any writer in England" (5.88). The emphasis on help to the self-educated suggests that Hunt had briefly played a role that John Dickens had neglected.

By this time, however, Dickens had already distanced himself from the Hunt who resembled John Dickens. By 1842 Hunt had asked for and received a loan, which Dickens begged him to forget. The occasional notes remain cordial but suggest impatience with Hunt's inability to do something as simple as make a firm dinner date. Not long after Hunt had received a government pension in 1847, making the benefit performances unnecessary, he found himself once again "in difficulties," and asked Dickens whether he might revive the performances on his behalf. Dickens refused, though he added a little box at the top of the letter, enclosing his sense of guilt: "If I could think of the 'KINDEST' WORD in the language, I'd put it here, to begin with" (5.447). Kindness was one of Hunt's watchwords. Improvidence was, of course, one of Dickens's greatest fears.

Dickens's inward association of Leigh Hunt with John Dickens made its way into the note Dickens wrote to calm down Hunt's distress about Skimpole. It is an uncomfortable performance, in which Dickens apologizes for giving Hunt pain and tries to dissociate him from the fictional character even as he admits that Hunt was his model. He ends, "The character is not you, for there are traits in it common to fifty thousand people besides, and I did not fancy you would ever recognize it. Under similar disguises my own father and mother are in my books, and you might as well see your likeness in Micawber" (7.460). As in the writing of Skimpole, Dickens is driven to tell his feelings in spite of himself. Somewhere in the life of his psyche, Hunt might as well have been his father.

After Hunt's death in 1859, memories of the Skimpole-Hunt connection began to circulate in the press. Hunt's eldest son Thornton requested that Dickens publish some comment in *All the Year Round* that might quell the revived rumors. Dickens graciously complied, telling Thornton through Forster that he would say what he had earlier said to Leigh Hunt: "that there are many remembrances of Hunt in little traits of manner and expression, in that character and especially in all the pleasantest parts of it, but that is all" (9.141). On Christmas Eve 1859, Dickens published "Leigh Hunt: A Remonstrance," in which he chides newspapers for reviving the "false" notion that Leigh Hunt was the original of Harold Skimpole. His method in the piece offers further evidence of the familial connection in his imagination: much of the article consists of quotations from Thornton Hunt's introduction to a new edition of his father's autobiography. Dickens gets much of his work done by corroborating the son's words of praise about the father; this section fills about two-thirds of the article.

Turning finally to his own responsibility for the Skimpole connection, Dickens, writing in the third person, admits that he had "yielded to the temptation of too often making the character *speak* like his old friend." Then he has a happy thought: "He no more thought, God forgive him! that the admired original would ever be charged with the imaginary vices of the fictitious creature, than he has ever thought of charging the blood of Desdemona and Othello, on the innocent Academy model who sat for Iago's leg in the picture" (Dent 4.18). It is others, it seems, who are guilty of suspicion, not this innocent author. Dickens concludes the article with a turn to the sentimental: "He cannot see the son lay this wreath on the father's tomb, and leave him to the possibility of ever thinking that the present words might have righted the father's memory and were left unwritten. He cannot know that his own son may have to explain his father when folly or malice can wound the heart no more, and leave this task undone" (18–19). Recently fallen from the respectability of his bourgeois marriage, full of his own need to be "righted" in his abandonment of Catherine, Dickens now reads Hunt, father and son, through the lenses of his own life, his own father, and his own son.

Skimpole is Dickens's most profound and terrifying portrait of a dissociated character. Esther comments that he speaks of himself as if he were describing another person; he boasts of himself as a lover of beauty, nature, and universal harmony who knows nothing of money, nothing of business, nothing of practicality, responsibility, or principle. In his professed view, the universe exists in order to give him pleasure, and he manages to imply that those who are occupied with responsibility, enterprise, and effort are delightful to contemplate and exist to exercise his sensibility and admiration. Slaves on an American plantation, for instance: "I dare say theirs is an unpleasant experience on the whole; but, they people the landscape for me, they give it a poetry for me, and perhaps that is one of the pleasanter objects of their existence" (*BH* 18). As for those whose generosity keeps him afloat, he is, in his own view, their benefactor: "I almost feel as if *you* ought to be grateful to *me*, for giving you the opportunity of enjoying the luxury of generosity" (*BH* 6). His response to chronic indebtedness is simply to deny that he can have anything to do with payment; instead he makes up entertaining stories about his dialogues with creditors who persist in misunderstanding his nature.

Dickens attacks the sinister aspects of Skimpole's "philosophy" through his ruthlessness to real children, who threaten to steal his thunder and others' charitable attentions. The orphaned children of the debt-collector Neckett of Coavinses give rise to his fantasy that "he had been giving employment to a most deserving man; that he had been a benefactor to Coavinses; that he had actually been enabling Coavinses to bring up these charming children in this agreeable way, developing these social virtues!" (*BH* 15). When Jo turns up at Bleak House with smallpox Skimpole advises Jarndyce to turn him out immediately. Jo, he argues, should turn criminal and get himself taken care of in prison: society owes him a spoon and he should insist on getting it. Skimpole, who thinks the world owes *him* a living, is perfectly willing to sacrifice a child who threatens his health; later that night he accepts a bribe from Inspector Bucket, tells him where Jo is hidden, and lies about Jo's departure to his benefactors. Meanwhile, he amuses himself by inventing a sad song about an abandoned orphan.

Insisting on this "childlike" version of his character in every scene, Skimpole becomes virtually unassailable by others. Every unwelcome part of himself is cannily projected onto someone else. When Esther and Richard keep him out of jail by paying his debts, Esther remarks, "Richard and I seemed to retain the transferred impression of having been arrested since dinner" (*BH* 6). The "enchantment" he spreads—at least in his early appearances—makes Esther feel that it is she, not Skimpole, who is worldly and designing. By such means Skimpole manages to abuse those who help him; there are serpents lurking in his "light and airy" pastoral monologues. The morning after being bailed out by Richard and Esther, he attacks the busy productivity of bees and praises the idle Drone, who will be fed by the labor of the bees. All will be well, he suggests, "always supposing the Drone to be willing to be on good terms with the Bee: which so far as he knew, the easy fellow always was, if the consequential creature would only let him, and not be so conceited about his honey!" The choice is his, whether to grace his self-satisfied hard-working friends with his dependency. His actual shrewdness, along with his hostile resentment of his benefactor, is neatly expressed in the observation that no Manchester manufacturer would allow his product to be taken from him, as bees do—and as Jarndyce does when he pays for Skimpole (*BH* 8).

The emphasis in *Bleak House* returns to the con game, and to the ways that Skimpole's friends try not to know that they are being manipulated by the apparent innocence of his discourse. Even before we meet Skimpole we meet Jarndyce's defense against his own suspicion: Skimpole is presented as a grown-up child "in simplicity, and freshness, and enthusiasm, and a fine guileless inaptitude for all worldly affairs" (*BH* 6). He protects Skimpole, while the young characters protect Jarndyce from his unacknowledged knowledge that Skimpole is a very clever con man. When Jarndyce gets worried, they assure him that Skimpole is only a child. The silliness of his relief at such junctures is not simply comic at his expense; Dickens successfully suggests that it is sometimes difficult to distinguish between true incapacity and a con game. Nevertheless Skimpole damns himself as a self-regarding leech whenever he opens his mouth, and Jarndyce's deafness is complicit to a dangerous degree—as it later appears when Skimpole systematically bleeds the dying Richard of his ever-waning funds.

Because Skimpole is presented through Esther's narrative, we get a mediated view of Jarndyce's culpability. When it comes to Skimpole, Esther is a strong guide who can think like a Dickens narrator; from the start she records her "confusion" at Skimpole's "contradictions" and "inconsistencies"; as the novel proceeds she moves to outright suspicion and finally to stern rebuke. Esther ventures to point out Jarndyce's yearning "to find one perfectly undesigning and candid man . . . I should be sorry to imply that Mr Skimpole divined this and was politic: I really never understood him well enough to know" (*BH* 15). That is what makes Skimpole a scary character. Exactly because his apparently honest self-description is his rhetorical weapon, he defies knowing or understanding; Dickens offers no clue as to what he might feel or need to protect. His speeches are so audacious as to be simply unanswerable; arguing with him is useless because there is nothing in him that responds to any appeal. Not unlike Dickens in his defensive mode, he cannot be in the wrong.

Dickens makes the heartless advocate of sympathy a thoroughly unsympathetic character, but he retains the capacity to trouble the mind. Skimpole's power to dissociate himself from his doings extends to his final scene, where he agrees not to visit Richard and Ada not because he is damaging to them, as Esther tells him, but because they are damaging to him: they now see him as someone who owes them money, and so cause him pain. Then, with a look of "disinterested benevolence" that Esther finds "quite astonishing" he further agrees to stay away so as not to be the cause of pain to them either (*BH* 61). Richard and Ada no longer have a half-penny to give him, but he finishes his fictional career persuading himself that he is not an accomplice in slow murder but an emotional protector. In the same fashion, he argues that he is "above" taking bribes, and that the bribe is "more blameable in Bucket—because he is the knowing man." Esther well knows that the only answer is to take her departure (*BH* 61). Skimpole is the apotheosis of Dickens's conflict between innocence and knowingness; in his character the proclamation of innocence becomes an agent of aggression. And Dickens makes it clear that Skimpole can get away with all of it, at anybody's expense.

When Mr. Dorrit appeared, Dickens touched for the first and last time on the quick of his own injuries. Dorrit is not one of Dickens's rhetorical stuntmen, so he may seem odd company in the sequence I have been tracing. But he gathers up strands that run throughout this history. His carefully polite speech is a mode of psychological survival during his undeserved twenty-five-year incarceration in the Marshalsea Prison; it nurtures and preserves his sense of continuing gentility. Dorrit's speech is strongly marked through the perfectly placed "hems," "ahems," and "ha's" that precede the utterance of his euphemisms. As he begins to beg from Arthur Clennam, he refers discreetly to the "Testimonials" that he extorts from others: "'Sometimes,' he went on in a low, soft voice, agitated, and clearing his throat every now and then; 'sometimes—hem—it takes one shape and sometimes another; but it is generally—ha—Money. And it is, I cannot but confess it, it is too often—hem—acceptable'" (*LD* 1.8). The shades of Micawber are audible, but where Micawber's interruptions are bursts of honesty within tracts of pompous circumlocution, Dorrit's suggest that the enunciation of each word is a painful stay against internal dissolution into shame or humiliation.

Dickens also gathers up the self-deluding egotism and the con-man effect from his earlier talkers, bringing them into an intimate realm of shared and unacknowledged shame that marks the pathology of Amy Dorrit's love for her father. Amy is offered the life-giving possibility of projecting an image of good fatherhood onto her beloved Arthur Clennam, but not before the reader experiences the damage her real father has done. Many critics have commented on the incestuous nature of this father-daughter bond, and on Amy's role as the nurturing mother of her father. What speaks most of incest in the connection, however, is Dickens's emphasis on the disavowed shame that creates the tightness of the bond in the first place. Observed by Arthur Clennam, Amy repeatedly insists that she feels no shame about her father; her insistence that he is "Such a good, good father!" (*LD* 1.9) draws no line at all between her own much-vaunted innocence and her neurotic denial. Her mind's methods rely on the third person as an internal antagonist: when she visits Clennam at midnight in inadequate shoes, the narrative situates itself somewhere between his mind and hers: "Little Dorrit had a misgiving that he might blame her father, if he saw [the shoes]; that he might think, 'why did he dine today and leave this little creature to the mercy of the cold stones!' She had no belief that it would have been a just reflection; she simply knew, by experience, that such delusions did sometimes present themselves to people. It was part of her father's misfortunes that they did." This treads a very thin line between knowing and not knowing, which Amy negotiates by feeling that her father truly belongs only to her. She imagines that she knows him better than anyone else does, yet "what he really is" is someone she could never have known: the person Dorrit believes himself to have been before his incarceration (*LD* 1.14).

In fact, she knows how bad he is. In the great scene between them (*LD* 1.19), her father attempts to manipulate her affections, making a devious attempt to get her to allow the affections of the turnkey's son John Chivery, and so to provide Dorrit with special favor from the prison authorities. In effect he desires to prostitute his daughter for the sake of his own comfort. As he speaks, Dickens writes, "he was opening and shutting his hands like valves; so conscious all the time of that touch of shame, that he shrunk before his own knowledge of his meaning." Amy responds only with a hand on his lips, and a "a dead silence and stillness." She will not put into words what they both know. And then, in the classic manner of the abused, she is punished for what she has heard by her father's protracted display of abject self-pity, which ropes her back into his service. During that display Amy has, for the first and only time in the novel, made a plea for herself: "Only think of me, father, for one little moment!" By the end of the scene, however, his methods have done their work, and Amy has taken on herself the role of the guilty party: "As if she had done him a wrong which her tenderness could hardly repair," she lavishes affection on what the narrator has earlier called "his degenerate state." It is little wonder that Amy's "burst of sorrow and compassion" at the end of the chapter is so double-edged: "No, no, I have never seen him in my life!" She refers to the fantasy of "what he really is," but expresses it in the familiar phrase that disavows any personal connection.

Dickens does not stint on the evidence of Mr. Dorrit's abusiveness and Amy's collaboration. She is the subject of his rages when she consorts with the poor, breaking the family illusion that the Dorrit family is still as genteel as it once was. She helps maintain the family fiction that Mr. Dorrit's children do not work for wages, and she knows it; as she tells Clennam, "I could never have been of any use, if I had not pretended a little" (*LD* 1.14). What she so diligently protects, her father secretly knows: we discover at the time of his release that he is perfectly aware of his children's employment. When he is suddenly rich, one of his first concerns is to erase that stain: "We owe it as a duty to them, and to ourselves, from this moment, not to let them— hum—not to let them do anything" (*LD* 1.35). The narrator acknowledges his pretense; Little Dorrit does not.

Dickens displays here an impressively acute knowledge of the dynamics of intra-familial psychological abuse. Whether he arrived at it from his experience as a child or from his experience as a husband—or both—we cannot be sure. He covers the knowledge the way Amy does, with protestations of her innocence. Yet she is allowed the classic Dickens kind of self-recognition: she sees in Pet Meagles's devotion to Henry Gowan what she will not say about herself. As she writes to Clennam, "you may be certain she will love him, admire him, praise him, and conceal all his faults, until she dies. I believe she conceals them, and always will conceal them, even from herself. She has given him a heart that can never be taken back; and however much he may try it, he will never wear out its affection" (*LD* 2.11). Like Dickens, she can articulate what she sees in someone else.

When he dramatizes Dorrit's extreme sensitivity to any real or imagined slight to his class status, Dickens writes from the most volatile part of himself. In the second half of the novel Dorrit's pretensions are wedded to his extreme terror lest others know of his prison past. The random look on a servant's face can make him feel that he has been found out. When a domestic attendant pauses for an instant before obeying an order, Mr. Dorrit, "seeing the whole Marshalsea and all its Testimonials in the pause, instantly flew at him" (*LD* 2.15). As Dorrit declines inside this mental prison, his tendency to project his own suffering and abjection onto his brother Frederick becomes more pronounced; when his daughter looks at him with concern he denies that he is tired and immediately assumes "an astonishing superiority to his brother's failing powers" (*LD* 2.19). Dickens has perhaps never been quite so clear about how such projections work to protect a character's threatened image of himself.

It is not long before Mr. Dorrit's lifelong self-delusion attacks him from the inside, and he reverts to his prison identity during an elegant dinner party. His secret is Dickens's secret; his extreme irritability, as well as his ability to feel ashamed of it, is Dickens's own. Had Dickens not known that, he could not have written this: "He had a sense of his dignity which was of the most exquisite nature. He could detect a design upon it when nobody else had any perception of the fact. His life was made an agony by the number of fine scalpels that he felt to be incessantly engaged in dissecting his dignity" (*LD* 2.3). It is a perfectly rendered description of the paranoid letter writer with whom this chapter began, a testimony to the self-knowledge Dickens could enclose in the safety of his fiction, and to his recognition that the prison of the mind is inescapable.

✍ The Pleasures of Suspicion

Little Dorrit as a whole is filled with contrasts between suspicion and generosity. Clennam fights that battle within himself, speaking generously, for example, against Mrs. Gowan's fraudulent suspicions of the Meagleses while feeling guiltily suspicions of his own parents. As if to inoculate himself and his readers against the disease of suspicion, Dickens includes the extreme case study of Miss Wade, whose self-explanation appears in the chapter called "The History of a Self-Tormentor" (*LD* 2.21). Miss Wade, an illegitimate orphan surrounded by improbably kind friends, is knowingness personified to the point of perversity. "From a very early age," she begins, "I have detected what those about me thought they hid from me. If I could have been habitually imposed upon, instead of habitually discerning the truth, I might have lived as smoothly as most fools do." The moment of her enlightenment comes at the age of twelve, the time of Dickens's own disillusionment. From then on, Miss Wade interprets every word and act of generosity or compassion as "insolent pity," condescension designed to make her friends and employers feel good about their patronage. Like a Harold Skimpole turned inside out, she bites back against any sign of social dependency by attacking the motives of anyone who becomes attached to her. Having reduced the world to nothing but pretense, she condemns herself to isolation supported by a false sense of empowerment. Her chapter, which Dickens thought of as central to his novel's themes, aims to expose the endpoint of knowingness as a kind of self-delusion powered by class resentment.

Dickens's discomfort with his own propensity to "detect designs" everywhere led him to overvalue innocent characters who manage to blind or deafen themselves to the ways others make use of them. He came to more direct terms with the subject in the story "Hunted Down," first published in the *New York Ledger* in late August 1859. Sampson, the story's narrator, is an insurance executive whose suspicions of the smooth-talking Julius Slinkton lead him to organize an elaborate counterplot that finally unmasks Slinkton's designs to poison his victims and inherit their money. The tale followed from two articles on current poisoning cases that Dickens had published in *Household Words*. "The Demeanour of Murderers" (14 June 1856) concerns the trial of the surgeon William Palmer for poisoning a racing associate; "The Murdered Person" (11 October 1856) was set off by the case of William Dove, who had gradually poisoned his wife with strychnine. Both murderers aroused interest because of their behavior during and after trial—Palmer for his calm assumption of innocence, and Dove for his extreme Methodist piety. Dickens, of course, goes after the notion that such behaviors were evidence of lingering sensibility; the two provided good examples for his crusade against members of the public who are taken in by con men. "The Demeanour of Murderers" is especially interesting for its claim that the faces and bodies of murderers are legible, if their words are not: "we will express an opinion that Nature never writes a bad hand. Her writing, as it may be read in the human countenance, is invariably legible, if we come at all trained to the reading of it" (Dent 3.378). Dickens proceeds quite convincingly to read every move of Palmer's as part of the structure of villainy that allowed him to plan and carry out the murder in the first place.

In "Hunted Down" Dickens establishes a tension between belief and suspicion in the person of his narrator Sampson, who opens the tale repeating the mantra of the *Household Words* piece: "There is nothing truer than physiognomy, taken in connection with manner." We have all learned to read faces, he suggests; we "are not to be taken in." And yet he has been taken in, "over and over again." Why? Because, although his "first impression of those people, founded on face and manner alone, was invariably true[,] My mistake was in suffering them to come nearer to me and explain themselves away." Sampson plays out the clash between watching and listening in his responses to Julius Slinkton, a smooth, well-dressed fellow who arouses his suspicion because of the way his hair is parted straight up the middle, as if to say "'You must take me, if you please, my friend, just as I show myself. Come

straight up here, follow the gravel path, keep off the grass. I allow no tres-
passing'" ("Hunted Down" 175–76). The dubious parting that defies investigation keeps Sampson's suspicions alive, but during his pleasant dialogues
with Slinkton he chastises himself for coldness and distrust. We seem to be
in the midst of Dickens's own struggle with the problem of innocence and
knowledge.

By the third section, however, the story turns; now the reader becomes
the dupe while the narrator dramatizes his own machinations to ensnare
Slinkton, as if he were innocent of them. The discerning reader, alert to clues
planted by the author, experiences the usual seduction of half-knowledge,
while the story goes about its business of saving Slinkton's intended victims
and exposing the murderer in a scene featuring a former victim, thought
to be dead, who has plotted behind the scenes with the narrator to get his
revenge. As usual, the collusion of several other "virtuous" plotters is required
to bring the designing plotter to bay. But the first-person narration gives the
story an additional twist. Sampson the teller is marked with the same brush
as Slinkton the swindler: both tell and withhold for the sake of their own
profits. In the tale Dickens gets as close as he ever does to the admission that
his profession depends on playing with his readers' willingness to be duped.

That sense of his art had led him earlier to idealize and identify with the
detective police: what could be more tempting than a profession that relies on
perpetual suspicion and full-time distrust of what other people say? Inspector
Bucket of *Bleak House* nails Skimpole's character seconds after meeting him,
and makes use of Skimpole to extract information for his own purposes; he
narrates that story to Esther with an easy, offhanded self-regard. Dickens,
I suspect, envied the freedom in this artful knowledge; police need not pretend to value dangerous innocence, or write novels that would appeal to the
sentiments of a polite middle-class public.

The Scotland Yard detective branch of the London Metropolitan Police
had been created in 1842. Dickens spent several years in the 1840s fantasizing about becoming a Police Magistrate who would hear cases brought by
members of the force. In both 1843 and 1846 he wrote flattering letters to
noblemen mentioning this desire, in the hopes that they would help him to
a post for which—not being a barrister—he was unqualified. There may
have been various reasons for this fantasy during the decade when Dickens
thought about alternatives to full-time novel writing: a desire to emulate his
admired predecessor Henry Fielding, a notion that he could understand and
educate the poor from a position on the bench, or a wish to gather material
at first hand from actual incidents of cops-and-robbers' con games. By the
end of the decade, his energy for direct social reform had been channeled

into the Home for Homeless Women that he ran for the rich philanthropist Angela Burdett-Coutts, and into the social writing he did for *Household Words*. In July 1850 he began a series of *Household Words* articles on the detective police that begin to reveal the intensity of his admiring fantasy.

"A Detective Police Party" ran on two successive weeks, and was based on a group interview arranged by Dickens with several members of the detective force, including Inspector Charles Frederick Field, who became Dickens's special friend and served as a model for Inspector Bucket. As Dickens tells it, the group met in the *Household Words* office: "Every man of them, in a glance, takes an inventory of the furniture and an accurate sketch of the editorial presence. The Editor feels that any gentleman in company could take him up, if need should be, without the smallest hesitation, twenty years hence" (Dent 2.268). It's hard to tell who's doing the keenest watching here, and that is the point throughout: the detectives are represented as ideal versions of Dickens himself. It isn't long before Dickens is performing a bit of competition on the page, asking several questions in which his obsession with con games and character reading is instantly recognizable. He asks whether there are actual highway robberies in London, or whether "circumstances not convenient to be mentioned by the aggrieved party" usually precede them. He asks whether in servants suspected of household robbery "innocence under suspicion ever becomes so like guilt in appearance" that officers have to take special care. He asks whether thieves and officers know each other when they see each other in a public place, "because each recognizes in the other, under all disguise, an inattention to what is going on, and a purpose that is not the purpose of being entertained?" (269). Of course the answers to all these clever questions affirm that Dickens is right; in effect, he is one of their order. Soon the police become storytellers, with Dickens "transcribing" the stories complete with dialogue in various voices. Much of the second article is a story told by an officer who disguises himself as a simple butcher from the country so he can infiltrate—over a period of ten weeks—a gang of warehouse thieves. "Even while he spoke," Dickens writes, "he became a greasy, sleepy, shy, good-natured, chuckle-headed, unsuspicious, and confiding young butcher" (277). Who could be more like Boz himself, in the process of creation? What more Boz-like plot than this story of faked innocence vanquishing the criminal at its own game?

About a year later Dickens published another article called "On Duty with Inspector Field" (14 June 1851), in which his identification takes on more troubling political overtones (Dent 2.359–69). As he accompanies Field through the lowest haunts of London, visiting one foul den after another, he focuses on the power of Field's personal knowledge of individual criminals in dark scenes of mass disorder. Time and again "the flaming eye" of the sergeant's lamp singles out a face and body from the crowded, shadowy dark. Field addresses these men as if he were a tough schoolteacher among children or the warden of a lunatics' asylum, expecting and finding subservience and obedience. Dickens represents the poor and the criminals among them as if they were entirely subject to Field's paternalist domain. As the detective's "roving eye" reaches every corner, there is—or so Dickens would have it—nowhere to hide from his all-encompassing knowledge. Field himself had been an amateur actor in his youth, and may have contributed his share of exaggeration as he showed his tricks to the famous novelist. But Dickens's attraction to the notion of absolute knowingness wedded to paternalist control colors his point of view throughout the article. Nothing can fool Inspector Field; allied with him Dickens is safe from the world of con men who raise the ancient specters of deceit and betrayal.

For one paragraph, however, the novelist disentangles himself from the police detective. Inspector Field is "at home wherever we go. *He* does not trouble his head as I do, about the river at night. *He* does not care for its creeping, black and silent, on our right there, rushing through sluice gates, lapping at piles and posts and iron rings, hiding strange things in its mud, running away with suicides and accidentally drowned bodies faster than a midnight funeral should, and acquiring such various experiences between its cradle and its grave. It has no mystery for *him*" (Dent 2.367). Dickens asserts here the claim of the emotional imagination that knows of things it does not know. He recalls the artistic power that gives humanity, biography, and mystery to a river that had haunted him since he was a child working on its edges. Inspector Field cares about what he can see. Dickens also cares about what he can't quite see or know, the strange things hiding in the mud at the bottom of the river as it takes its course through life.

❧ CHAPTER 3

Memory

In Dickens's first fantasies about editing the periodical that was to become *Household Words*, he imagined a collective narratorial presence called "the SHADOW," calling it "a kind of semi-omniscient, omnipresent, intangible creature." He elaborated his idea in a letter of October 1849 to John Forster, after completing the sixth number of *David Copperfield*, in which David tries to forget the dark knowledge of his childhood sufferings, and becomes "A New Boy in More Senses Than One" (*DC* 16). The capitalized and personified Shadow adumbrated in the pages of Dickens's letter is a very odd creature indeed. Despite its ominous name, it is, Dickens claims, "a cheerful, useful, and always welcome Shadow." Then again, it is a "Thing" that clings and won't let go: "the Thing at everybody's elbow, and in everybody's footsteps. At the window, by the fire, in the street, in the house, from infancy to old age, everybody's inseparable companion" (5.622–23). Omnipresent, then, both spatially and temporally, this Shadow-Thing emerges hot from Dickens's inner life at the moment when he has figuratively pulled the curtain on Copperfield's painful past. His insistence on its cheerful and companionable qualities reads as a willful desire to wrest new narrative life from the stubborn persistence of old grief.

Forster immediately saw the murkiness in his friend's idea, and the Shadow was banished from the prospective title page of the new journal. It quickly turned up again in a new guise, as Shadows tend to do. Once *Household Words* was launched, Dickens invited Charles Knight to write a series of papers entitled "Shadows," which treated early English letter-writers and memoirists whose manuscripts had been published in the nineteenth century. Knight began with the memoirs of Lucy Hutchinson and went on to the letters of Margery Paston. On receiving the second paper, Dickens intervened, urging Knight to use the present tense rather than the past. "I understand each phase of the thing to be *always a thing present, before the mind's eye*—a shadow passing before it. Whatever is done, must be *doing*. Is it not so?" (6.446). The shadow appears this time in a more recognizable shape, as a visual image cast by the imagination, or a shape projected by a magic lantern. Yet it retains the omnipresence of the earlier image, along with its refusal to go away: what is done, completed, must be doing, its action ongoing. Knight's project, as Dickens saw it, was to bring back a long-dead life history that had been hidden in various forms of autobiographical writing. As Dickens had done in the markedly retrospective sections of *David Copperfield*, Knight was to preserve his subjects by memorializing them in the present tense. At this point editorial advice begins to shade into a theory of autobiography:

> For example. If I did the Shadow of Robinson Crusoe, I should not say he was a boy at Hull... but he *is* a boy at Hull—there he is, in that particular Shadow, eternally a boy at Hull—his life to me is a series of Shadows, but there is no 'was' in the case. If I choose to go to his manhood, I can. If I choose to go to his boyhood, I can. These shadows dont change as realities do. No phase of his existence passes away, if I choose to bring it to this unsubstantial and delightful life, the only death of which, to me, is *my* death—and then he is immortal to unnumbered thousands. (6.446–47)

This is not just an instance of Dickens's desire for immortality through the "unsubstantial and delightful life" of writing. His insistence that "there is no 'was' in the case" asserts that boyhood and manhood exist simultaneously and eternally in Shadows that are always accessible by choice. Shadows, then, are memories eternalized by writing; at the same time the passage suggests a reluctance to admit either loss or change. To be "eternally a boy at Hull"—or, in Dickens's case, eternally a boy at Chatham—is to freeze time at a moment before chaos strikes: before Robinson Crusoe goes on his disastrous voyage, before Charles Dickens goes to London and works in a blacking factory. The boy and the man coexist; how the boy becomes the man is elided.

I have begun with these letters of 1849 and 1851 because they are so suggestive about complications in Dickens's ideas about memory and the past. It is often said that Dickens uses memory in a regressive way, in the form of a yearning for innocent pastoral childhood or a bachelor world of male camaraderie. Dickens's habit of conflating past and present, and other instances of suspended temporality in his writing, have been noticed in a variety of critical contexts. I want to redirect these observations by positing a complex fracture between Dickens's valorized idea of memory and the unwilled, negatively inflected recollections that return again and again to shape his work.

This distinction between memory and remembering makes it possible to revisit Dickens's most famous recollection, the autobiographical fragment narrating the story of his employment as a twelve-year-old child worker in a blacking warehouse during and after his father's three-month incarceration for debt. My interest lies primarily in the autobiographical fragment as a piece of writing shaped by the particular contexts of the 1840s and finally set down by the thirty-six-year-old novelist, probably during the late months of 1848. Yet the actual context of this document extends from the beginning to the end of Dickens's career. The memory Dickens wrote for Forster is indeed a "fragment," not of an uncompleted memoir, but of a lifetime writing project that included fictional portraits of traumatized children, doubts and fears about the act of autobiographical telling, evocative memory-writing, and a series of novels that turn on differences between resentful remembering and strategic forgetting.

The Dangers of Autobiography

Dickens took pride in the accuracy of his visual and verbal memories, and cultivated them rigorously. As Peter Ackroyd tells us, he would give long speeches without notes by mentally organizing his topics as if they were the spokes of a wheel; as he finished each section he would mentally flick away its imaginary spoke (423). Dickens's letters also make it clear that he had absorbed current theories of memory, both through his reading and through his close association with Dr. John Elliotson, whom he met in 1838, and from whom he learned theories of mind and the practice of mesmerism. He was quite aware of the distinction between spontaneously occurring memory and willed recollection, established by the philosopher Dugald Stewart in 1792. In the 1840s psycho-physiological work on memory and amnesia had not yet brought the distortions and erasures of memory to center stage. However, as Jenny Bourne Taylor explains, debates about double consciousness and its shaping of the self were well underway in the early part of the century, and they "focused principally...on patterns of hidden memory within the individual" (Taylor 2000, 580). Dickens was fascinated by work on the unconscious reservoir of inaccessible memory traces that might be called up through the association of ideas. He owned a copy of Robert Macnish's *The Philosophy of Sleep* (1830), which emphasized the in-between state of dreams, and their capacity for "renewing long-forgotten ideas" (Taylor and Shuttleworth 103). Such fascinations shape many an uncanny fictional moment, but they cohabit with Dickens's equally intense desire to employ memory as a handmaiden of willed and willful consciousness.

In letters written before and during the 1840s, Dickens made no hard and fast distinction between the terms "memory" and "recollection," although he shows a general tendency to "recollect" when he is talking about social matters like forgetting dates or recalling friends to mind. After his sister-in-law Mary Hogarth died in 1837, Dickens began to write of memory as a sacred power; at times he imagines, in letters of condolence to others, that memory overrides the break between life and death, bringing the affections of the living and the dead closer than ever. By the late 1840s the idea of memory is more often linked with the association of ideas, as if Dickens were growing increasingly interested in the independent process of memory and its selection of associations. Thus, for example, he writes to his Lausanne friend W. F. de Cerjat, in 1850: "When I write your name, I have always an association with that night at Martigny when we walked up and down before the Inn, smoking Cigars, and our party were singing inside.—You remember? Why my memory should select that particular time, I don't know—but it always does" (6.184). Writing Cerjat's name triggers a memory endowed with an unnamed emotion that links the two men in the past, and again in the present appeal. The point of the pen, Dickens implies, is an important actor in the associative process.

The letters also reveal Dickens's repeated articulation of a wish to erase bad memories or to replace them with good ones. The impulse emerges in a comically exaggerated apology Dickens wrote in 1839 to one William Upcott. "As antiquaries *do* sometimes suffer themselves to be deceived and take new lamps for old ones," Dickens wrote, "so I am not without hope that you will ante-date my apparent neglect and consider it so old as to be quite beyond the memory of man" (1.623). New memories for old: the plot of *David Copperfield* was to enact just such a "deceiving" exchange. Closer to home, Dickens rather ingenuously proclaimed to his friend Douglas Jerrold that a bad review "will throw me into a violent fit of anger for the moment, it is true—but his acts and deeds pass into the death of all bad things next day, and rot out of my memory. Whereas a generous sympathy like yours,

is ever present to me, ever fresh and new to me" (4.642). In other letters of
the mid-1840s good experiences "blot out" or "drown" the recollection of
unpleasant ones (4.280; 4.664). Perhaps the most stunning example of Dickens's will to erasure may be found in a later letter of February 1864, in which
Dickens responds to Angela Burdett-Coutts's suggestion that the death of his
son Walter might bring him into greater sympathy with his wife Catherine
Dickens, from whom he had separated six years earlier. Dickens denied that
emotional connection of any kind was possible, insisting "that a page in my
life which once had writing on it, has become absolutely blank, and that it
is not in my power to pretend that it has a solitary word upon it" (10.356).
The strange writing metaphor implies that a part of the mind over which he
has no control had written his marital page in disappearing ink.

   Time traveling, or making the past present, was another persistent trick in
Dickens's negotiations with his own history. Confronted with a voice from
the past, Dickens sometimes liked to pretend that the intervening years had
vanished. When at forty he writes to George Beadnell, the father of his first
love Maria, he sends love to the Beadnell daughters, noting, "I am exactly 19,
when I write their names" (6.660). In a similar vein, he writes to his former
Chatham schoolmaster, the Rev. William Giles, in October 1848, "I half
believe I am a very small boy again; and you magnify, in my bewildered sight,
into something awful, though not at all severe. I call to mind how you gave
me Goldsmith's Bee when I left Chatham (that was my first knowledge of
it) and can't believe that I have been fledging any little Bees myself, whose
buzzing has been heard abroad." Such time traveling connects his Chatham
childhood directly with his literary success, eliding the years between. It is
also a way to cover his current domestic frustration with epistolary charm:
"—As to Mrs. Charles Dickens, there is manifestly no such person—It is
my mother, of course, who desires to be cordially remembered to yourself"
(5.432–33). Pretending that he is still a child living with his parents allows
him to eliminate his wife for the space of a sentence; his invocation of cordial
memory covers a powerful desire to forget the present.

   In Dickens's correspondence, autobiographical writing of one sort or
another was usually triggered either by moments when he was compelled to
defend himself from what he perceived as attack, or by incidents in which
the stresses of daily life could be transformed by writing himself up as a sort
of third-person comic hero called the Inimitable, the Sparkler, or Dick. The
comic mode provides much of the energetic charm in the letters, whether
Dickens is describing himself as a lurching body on board an Atlantic steamer,
or as an anxious householder fretting about repairs to the drainage system at
Gad's Hill. The idea of autobiography itself was, however, always a troubled

one. Dickens's fear of it may be discerned in a letter of advice he wrote to his fellow-novelist Elizabeth Gaskell in 1850 about a young ex-prostitute and thief she was readying for emigration to a new life in Capetown: "Let me caution you about the Cape. She must be profoundly silent there, as to her past history, and so must those who take her out . . . this caution is imperative, or she will either be miserable or flung back into the gulf whence you have raised her" (6.29). Dickens was, of course, thinking practically about the girl's prospects. But his phrasing and emphasis suggest his identification with the notion that telling the past is dangerous, not only to the aspirations of the teller but also to his or her psychological condition.

Like all famous writers, he was harassed by requests for biographical information from various quarters, but he rarely provided it. As he wrote to Wilkie Collins in 1856, "I do not supply such particulars when I am asked for them by editors and compilers, simply because I am asked for them every day." For Collins, he went on to violate his rule, but the emotional effect of constructing even a brief *curriculum vitae* emerges at the end of the letter: "This is the first time I ever set down even these particulars, and, glancing them over, I feel like a Wild Beast in a Caravan, describing himself in the keeper's absence" (8.130–32). The image is resonant in more ways than one. The absent keeper is presumably Dickens the secret-keeper, the part of himself who carefully controls the public displays of the circus animal, Dickens the performer. The sense of guilt and danger suggests as well that Dickens knew he was lying: the curt summary of his early years rewrites his childhood, extending the years of schooling and eliding the period of family debt, bankruptcy, and blacking. He was also wrong when he claimed to be breaking his rule for the first time, though it would not be altogether surprising had he forgotten a letter written eighteen years earlier to the German journalist J. H Kuenzel, which offers a similarly pruned mini-autobiography (1.423–24). In both accounts, Dickens emphasizes his extraordinary success as a parliamentary reporter, his precocity as a child reader, writer, and actor, and the fact that he was married to the daughter of a man who was a great friend of Walter Scott. In both cases his autobiographical "particulars" were destined for publication in foreign-language publications, which may have mitigated his usual fears of exposure to the class prejudices of English society.

On the rare occasions when Dickens responded to the curiosity of his (usually foreign) correspondents, he exudes "manly" pride about his youthful physical condition or about the status he has fairly won through the independent profession of Literature. Yet despite his deeply determined rule of reticence, he flirted intermittently with the idea of autobiography, if only as a way to correct the many inaccurate accounts of his life that found their ways into journals. Responding to one of these during his 1842 tour of the United States, Dickens jokes, "If I enter my protest against its being received as a veracious account of my existence down to the present time, it is only because I may one of these days be induced to lay violent hands upon myself—in other words attempt my own life—in which case, the gentleman unknown, would be quoted as authority against me" (3.61). The image of autobiography as suicide, emerging as it does from Dickens's word play, suggests that he was holding the terror and self-division associated with the story of his life on a comically distanced verbal plane.

From then on, Dickens spoke of autobiography only in connection with his own death. In November 1846, as he invented Paul Dombey and Mrs. Pipchin, he confided to Forster that he had been pulled back into his own childhood. Characteristically, he backdates the Pipchin memory that properly belonged to his twelve-year-old self: "It is from the life, and I was there—I don't suppose I was eight years old." And then, abruptly, he swerves toward the prospect of further confession: "Shall I leave you my life in MS. when I die? There are some things in it that would touch you very much" (4.653). Since Forster was exactly his own age, there was no reason for Dickens to assume that he himself would die first. It was simply that autobiography had to be linked with a posthumous time. Some years later he twice refused material to the classicist and editor Edward Walford, who hoped to include his story in a collection of contemporary biographies; one of his reasons was his plan "to leave my own auto-biography for my childrens' information" (8.200; 8.612). By this time Dickens had given Forster the narrative describing his father's imprisonment for debt and his own dark days as a child factory worker. He may have wished his children to read a version of that narrative after his death, before Forster published it in his biography. Or, he may simply have been staving off yet another hungry journalist with a version of his long-standing formula.

Whether he hid it or idealized it, Dickens's childhood would always feel to him like a Shadow that clings and will not be forgotten. No matter how often he transformed it from a bad memory into a good fiction, it persisted, repeating itself in a series of ever-ingenious guises. Sometimes it appeared in the all-too-familiar form of his feckless father, John Dickens. In a letter of September 1843 to his old family friend and lawyer Thomas Mitton, the outraged son writes, "Even now, with the knowledge of him which I have so dearly purchased, I am amazed and confounded by the audacity of his ingratitude," and describes his family as exploiters: "He, and all of them, look upon me as something to be plucked and torn to pieces for their advantage.

They have no thought of, and no care for, my existence in any other light" (3.575). This ancient anger about being unknown and unappreciated by his nearest relations was to erupt again in the autobiographical fragment. Meanwhile, Dickens gave specific body to the figure of the unwelcome Shadow in another letter to Mitton of February 1844, exactly twenty years after he had begun his stint at Warren's Blacking: "For anything like the damnable Shadow which this father of mine casts upon my face, there never was—except in a nightmare" (4.45). The restless desire to live away from England that overtook Dickens during the 1840s may suggest attempts to run away from that shadow. Yet his wanderings abroad correspond with his growing attention to memory itself, both in the letters I have mentioned and in the Christmas Books written between 1843 and 1848.

Several personal experiences stimulated recollection during this period, as Dickens was heading toward the autobiographical fragment. He shared early memories during frequent visits with his sister Fanny Burnett as she lay dying of tuberculosis in 1848. In that year his carefully protected, well-educated eldest son Charley was approaching the age at which Dickens had been sent to work. Nostalgia for the reporting exploits of his youth is on display during his brief flirtation with editing *The Daily News* in 1845–46. Before beginning the editorship Dickens bragged about his extensive "express and post-chaise experience" in a letter to Forster; after resigning, he proclaimed to his Genoese friend Emile de la Rue, "I am again a gentleman" (4.460–61; 4.498). The whole affair, which included working with his father as a staff member, seems to have awakened troubling memories; he wrote to Forster months later that he feared to publish his new novel with Bradbury and Evans, who put out *The Daily News*.

Dickens's unconscious memory also came into play in the quite different arena of public affairs. A striking complication of his expanding social conscience during the 1840s was his inability to respond to the plight of child workers in mines and factories. Under the leadership of Lord Ashley, the Commission for Inquiring into the Employment and Condition of Children in Mines and Manufactories issued reports and drawings substantiating the abuses of young children and women in industrial settings. Dickens was sent preliminary versions of two reports (December 1840 and February 1843) by one of the commissioners, Dr. Thomas Southwood Smith. Smith hoped to enlist Dickens's voice in support of protectionist legislation—a natural subject for the creator of Oliver Twist, Smike, and Little Nell, he might justifiably have thought.

Dickens's actual response, full of conflict and unkept promises, is the more interesting for being unexpected. The drawings of small children laboring alone in dark mines, and the testimonies of uneducated young voices led on by questions from grand commissioners may have touched him painfully, perhaps in ways he did not fully understand. He announced to Forster, during a trip to Scotland in the summer of 1841, that he had "made solemn pledges to write about mining children in the *Edinburgh Review*, and will do my best to keep them" (2.317); his phrasing suggests both duty and doubt. Over the course of the next year Dickens wrote three times to the *Review*'s editor Macvey Napier, requesting delays and finally suggesting in July 1842 that "our subject was too stale" (3.288–89). The *Edinburgh Review* was not Dickens's sort of periodical; clearly he was both tempted by and resistant to a higher class of journalism than he normally practiced. But the greater resistance was lifelong: Dickens simply did not write about children who worked—as he had done—in nondomestic jobs for regular wages. (The exception is of course chapter eleven of *David Copperfield*, partly transcribed from the autobiographical fragment). In fact, when it came to wage-earning children, he discovered he was not a protectionist at all. When he responded to the second Commission report on 1 February 1843, he wrote to Southwood Smith that, while he saw the need for a "mighty change," he could not "reconcile it to myself to reduce the earnings of any family—their means of existence being now so very scant and spare" (3.436). His anti-protectionist stance may have served to protect his own memory against the shame of his childhood employment, by constructing the family past as a story of economic necessity.

It is also quite likely that the public exposures of child exploitation activated Dickens's own deeply held secret in a way that led him both to associate himself with and to dissociate himself from the uneducated mass of working-class children whose stories were coming to light. How could his most painful memories compete with such unendingly downtrodden lives? Leaving that difficult problem aside, Dickens turned instead to champion the Ragged School Movement. Early in March 1843, he had promised Southwood Smith a cheap pamphlet, an "appeal to the People of England, on behalf of the Poor Man's child." Four days later he withdrew the promise, alluding to some other form of writing in which "you will certainly feel that a Sledge hammer has come down with twenty times the force—twenty thousand times the force—I could exert by following out my first idea" (3.459; 3.461). A long critical tradition supposes that the blow was struck in *A Christmas Carol* and *The Chimes*, published in 1843 and 1844. But neither story is about children who work, and the child-figures of Ignorance and Want, who appear at the end of Stave Three of the *Carol*, are the nightmare fantasies who replaced child workers in Dickens's imagination. They are specters of the children Dickens encountered in his visit to a Ragged School in September 1843, who make money or steal it on the streets, resisting education and civilization. In his support of Ragged Schools he appeals to fear: these children are savages who need basic teaching about the most essential differences between right and wrong. During his actual school visit, however, Dickens warmed to the Ragged School children, loved their laughter at his brightly polished boots, and found among them a very bright boy whose age he estimated in relation to his son Charley's (Dent 2.359–69). They were children of the London streets—his world, his companions of old. When he came among them, he was, in an odd way, at home. Too much at home for comfort, clearly: when he turned them into fearful specters in his public writing he made sure to dissociate himself from such children in every possible way.

The "Sledge hammer blow," with all its implicit rage and violence, never did land on behalf of working children. Instead it fell, first, on the head of a certain Lord Londonderry who opposed factory legislation in the House of Lords, a father figure it cost Dickens nothing to revile. What he *could* write about the Factory Movement appeared in a letter and a review published in *The Morning Chronicle*, the newspaper he had worked for in his reporting days. On 25 July 1842 Dickens intervened anonymously in the debate about Ashley's Bill on Mines and Collieries, which excluded women and girls from mines and set minimum ages for the employment of boys. His letter follows a single rhetorical strategy: not to support the bill as such, but to dismantle and undermine the self-serving arguments raised against it by members of the House of Lords. Later that year he reviewed Londonderry's *Letter to Lord Ashley, MP, on the Mines and Colliery Bill* (20 October 1842). In both pieces, the bill itself becomes the abused child, while the resisting Lords play the role of its cruel masters. As Dickens writes in July, the bill "will arrive tonight at that stage in which the tender mercies of the Colliery Lords will so distort and maim it, that its relations and friends elsewhere will be sorely puzzled to know it again when it is returned to them" (3.278–79). The October review, a deeply facetious *ad hominem* attack on Lord Londonderry, opines that measures for improving the public condition "are very troublesome children to their fathers in the House of Lords. They cost a world of trouble in the bringing up; and are, for the most part, strangled by the Herods of the Peerage, in their cradles" (Dent 2.47). The pain and rage that fuel these metaphors of maimed and strangled children may be our only clues to the actual nature of Dickens's unarticulated responses to a public controversy that touched his private memory in intense but incalculable ways.

In one especially telling moment, Dickens parodies Londonderry's ideas about the easy life of the six-year-old trapper in the mines, who sits alone in the dark to open and shut trap doors: "If I were not this great peer, quoth Lord Londonderry, I would be that small trapper. If I were not a lord, doomed unhappily in my high place to preserve a solemn bearing, for the wonder and admiration of mankind, and hold myself aloof from innocent sports, I would be a jolly little trapper. Oh, for the cindery days of trapper infancy!... Jolly, jolly trappers!" (3.281). Conflating the trapper and the lord in one person, this little riff suggests a personal investment above and beyond the Carlylesque denunciation of the letter as a whole. The "I" is Dickens's "I" disguised as Londonderry's. The writing moment discovers the grotesque connection between a self-serving nostalgia for childhood and Dickens's haunting fantasy: were he not this great author, he would be that small trapper.

Dickens did little for the Factory Movement, but the Factory Movement may have done quite a lot for Dickens, by providing external images that stirred up internal memories in disturbing ways. The Christmas Books of the 1840s begin to respond to the specific content of such memories, as well as to the act of remembering itself. The Spirit of Christmas Past in *Carol* is ingeniously constructed to represent the altered perspective from present to past that characterizes the act of memory. He looks both like a child and like an old man with "the appearance of having receded from the view, and being diminished to a child's proportions." From his head springs "a bright clear jet of light," but this human candle of memory carries its own extinguisher cap, representing the repression of memory that Scrooge has imposed on himself. Like memory, "the figure itself fluctuated in distinctness," changing shape, melting away, and reappearing "distinct and clear as ever" (*CB* 25–26). The domestic action of *The Battle of Life* is set on darker ground: an old and "guilty" battlefield that lurks, largely forgotten, directly below the surface of its present pastoral beauty (*CB* 239).

The Haunted Man, last of the Christmas Books, was—so far as we know—written almost in parallel with the autobiographical fragment during the fall of 1848. The Phantom who exactly doubles its protagonist Redlaw is the internal voice of pained and resentful memory that finally surfaces with a version of Dickens's own story. The Phantom appears to Redlaw with the announcement "I come as I am called." "Unbidden," Redlaw replies. "Unbidden be it," the Spectre replies. "It is enough. I am here" (*CB* 331). In its uncanny way, the split figure dramatizes Dickens's struggle with old memory that returns unbidden yet half-consciously invited. Although the Phantom is represented as a demonic tempter who promises to erase Redlaw's memory, it speaks in powerfully personal ways, its sense of abandonment audible in the iambic cadence of "a stranger came into my father's place when I was yet a child' (*CB* 332). The same voice that tells the resentful tale aloud promises freedom from it, as the temptation of autobiography might promise exorcism. The condition of that freedom is a kind of publication, a mysterious diffusion that blights the memory and the moral capacities of everyone in Redlaw's life. He does not know exactly how his blighting power works; like publication, or infection, it spreads beyond his control or knowledge. *The Haunted Man* might then be read as an allegory of auto-biographical anxiety: what uncontrollable damage might result from giving away ineradicable memories? What would happen to Dickens's relationship with his audiences if he revealed his low past, or his personal anger and shame?

Redlaw's acceptance of the Phantom's bargain precipitates the appearance of a monstrous child, a second double figure who follows Redlaw as his shadow. This beast-like wild child, another of the savage children that haunted Dickens's writing during the 1840s, is immune to all fellow feeling, and cares only about accumulating money and food. He is a recognizably guilty version of the child in the autobiographical fragment, obsessed with counting shillings and meals, who "might easily have been, for any care that was taken of me, a little robber or a little vagabond" (Forster 28). The wild child's only sign of humanity lies in his frantic desire to be near the redemptive woman: maternal love, like money and food, is counted among his basic deprivations. Enclosed within the story's allegory, the figure of the wild child emerges as an acknowledged part of Dickens's own psyche.

While the Christmas stories venture ever more deeply into memories of abandonment, their plots struggle to maintain a moralized account of memory as a benevolent power. In *A Christmas Carol*, it is relatively simple: Scrooge's ability to look upon his abandoned young self in the schoolroom brings self-pity; self-pity brings tears, awakening feeling; feeling leads to sympathy for others. Five years later, in *The Haunted Man*, memory is a curse, and brings with it a powerful desire to forget. Redlaw accepts the Phantom's Faustian bargain to destroy painful memories, including "the inter-twisted chain of feelings and associations, each in its turn dependent on, and nourished by, the banished recollections" (*CB* 335). When Redlaw finds that he has the power to destroy memory in every person he encounters, the results are predictably chaotic: as failures of memory lead directly to failures of sympathy, all bonds of love and friendship are threatened. A good deal of highly sentimental plot machinery goes into action to cover up the damage. The moral of the story is that one must live with those enchained associations of dark and tender memories, at least for the sake of maintaining the cheerfulness of lives more innocent than one's own.

Chastising its hero for dwelling in old resentments, the story picks up a thread begun in the earlier fantasy of *The Chimes*, which punishes its working-class hero for allowing the ideas of upper-class social reformers to haunt and depress his simple mind. This story has conventionally been read as a sign that Dickens had moved away from portraits of individual villainy to a systemic view of social evil. Indeed, the story pillories the rhetoric of upper-class reformers, whether they are political economists or paternalists, with consistent venom. They are all accused of erasing the humanity of the poor, of imagining them as a threatening blight that has to be controlled or cleaned up, and of creating despair in the minds of the very people they claim to be helping. This, finally, was Dickens's nullifying response to Lord Ashley and the Factory Movement. But the story is stranger and more confused than this account suggests. The villains are the reformers who make the poor feel that they are "born bad" and can only get worse. Yet the wrong takes place inside the head of the childlike old man Trotty Veck, when he allows himself to absorb and believe what the reformers say. The chimes that represent his obsessional thoughts turn from voices of cheer into echoes of the reformers' contempt. They generate a dream vision of the future in which his family and friends come to ruin in just the ways the upper classes predict. Then the Bells themselves become chastising agents that accuse him of participating in the reformers' wrong through his unconscious internalization of their attitudes.

The story makes the victim take the responsibility for the perpetrators' crimes against human nature. Its message seems to be that it's the job of the poor not to believe the way they are portrayed, but to manufacture hope and optimism out of themselves. Read autobiographically, the fable raises a number of questions. Did Dickens blame himself, as the story rebukes Trotty, for allowing the recurrent nightmare of his early poverty and shame to take over his thoughts like bells that clanged and could not be stopped? Did he recognize in Trotty's alternation between sentimental cheer and anxious despair the poles of his own psychology? Or, did he sense his collusion with the reformers in his own fearsome images of savage, uncivilizable children? The guilt of the fathers pervades and infects the world of *The Chimes*, but it runs parallel to the guilt of the oppressed psyche that cannot get on with ordinary "trotting" about its business. All three of the Christmas stories seem split between the desire to tell their memories of woe and stern rebukes to the anxieties and depressions that are produced by the woes themselves. The interior conflict that Dickens pursued through the writing of these phantasmagoric fictions served as the prelude to the brief, fragmented set of autobiographical reminiscences he designed for a private audience of one.

🍂 The Autobiographical Fragment

We come, then, to the question of childhood trauma. Was it or wasn't it? Why did Dickens remain silent about it for so long—was it social shame, or was he loyal to the family policy of pretending it hadn't happened? Does the fully conscious experience of a twelve-year-old qualify as formative trauma? And where does the biographical emphasis properly fall: on the moment of a boy's psychological development or on the act of writing about it that occurred more than twenty years later? Can a twentieth- or twenty-first-century critic make a psychoanalytic diagnosis of a nineteenth-century child? If so, what were the pubescent child's dominant emotions: guilt at repressed aggression against the father, anguish at abandonment by the mother, the confusion and the heightened sense of being looked at that accompany shame? Was the fragment itself a deep indulgence in self-pity written by an adult who was too self-absorbed to recognize the pressures that had acted upon his own parents? Were those four or five months at Warren's Blacking—give or take a number, depending on your critic—really so unusual? Was the fragment a retrospective reevaluation of the early event as a trauma? Was it a document written from the pride and stability of his present success, as an explanation of his aggressive ambition?

These questions constitute a very brief summary of a critical history familiar to students of Dickens. The most recent twist in the tale has been provided by John Drew, who discovered an advertising jingle for Warren's Blacking written by the twenty-year-old Dickens for the *True Sun* in 1832. "The Turtle Dove," as the verse parody is called, tells of a mourning dove who, seeing its own reflection in the mirror of shiny blacked boots, is deluded into thinking she has found her true love (Drew, *Dickens* 18). Drew's discovery makes it clear that Dickens had contact with Warren's well after his release from the warehouse. Indeed, sly references to poets who wrote for Warren's Blacking crop up frequently in Dickens's early works. "Seven Dials" features a "shabby-genteel man in a back attic" who, it is rumored, "writes poems for Mr. Warren" (Dent 1.74). Tony Weller's idea of the "unnat'ral" quality of poetry comes from reading "Warren's blackin'" poets among others (*PP* 32). The well-named Mr. Slum offers, for a mere five shillings, to revise his Warren poem to suit Mrs. Jarley's Waxworks (*OCS* 27). Like the many references to blacking, blacking bottles, blacking brushes, and highly polished boots that Dickens sprinkled through his work, such moments suggest his private amusement in little games of telling and not telling. John Drew, however, concludes in a *Guardian Review* piece that Dickens's willingness to write for Warren's "threatens to undermine the legend" of his traumatic servitude there. His comment lines up neatly with the question raised by Alexander Welsh: at what point did Dickens decide that the blacking warehouse was traumatic?

I'm not at all sure these are the right questions. There is no point at which Dickens made a change from comic parody to pathos in his repeated fictional projections of the feelings connected with the blacking period. He practiced both modes, usually in the same text, throughout his career. Some years after writing the autobiographical fragment, he was more than ready to make savage fun of it in *Hard Times*, which features Bounderby's boastful and deluded retrospective tales of childhood abandonment. (Bounderby's memories include the claim that he saw only one picture: "engravings of a man shaving himself in a boot, on the blacking bottles that I was overjoyed to use in cleaning boots with" [*HT* 2.7]). This exuberant self-parody does not mean that Dickens had come to disavow his own story, only that the story simply refused to go away. Writing the fragment, writing *David Copperfield*, did not exorcise the pain or settle it down with a cup of tea in a comfortable corner of memory. That, finally, is why the blacking period might be called traumatic, at least in the light of recent attempts to discuss the intersection of literature and psychoanalysis. As Daniel Albright points out, we remember memories, not events (Albright 34). And, as Cathy Caruth reads Freud, trauma is a "wound of the mind—the breach in the mind's experience of time, self, and the world" that is "experienced too soon, too unexpectedly, to be fully known." Trauma is not locatable in the past event, "but rather in the way that its very unassimilated nature—the way it was precisely *not known* in the first instance—returns to haunt the survivor later on" (Caruth 4). Trauma is recognizable, then, in the repetitive returns of memory fragments. There is no way to count the variety of metaphors, moods, or tones through which such fragments could be evoked by a writer like Dickens.

What Dickens wrote for Forster is just one of many stages in his attempt to take rhetorical command of those memories and the feelings that had attached to them over the course of twenty-four years. It is composed of three prominent kinds of writing: first, highly detailed memories of places, food, and people; second, moments of specular drama when the narrator in the present watches the child being watched by others in the past; and, finally, the interpolated passages of anger and outrage in which the present narrator heats up the emotional temperature of the piece. The three kinds of writing sometimes blend into one another, of course. And any interpretation has to recognize the instability of the account that Forster organized and edited for his own purposes after Dickens's death. I will work only with the material that Forster puts in direct quotation, but it's worth noting that Forster sometimes calls attention to "blanks" in the written narrative, and tries to fill them in. The very form of the fragment may attest to a failure of sequential storytelling, and thus to an eternally present experience that would resist integration with a full-life narrative.

As he renders the minute details of places, eating houses, food shops, and shillings, Dickens frequently draws attention to the act of memory. The rat-ridden warehouse and its dirt and decay "rise up visibly before me, as though I were there again." He can't quite recall whether he earned six or seven shillings a week, but decides, since both numbers are in his head, that it was first one and then the other (Forster 25). He locates the two pudding-shops and the three coffee-shops he frequented by their street addresses as well as by other distinguishing details. Of one coffee-house he can "only recollect that it stood near the church, and that in the door there was an oval glass-plate, with COFFEE-ROOM painted on it, addressed toward the street." When he's now in a coffee-room with the same inscription, the present narrator says, "a shock goes through my blood," and he recalls the "dismal reverie" of the child inside the coffee-room reading the word "backward on the wrong side" (Forster 28). The shock might be read as a shock of fright at the identity of this adult and that child, stuck on the wrong side of the glass. At the same time it's the verifying shock of truth. In this kind of writing, Dickens is clearly enjoying the opportunity to remember; he is also determined to persuade himself and his reader that the incident happened exactly the way he tells it. He succeeded brilliantly: these details form the "factual" basis of every subsequent biographical account. When Dickens tells us that certain shops—and the warehouse itself—are presently razed or gone, he only adds to the apparent authenticity of the evidence. So does his capacity for ironic humor, which does not desert him even in moments of pathos. For example, he describes pretending to co-worker Bob Fagin that a house far from the prison is his home: "As a finishing piece of reality," he jokes, he rings the bell and asks "if that was Mr Robert Fagin's house" (Forster 30). In these sections humor and observation blend lightly with the adult narrator's message: all of this happened too soon; a child should not have to attend so early to details of food, or money, or shame.

In the scenes of specular encounter, Dickens complicates the relation between the adult narrator and the child: the staged child, and those who look at him in the past, become objects of the narrator's present gaze. Eating-houses in particular are theaters for the display of the child-as-spectacle. When the child goes into "the best dining-room in Johnson's alamode beef house," the narrator comments, "What the waiter thought of such a strange little apparition, coming in all alone, I don't know; but I can see him now, staring at me as I ate my dinner, and bringing up the other waiter to look" (Forster 26–27). When the child goes into a pub and demands a glass of "your very best—the VERY *best*—ale," the landlord calls his wife, who "joined him in surveying me. Here we stand, all three, before me now, in my study in Devonshire-terrace." When the staring adults ask questions, the child fictionalizes: "that I might commit nobody, I invented appropriate answers" (Forster 32). The child's sense of incongruity is acute: he is not what he appears to be, or—far worse—perhaps he is. The uncertainty creates the necessity for fiction, a way of substituting something else for what he secretly knows and what he secretly fears.

In little scenes reminiscent of his own fiction, Dickens shows us the lonely, canny child along with the curiosity and pity of his observers, all contained within the wider gaze of the present-day narrator. He attests again to the immediate presence of the past, but in these cases the child becomes less a subject than an object of memory. The narrator dramatizes pathos in terms of the child's helpless visibility, and flaunts his adult power to protect the child by controlling and staging the visual field of the narration. Here the implicit split between retrospective narrator and child-character becomes explicit as a kind of dissociation: the adult inhabits the stable perspective from his study at the cost of eliding the emotional continuity between child and adult.

Both kinds of memory writing are concrete and persuasive. The anger and resentment that play leading roles in most biographical interpretations are largely cordoned off in four or five hyper-rhetorical, present-tense passages that reveal an internal split between memory writing and trauma writing. They are the ones most often quoted, the ones that begin: "It is wonderful to me how I could have been so easily cast away at such an age," or "No words can express the secret agony of my soul as I sunk into this companionship," or "I know that I do not exaggerate, unconsciously and unintentionally, the scantiness of my resources and the difficulties of my life" (Forster 25, 26, 28). The writing is characterized by the mantra-like repetition of sentence beginnings and the buildup of clause on clause that Dickens uses when he is going for a direct assault on his reader's emotions. It sounds exaggerated and defensive, as Dickens sounds elsewhere in his letters when he is justifying his sensitivity to a remembered slight or defending his exemplary motives when he believes he has been cheated of his due. In the fragment, these moments suggest a specific anxiety: someone doesn't believe me, and I must convince him—or her—that my suffering was overwhelming and endless. Present and past merge into the same time zone: Dickens is just as concerned to defend his feelings now as then. "The deep *remembrance* of the sense I had of being utterly neglected and hopeless," he writes, "cannot be written" (emphasis added). In dreams, he writes, he becomes the child again, forgets that he has an adult existence and "wander[s] desolately back to that time of my life" (Forster 26).

The sudden loudness of Dickens's voice in these passages might suggest that he fears not being heard, or perhaps that he labors against some uncertainty or doubt about the significance of his early experience. The internal audiences he wants to convince inhabit both present and past. They include the parents who were blind enough to "throw away" so sensitive and talented a child; the unforgiven mother who wanted him to return to work after his release, the friend—Forster—who could be skeptical about Dickens's intensities; perhaps even the Factory Commission reports that cast his individual suffering in a stern social perspective. Of course it is exactly the loudness of voice that creates doubt—or its counterpart, the urge to diagnose and interpret—in Dickens's biographers.

But let's take it another way. This writing is not just about being unseen or unheard by others. It is also about the impossibility of speaking about something that eludes the knowledge and control conferred by the narration of specific memories. "How much I suffered, it is, as I have said already, utterly beyond my power to tell," Dickens writes, calling attention to futile but necessary repetitions of attempts to speak the unspeakable (Forster 29). As he approaches the end of his reminiscences, he feels that the writing has been a failure: "It does not seem a tithe of what I might have written, or of what I meant to write" (Forster 35). Such utterances call up the aspect of trauma that Cathy Caruth calls "a wound that cries out, that addresses us in the attempt to tell us of a reality or truth that is not otherwise available. This truth, in its delayed appearance and its belated address, cannot be linked only to what is known, but also to what remains unknown in our very actions and our language" (Caruth 4). In the act of writing, for once, directly about himself, Dickens discovered the critical disconnect between trauma and language. The silencing enforced by autobiography may well have turned him toward the fiction of David Copperfield, where he could re-bury—and in effect forget—his story within a context he invented and controlled.

The quality of Dickens's unknown knowledge comes through especially well in a series of sentences that start with the phrase "I know." The paragraph begins with an effort to claim mastery over unknown parts of the mind: "I know I do not exaggerate, unconsciously and unintentionally, the scantiness of my existence and the difficulties of my life." It ends with the greatest exaggeration of them all: "I know that, but for the mercy of God, I might easily have been, for any care that was taken of me, a little robber or a little vagabond" (Forster 28). There's plenty of evidence within the fragment itself that the claim is not literally true: his parents did provide young Dickens with lodging, clothes, and family company. In the very next sentence, in fact, Dickens restores his social status and tells us that he was treated differently from the other working boys, as a "young gentleman." The hyperbolic assertion of neglect is a kind of figuration that bears witness to the crisis of interpretation displayed in the rhetorical oscillations of the fragment. Dickens remembers himself among working boys, connected, observant, skillful at his work. The passages of outrage deny the connection, swearing that the whole experience was one of internal dissociation. The wound speaks, perhaps, in the veering between. Dickens transforms himself, as he transformed the Ragged School children, into a specter of uncouth crime, a little robber or vagabond. His concrete memories of association engender violent assertions of dissociation, both from his working-class companions and from the parents who put him into their company.

The sense of flailing frustration in these rhetorically over-controlled passages shows the adult in an active replay of the baffled child's suffering. But I think it also arises from the unsatisfying and ultimately meaningless end of the story. Dickens does not know why he was released from Warren's when he was. His father had left the prison after three months, but apparently expected his son to go on working. When it finally came, the release felt accidental; Dickens speculates that it might have followed from his father seeing him at work in the warehouse window, or perhaps from an argument between family members that remained obscure. "With a relief so strange that it was like oppression, I went home," he writes in a moment of notable emotional accuracy (Forster 35). After that, family silence prevailed; no apologies or explanations were offered or at least remembered. His repeated intention to "drop the curtain," expressed in both the fragment and *David Copperfield*, is not just a wish to forget, but a wish for an ending that makes sense and stays in place. As it was, the memory had, so to speak, no solution; it muffled both the feelings and the motives of all its chief participants, presumably generating an endless series of attempts to transform it into a narratable story. So it was that the curtain went on rising year after year, on newly displaced versions of the drama in which Dickens was free to invent his own meanings and his own endings.

❧ Fictions of Memory

By the time he came to incorporate fragments of the autobiographical story into the narrative of *David Copperfield*, Dickens could afford the lightness of touch which graces that novel. He had been writing about painful memory since his birth as a novelist. The interpolated tales in *The Pickwick Papers* are Gothic family melodramas that sit in the main body of comic text like unintegrated pieces of traumatic memory. Mr. Pickwick sleeps through them, and wakes up to newly sunny days with no disturbing traces in his consciousness. When Pickwick goes to the Fleet Prison, he does so by principled choice, while his money, his benevolence, and his curiosity shield him from the prison taint that transforms the other characters within the prison walls. Yet, for two chapters, Pickwick's sunny character is jolted into shock, depression, and anger. He is "alone in the coarse vulgar crowd, and felt the depression of spirit and sinking of heart, naturally consequent on the reflection that he was cooped and caged up without a prospect of liberation" (*PP* 41). The word "coffee-room" floats everywhere in the narrative like a signpost pointing to suppressed memory. Momentarily transformed into Dickens the journalist, Pickwick "gradually worked himself to the boiling-over point" as he reflects on the poor side of the prison; Dickens connects his state with memory when Pickwick is said to enter the room "before he had any distinct recollection either of the place in which he was, or of the object of his visit" (*PP* 42). This odd, not-quite-integrated clause may signal Dickens's own confusion about writing himself into memory-land in the course of a picaresque comedy.

Oliver Twist, the first of many traumatized children, also seems to have been endowed with a Teflon-covered soul that allows him to bounce back and forth between the thieves and the genteel world without incurring permanent damage. For the most part memory in *Oliver Twist* is treated as a cranked-up Wordsworthian pastoral automatically associated with nature, escape from trouble, and the yearning for peaceful death. As in *Pickwick*, however, traumatic memory briefly invades the very heart of the pastoral when Fagin and Monks appear at the window of Oliver's pastoral retreat. The narrator sets up the scene as if he were an expert in the relations between the conscious and the unconscious mind: "There is a kind of sleep that steals upon us sometimes which, while it holds the body prisoner, does not free the mind from a sense of things about it." It sounds like mesmeric slumber, in which "words which are really spoken, or sounds which really exist at the moment" merge with internal visions, "until reality and imagination become so strangely blended that it is afterwards almost a matter of impossibility to separate the two." Having put his subject into a trance, Dickens represents what happens as an instance of traumatic return: suddenly Oliver is back "in the Jew's house again," listening to Monks make threats on his life (*OT* 2.11).

Then, Dickens makes his most interesting move: Oliver wakes up in terror, and "actually" sees the two dark figures staring at him through the window. "It was but an instant, a glance, a flash before his eyes, and they were gone." It might be a textbook case of flashback, especially when it appears that the two figures could not have been there; they have not bent down a single blade of grass in their passage. In fact, Dickens suggests that the new vision has always already been there: "But they had recognized him, and he them, and their look was as firmly impressed upon his memory as if it had been deeply carved in stone, and set before him from his birth" (*OT* 2.11). It is an astonishing passage, attesting to Dickens's almost uncanny ability to imagine the terror of a memory-hallucination of events that take place before the conscious activity of memory begins to function in the young child.

Little Nell also inhabits a novel in which, most of the time, memory, pastoral, and death blend into a single stylistic activity. She too gets one brief moment of traumatic experience as she lies powerless to move, watching as a dark figure enters her bedroom and steals her money. When she follows the figure and discovers that it is her beloved grandfather, the terror is "immeasurably worse" and turns into traumatic haunting: she is forced to re-experience the dread in a state that blends imagination and reality: "it was worse, for the reality would have come and gone, and there an end, but in imagination it was always coming, and never went away." Instantly, as if to protect herself, the child dissociates her grandfather from the haunting phantom, which becomes "another creature in his shape, a monstrous distortion of his image, a something to recoil from, and be all the more afraid of, because it bore a likeness to him, and kept close about her, as he did" (*OCS* 31). From the moment this Shadow descends, Nell becomes a dissembler with a secret she can neither voice nor escape; she acts to nurture and protect her grandfather, but begins to fade in health until she dies, as if inevitably, from the burden of her split consciousness. Both *Oliver Twist* and *The Old Curiosity Shop* display radical and unacknowledged divisions between the idea of memory and the damaging potential of traumatic experience.

Nicholas Nickleby treats the aftermath of painful experience in a more sustained way that includes Smike's permanently damaged memory, the distorted personality of Newman Noggs, and the associative ramblings of Mrs. Nickleby. Noggs, whose dreary lodging displays broken blacking bottles, expresses through a set of physical contortions the agony of an enforced silence about his past; his only relief lies in pugilistic encounters with the empty air. "Once nobody was ashamed—never mind that. It's all over," he observes "in cramped and crippled writing" as he offers Nicholas aid in time of need (*NN* 7). Becoming "somebody" who can write freely in his own person would require some way of negotiating with that suppressed shame; Noggs can do so only by acting to rescue the younger generation from a similar plight. Smike's traumatic imprisonment in Ralph Nickelby's attic occurs in early childhood; followed by prolonged brutal treatment at Dotheboys Hall, it leaves his memory damaged beyond repair. When Nicholas gently prods him, Smike claims, much like Newman Noggs, that he once had a good memory, "but it's all gone now—all gone. . . . I was always confused and giddy at that place you took me from; and could never remember, and sometimes even couldn't even understand what they said to me." When Nicholas draws him back to early childhood, Smike reveals the original trauma, the imprisoning, frightening, almost empty room: "when I have terrible dreams, it comes back just as it was" (NN 22).

At this point we hear Nicholas "abruptly changing the theme." Changing the subject is a repeated recourse in Nicholas Nickleby; it happens often when something shameful comes along, as if it were the only useful remedy. It is, for example, the only way to divert the streams of association that tumble out when Mrs. Nickleby cheers herself up by falling into "one of her retrospective moods" (NN 35). Mrs. Nickleby may be wonderfully and horribly ridiculous, but she is part of the novel's meditation on the uses of memory. In her case conjuring up the most trivial details of a lost daily life is an exercise in nostalgia that helps to soften the blow of her present houseless and penniless condition. Present and past mix freely in her mind, so that the family's bankruptcy is covered with a filigree of remembrance that denies the existence of permanent change. Her blind desire for social status makes her a dupe in ways that put her children in danger, but her method of self-protection forms a clear counterpoint to the more damaging forms of enforced forgetting dramatized in Smike and Newman Noggs.

In these and many other ways the early novels attest not only to Dickens's repeated representation of isolated traumatic experience, but also to his keen interest in the mental processes that follow from it. During the 1840s, Dickens became more occupied with his personal memories and with the problem of whether and how to tell them. His decision in David Copperfield to link the exploration of memory with a retrospective first-person voice suggests his willingness to confront both the memory that erases and the memory that persists.

Late in his life, in the Preface to the 1867 edition, Dickens referred to David Copperfield as the "favourite child" among his novels. His impulse to imagine the novel as a child suggests that he associates it with a fond remembrance of things past. But his preference for this narrative may also rest on a sound artistic judgment: he had achieved in it the most perfect tonal and structural balance between his nostalgic love of memory and his fear of uncontrollably intrusive memories. From the start, the faculty of memory is a hero of the novel: it is associated with the keen perceptiveness of children and with the gentleness of people who sustain the childlike capacity of observation into adulthood. The narrator repeatedly calls it up at will, and it obediently produces, in present-tense images, vivid yet dreamlike snapshots that represent certain periods of his life. More dubiously, memory is said to superintend wonderful feats of erasure. When David's mother dies, after ruining David's young life through her remarriage, he claims that he remembered her from then on only "as the young mother of my earliest impressions." "In her death," he claims, "she winged her way back to her calm untroubled youth, and cancelled all the rest" (*DC* 9). When James Steerforth disappears, betraying David and ruining Emily, David claims that his memories "were as the remembrances of a cherished friend, who was dead" (*DC* 32). Once free from his working-class slavery at Murdstone and Grinby's, David expresses his relief that "a curtain had for ever fallen" on that painful life. "I have lifted it for a moment, even in this narrative, with a reluctant hand, and dropped it gladly" (*DC* 14). It would seem that the narrative is quite deeply invested in denying the force of haunting painful memories, if only for the purpose of creating David as a figure free from the anger and resentment such memories might call up.

In fact, the reader is allowed to witness such acts of deliberate suppression precisely because we know so well what they attempt to cover and how unsuccessful they are. The moments that "tell" of the nostalgic suppressions contain within them the recognition of unalterable pain. When David tells us of his mother that his memory "cancelled all the rest," the reader knows the "rest," and is hardly surprised when David has to renegotiate his childhood feelings through his marriage to the Clara-like Dora Spenlow, or when he projects his shame about his mother's remarriage into his suspicions of Annie Strong's fidelity. When David mentally "kills" Steerforth after his friend absconds with Emily, he writes that he cannot stop loving him: "I should have held in so much tenderness the memory of my affection for him, that I think I should have been as weak as a spirit-wounded child, in all but the entertainment of a thought that we could ever be re-united" (*DC* 32). The "spirit-wounded child," protected from shame and social disgrace by Steerforth's patronage at Creakle's school, is alive and trembling in the present, visibly re-protecting himself from the pain of naming the ways Steerforth has used him.

In moments like these, knowledge about the activity of suppression circulates on the surface of the narrative, although the narrator does not interpret it for us. The relationship between the retrospective narrator-David and the younger character-David hovers in a blurrily continuous time zone, quite different from the retrospective judgments enforced by Pip the narrator on Pip the younger in *Great Expectations*. Because of this difference, *David Copperfield* is often read as a narrative that refuses to confront the innocent hero's implication in the class injustices that surround him. Mary Poovey offers the most powerful formulation: she sees the duplicity of the class system reduplicated in the retrospective narrative's "splitting of the protagonist into an innocent hero, who does not know such deceitfulness because he is too young and too good, and a worldly narrator, who knows but will not tell" (Poovey 121). If, however, we read the whole narrative as a writing that creates David's consciousness and unconsciousness, it does nothing but tell. What it does not do is to tell us that it's telling; and it is exactly because of that, I suggest, that *David Copperfield* achieves its great uncanny power to render the human condition of knowing without knowing that we know.

That power is markedly on display in two scenes during which David plays the role of silenced witness: the firing of Mr. Mell (*DC* 7) and Rosa Dartle's attack on the seduced and abandoned Emily (*DC* 50). Both scenes play out, as in dreams, the contending voices of David's always shaky sense of his class identity. In the schoolmaster Mr. Mell, David encounters a grown-up version of the child in the autobiographical fragment: a shamed, anxious, and yet loving child of an indigent, institutionalized parent, who pretends to be no one's child in order to maintain his status in the eyes of his employer. David learns that the old almswoman is Mr. Mell's mother in one of those sleep-waking trances that figure unacknowledged knowledge in Dickens. Offstage and hidden from the reader, he tells Steerforth; Steerforth uses the knowledge to stage a dramatic and humiliating scene in which Mr. Mell is publicly fired for his association with a "beggar." Mell stands in for David/Dickens, receiving exactly the treatment that David fears from his mates when he arrives at school with a shaming placard on his back.

In the firing scene, Mell, David, and Steerforth all play out parts of the conflict between knowing and telling: the son who hushes up his parent's shameful dependence, the telling child who betrays the secrets, the arrogant public exposer who displays the secret, and the declassed adult whose hand on the child's head protects and forgives him for his betrayal. It is given to Mell to stutter out in uncanny repetitions the autobiographical work this episode performs: "I have not forgotten myself, I—I have remembered myself, sir." Remembering himself, David displays the split between his dependence on Steerforth's class power and his guilty identification with its victim. "I soon forgot him," he announces of Mr. Mell, marking once again a site of distressed memory.

Perhaps the most disconcerting scene in the novel occurs when David, hidden behind a door, watches Rosa Dartle attack the fallen Emily. The confrontation between the two women who share a history of loving Steerforth presents a case of excessive rage against one who mirrors back the self. Rosa vehemently denies that she and Emily have anything in common, although she is drawn to her because she wants to gaze upon, reject, and threaten to expose an image of her own helplessly abject love. David represents himself as frozen and mesmerized by the scene, through which he watches the drama of his complicity in Emily's fall and his mixed identifications with persecutor and victim. He is guilty like "innocent" Emily of attraction to Steerforth as to a promise of gentility conferred; he is guilty like Steerforth of the class contempt that Rosa vents in the scene. Throughout the surrogate drama we are reminded of the ludicrous position in which David hides, watching once again the punishment of a lower-class character who has been put in danger by David's failure to recognize what he knows about Steerforth.

The question of how to live with a painful, humiliating past is parceled out among many characters in the novel, with David's story just one among them. Rosa Dartle's scar writes her past on her body, and she makes the writing visible by inflaming it with rage. Betsey Trotwood obsessively purges her tiny lawn of donkeys, but cannot keep her exiled husband from making periodic returns. Mr. Dick transforms his traumatic memories into the metaphor of King Charles's head, but he cannot keep that head out of his memorial. Uriah Heep's class humiliation becomes a revengeful desire to humiliate the middle class in return. Mr. Micawber erases his past failures by living in an ever-hopeful present that condemns him to a life of cyclical repetition. Agnes Wickfield endures silently amid the humiliations of her father's alcoholism and the Heeps' predatory invasion of her private space. And so forth. Ultimately the right answer to the problem of living with past pain is to forgive rather than to revenge oneself, but the vengefulness of characters like Rose Dartle and Uriah Heep is essential to David's recording of those emotions he does not name in himself.

Such scenes of dreamlike displacement extend the narrative resources with which Dickens creates his innocent yet knowing protagonist. Early in the novel the distinction between knowing child and telling adult is based on the adult's acquisition of reasoned argument. David's instinctive dislike of Mr. Murdstone "was not the reason that I might have found if I had been older...I could observe, in little pieces, as it were; but as to making a net of a number of these pieces, and catching anybody in it, that was, as yet, beyond me" (*DC* 2). The child knows, without having to articulate it, that Murdstone's "firmness...was another name for tyranny," while the adult narrator sets forth in Dickensian style what the implicit assumptions of the tyranny were (*DC* 4). In a description of the prisoners he met while his father was in the Marshalsea, Dickens had made similar claims about the sexual knowing-ness of the child. As he goes upstairs to borrow a knife and fork, he observes the family of one Captain Porter: "I knew (God knows how) that the two girls with shock heads were Captain Porter's natural children, and that the dirty lady was not married to Captain Porter. My timid, wondering station on his threshold, was not occupied more than a couple of minutes, I dare say; but I came down again to the room below with all this as surely in my knowledge, as the knife and fork were in my hand" (Forster 14). The inno-cent child, it turns out, is the knowing child in disguise.

The genial tone of *David Copperfield* might be read as a long effort to mitigate the shameful knowingness of this child, and to replace it with the polite charm of genteel nostalgia. Uriah Heep, who can see through this project, wonderfully parodies the strategy when he forces David, for the sake of old times, to call him by his given name: "Thank you, Mas-ter Copperfield! It's like the blowing of old breezes or the ringing of old bellses to hear *you* say Uriah" (*DC* 25). He knows what David does not tell, as well as the reader does. The hovering of the narration in the space between knowing and telling, or knowing and condemning, was Dickens's solution to the problem posed by the prospect of autobiography. In fiction he could continue to charm his audience, while allaying the anxiety about the damaging effects of autobiographical confession he had explored in *The Haunted Man*.

The mood of *David Copperfield* lingered in Dickens, as if he wanted to prolong its mixture of nostalgia and indirect confession. The Christmas issue of *Household Words* for 1850 included his most detailed sentimental memory, "A Christmas Tree," followed in 1851 by "What Christmas Is, As We Grow Older." "Where We Stopped Growing," which appeared on New Year's Day 1853, celebrates the idea that childhood passions may continue to be held by the adult in their "original" forms. Dickens recalls incidents from books he had loved as a child as well as places and figures that had fascinated him in the London streets; he even smuggles in a prison memory: "We have never out-grown the rugged walls of Newgate, or any other prison on the outside. All within, is still the same blank of remorse and misery." The "within" merges the insides of prisons with the mind of the narrator. Nonetheless the piece ends in gratitude for those moments of arrested growth: "If we can only preserve ourselves from growing up, we shall never grow old, and the young may love us to the last" (Dent 3.112). This mood would not have presented a problem had its sentiments remained in storybook forms. But when the object of Dickens's first infatuation showed up again in his life, he responded as if he were identical with the young David Copperfield.

Miss Maria Beadnell had flirted mercilessly with the susceptible Dickens in his youth; in 1855 Mrs. Maria Winter ventured to revive the excitement by getting back in touch with the famous novelist who had so touchingly portrayed David and Dora's young love. Dickens was already in a David Copperfield mood, writing to Forster early in February, "Why is it, that as with poor David, a sense comes always crushing on me now, when I fall into low spirits, as of one happiness I have missed in life, and one friend and companion I have never made?" (7.523). The three long letters he wrote to Maria in that month, after he had received her note but before he had seen her in person, are shocking to behold among the letters that Dickens wrote in the midst of his busiest decade. Without a thought he enters the time-traveling mode; when he sees the handwriting on her note, "Three or four and twenty years vanished like a dream, and I opened it with the touch of my young friend David Copperfield when he was in love." Memories spill out of him, proofs that she has never been absent from his thoughts. Like David Copperfield, he seems to feel that his virtue is dependent on having forgotten nothing: "What should I be worth, or what would labour and success be worth, if it were otherwise!" (7.532–33).

The second letter, written from Paris on 15 February 1855, accepts a commission to buy some jewelry for her and responds to her assurance that his letters will be read by her alone. Now Dickens is fully immersed in a David Copperfield vision of himself, minus the comic irony of the novel. "Whatever of fancy, romance, energy, passion, aspiration and determination belong to me, I never have separated and never shall separate from the hard hearted little woman—you—whom it is nothing to say I would have died for, with the greatest alacrity!" The sound of her name "has always filled me with a kind of pity and respect for the deep truth that I had, in my silly hobbledehoy-hood, to bestow upon one creature who represented the whole world to me. I have never been so good a man since, as I was when you made me wretchedly happy. I shall never be half so good a fellow any more." It is remarkable, if not downright terrifying, to observe Dickens so wrought up by an interior fantasy world that Maria herself has no existence except as the "Sun" who inspired what he mistakenly believes were the best, "the most innocent, the most ardent, and the most disinterested days of my life" (7.538–39). Why was it so essential to link memory with a loss of "deep truth" and virtue, when the memory referred to a period of blindness and torment?

Such a question could be answered in a number of different registers. Dickens was feeling the guilty death-throes of his love for Catherine, and the memory of being whole-hearted—if wrong-headed—may have struck him with particular force. The fantasy of a first wife (Dora) replaced by a wife he had known all along (Agnes) may have held his imagination in thrall. The occasion may have presented itself as an opportunity to convince Maria, once and for all, how much gold she had squandered when she toyed thoughtlessly with his young feelings. In the letters, as in *David Copperfield*, he was also tapping into a cultural love affair with the idea of sustained memory as the channel of continuity in the soul, which had manifested itself in such major literary events as Wordsworth's *Prelude* and Tennyson's *In Memoriam*, both published in the same year as *Copperfield*.

In this case Dickens's nostalgic rhetoric set him up for yet another disappointment from Maria. She seems to have replied by hinting that she sustained feelings for Dickens as well, and suggested that they meet privately before the date of their planned dinner with their spouses. Dickens responded with another long outpouring of memory, accepting her invitation to establish "a confidence between us which still once more, in perfect innocence and good faith, may be between ourselves alone." The "once more," was added over a caret, as if to emphasize a continuity of trust that had never existed, but was still wishfully cherished. As for a private meeting—Dickens was suddenly aware of the world he inhabited: "I am a dangerous man to be seen with, for so many people know me" (7.544–45). They may have met once, perhaps at her house, before the properly familial dinner took place on 27 February 1855.

Seeing Maria, middle-aged, fat, and silly, instantly cured Dickens of nostalgia. However ludicrous the collision between his epistolary fantasy and the reality of her presence, it was probably a great moment for his art. *Little Dorrit*, his next novel, is saturated in an anti-nostalgic view of memory. Set in 1825, at the time of Dickens's work at Warren's, the novel is famously obsessed with prisons the mind cannot leave behind. It is equally uncompromising in its insistence that children inherit their parents' pasts: both Arthur Clennam and Amy Dorrit are damaged survivors of their family stories. The earlier split between benevolent memory and isolated traumatic return disappears in a newly introspective narrative; here memory is persistent, anxious, and sad, creating depression rather than nostalgia or trauma. Arthur Clennam's return to his mother creates an unwelcome form of time travel; he's back in "the timid chill and reserve of his childhood" with "all the old dark horrors" ready "to overshadow him" (*LD* 1.3). For Amy the prison and its people are "all lasting realities that had never changed" (*LD* 2.3). Mr. Dorrit's attempt to erase his prison life after their release ends in psychic collapse, as does Mrs. Clennam's confession of long-suppressed events.

Little Dorrit retains Dickens's moral contrast between those who remember resentfully (like Miss Wade and Mrs. Clennam) and those who transform past pain into generous sensitivity (like Amy Dorrit and Arthur Clennam). But the costs of each procedure are evident as never before. Even the comic relief provided by Flora Finching, Dickens's hostile and generous tribute to Maria Winter, is based on her memory for every detail of her former love for Arthur Clennam; Flora's inability to separate the past from the present is wonderfully played out as a massacre of English syntax. The senile dementia of Mr. F's aunt renders any and every time as emotionally present; her sudden eruptions can be located nowhere in temporal sequence. Too much memory and too little memory come to the same thing: in this novel the present is relentlessly drenched in the past.

The mood of *Little Dorrit* also reflects Dickens's personal sense of resignation and imprisonment in marriage. Like Maria Beadnell, Catherine had grown very stout; her bodily presence may have been an unwelcome reminder that time was passing and transforming their lives. Destroying the marriage was a kind of prison break, an attempt to start afresh which the author of *Little Dorrit* already knew to be futile. So did the author of *A Tale of Two Cities* and *Great Expectations*, the shorter novels in weekly installments written soon after the breakup, to stimulate sales of Dickens's new journal *All the Year Round*. In *A Tale of Two Cities*, Dickens presented a case study of traumatic return. The story of Dr Manette's amnesia drew on contemporary writing about "double consciousness," which describes and attempts to explain patients who move between two states of identity, and who, when in one, cannot remember the other. Dickens connected this phenomenon with traumatic knowledge: when the recovered Doctor receives disturbing information about Charles Darnay's identity, he experiences a nine-day return of the silent shoemaker self he had become during his long imprisonment in the Bastille. Speaking as a doctor about his other self the patient, Manette reveals that he had both dreaded and expected the relapse because of "a strong and extraordinary revival of the train of thought and remembrance that was the first cause of the malady" (*TTC* 2.19). In *Great Expectations*, Dickens revised the narration of *Copperfield* in another fictional autobiography, this time exposing and derailing its narrator's fantasies of an ascent to gentility, and cutting off the possibility of nostalgic return. The reappearance of Magwitch as Pip's secret benefactor is a strong example of traumatic repetition, underlined by the distinction Pip makes when he recognizes his convict of old: "I could not recal a single feature, but I knew him!" The wind and the rain drive away all "the intervening years" and there they are again, "face to face on such different levels" in the classic Dickens position of mirrored identity (*GE* 2.20). Pip "knows" Magwitch, but he does not remember him because he has been there all along as an unintelligible tangle of innocence, sympathy, guilt, and shame, apparently buried but never left behind. Recognition does not open the way for nostalgia, however. After crushing Magwitch's own nostalgic desire to embrace the memory of the cherished child, the novel strips Pip of his final delusion, the fantasy that he might go home to the forge and Biddy.

Dickens was capable of turning the insights of these novels to personal purposes. Forster reports a fragment of a letter dated sometime in 1862: "I must entreat you, to pause for an instant, and go back to what you know of my childish days, and to ask yourself whether it is natural that something of the character formed in me then, and lost under happier circumstances, should have reappeared in the last five years. The never-to-be-forgotten misery of that old time bred a certain shrinking sensitiveness in a certain ill-clad, ill-fed child, that I have found come back in the never-to-be-forgotten misery of this later time" (10.97–98). The five years in question were the ones in which Dickens had left Catherine and entered into a "vagabondish" double life with Ellen Ternan in one compartment and his public readings in another. In a strange way he had invited the traumatic return, as if he could not help smashing through the appearance of bourgeois gentility he had so assiduously courted for many years. The "never-to-be-forgotten" misery is not quite a remembered misery; the phrase suggests both the impossibility of forgetting and the timelessness of experience that is never-to-be-forgotten even as it is occurring. Yet the fact that Dickens was making himself a character in a condensed version of one of his fictions invites further scrutiny. Because of the marital separation, the relationships with Ellen Ternan and Wilkie Collins, and the reading tours, Forster and Dickens were somewhat alienated from each other. But Dickens was still relying on Forster to act as his biographer, and to tell his story sympathetically. The letter is partly an appeal to their old confidences, partly an interpretation of his present behavior that casts him in the role of sufferer rather than the source of others' suffering. The narrative of traumatic return is a sad story, but it has its uses.

✒ Tales of Resentment

While Dickens's negotiations with memory and forgetting were developing in the ways I have outlined, he was also experimenting in fiction with the pleasures and dangers of telling one's own story. I refer not to the prolonged fictional autobiographies of David, Esther, and Pip, but to moments when a character momentarily stops the action of a novel to confront an audience with a story of past suffering. Until late in Dickens's career, such characters are generally female—women who are in some way tainted, physically or mentally "fallen." They are the vessels, marked by shame, that are allowed to carry the angry and resentful aspects of Dickens's autobiographical impulse. The stories, told by Nancy in *Oliver Twist*, by Edith Dombey and her cousin Alice in *Dombey and Son*, by Rosa Dartle in *David Copperfield*, by Louisa Gradgrind in *Hard Times*, and, in a different form, by Miss Wade in *Little Dorrit*, all make some connection between the release of a woman's suppressed story and the extinction of her life force.

Nancy, the thieves' moll, tells a tale at the cost of her life. Soon after her first appearance as a successful actress in Fagin's service, Nancy saves the kidnapped Oliver from a beating by falling into a passionate rage. While Fagin calls uneasily for "civil words," Nancy lashes out with the story of her childhood corruption and her twelve years of degradation at his hands. "Not speaking, but pouring out the words in one continuous and vehement scream," she turns language into a passional force that, in the act of accusing Fagin vindicates her own virtue (*OT* 1.16). The risk she takes to protect Oliver from her own fate is repeated and heightened when she goes secretly to Rose Maylie to report on the underworld plot. This act of tale bearing both betrays and reaffirms Nancy's loyalty to Bill Sikes and the life of the gang. As she refuses Rose's offer of asylum, Nancy tells her, "I am drawn back to him through every suffering and ill usage, and I should be, I believe, if I knew that I was to die by his hand at last" (*OT* 3.3). Dickens writes frequently of the loyalty of the abused woman in his early work, but in this melodramatic version, the loyalty that will culminate in Nancy's extinction is the final sign of her redemption.

Edith Granger of *Dombey and Son* is similarly trapped between the social roles pressed upon her and the "better feelings" elicited by the vicinity of an innocent child. "Burning" with "the indignation of a hundred women," Edith prepares for her unwilling engagement to Dombey by casting her mother's crimes in her face (*DS* 27). Telling in her own way the long-repressed story of her childhood, she accuses her mother of destroying it, of "giving birth to a woman," of turning her youth into "an old age of design" and shaping her as an object of barter in the marketplace. Edith sees her education as a kind of prostitution for which there is no redemption; her mother's social designs merge into a conviction of her own corruption. At the same time the accusatory telling is, paradoxically, her way of expressing loyalty to her mother, for the end of her story is an implicit acceptance of Mrs. Skewton's marital bargain. When Edith rebels against that bargain, she does so by manipulating her sexual reputation to destroy Dombey's good name. At the moment when Carker's long seduction is to be consummated, however, she substitutes the power of speech for the submission of sex, assailing Carker with pages of narrative in which she gives her own account of the emotional transactions that have led her to flee with him. This narrative, Dickens claims, is so ferocious and powerful that it successfully repulses and delays Carker, whose force is bent under the stream of words. As in Nancy's accusation scene, the violent outpouring of a woman's language unmans the villain who buys and sells women. It is also the kiss of extinction; after the speech Edith disappears from the world, surfacing only to clear her name with Florence and to send her away with the injunction to "think that you have left me in the grave" (DS 61).

The burst of narrative rebellion that is a tacit act of obedience is repeated in the story of Edith's cousin Alice Marwood, the literally fallen woman who mirrors Edith's emotional prostitutions. Alice tells her story first to her mother and then to Harriet Carker. Both narratives end in assertions of loyalty to those who have corrupted her; the first story reunites mother and daughter, the second warns Harriet about the dangers that threaten Alice's seducer and Harriet's brother James Carker. The woman with a past turns, in Dickens's hands, into a woman who can save her soul, though not her life, by telling her tale. Dickens compressed the pieces of Edith's story into a suffocating knot when he invented Rose Dartle, a heroine consumed "by some wasting fire within her" (DC 20). Rosa crashes through her long years of insinuating silence at the moment David tells Mrs. Steerforth of her son's death. She tells of her obsession with the man whose violence has disfigured her, accusing the stricken mother of the double crimes of distorting Steerforth's nature and of taking his love away from Rosa herself. The accusation of the parent and the repressed sexual secret are collapsed into one, and Rosa's fire burns out into a frozen final tableau of continued service to the object of her rage.

Louisa Gradgrind enacts a milder version of the pattern after she has submitted unwillingly to an arranged marriage with Bounderby, and then to the seductive powers of James Harthouse. At the climax of Hard Times she returns to tell her father the story of her emotional history and falls, senseless but saved from degradation, at his feet. Replacing the sexual fall that has already occurred in the craven fantasies of Mrs. Sparsit, this literal fall recharges and renews the father-daughter relationship that is the original source of Louisa's lifelong despair. "You have brought me to this," she accuses, and cries out against her father's attempt to hold her up, as if to enact before his eyes the connection between his educational system and her fallen inner world (HT 2.12).

These stories dramatize the disturbances that fed Dickens's deep ambivalence about autobiographical confession. Rages against parents who use children as capital and against seducers who use women as objects are closely conflated. Damaged children turn into women fallen, in name if not in fact. There is a clear emotional continuity between the repressed shame of the used child and the expressed sexual shame of the adult woman, whose narrative of fallenness is her only weapon of revenge. The act of storytelling is a proclamation of that continuity, a deliberate retrieval of the past in a narrative that insists on connections that a parental figure represses or denies. The story effects no liberation; instead it binds the teller more closely to the target of her rage. It channels the woman's passion in a narrative that successfully burns it out, leaving her either dead or deprived of a sexual future. This pattern of invention offers a remarkable unfolding of the fears hidden in Dickens's 1842 joke about autobiography as suicide: "I may one of these days be induced to lay violent hands upon myself—in other words attempt my own life" (3.61). Safely distanced in the figure of a woman, the repeated story also implies that shamed and vengeful autobiographical outbursts are unmanly, unfit for a gentleman's repertoire.

Dickens's abandonment of respectable married life shifted the tenor of his memory writing. Personal memories appear in a few of the *Uncommercial Traveller* pieces he published in *All the Year Round*, but they are now recalled in a context of changing times; the glossy sheen of time traveling disappears. The fiery outbursts of passionate women diminish: Estella has a minor outburst against Miss Havisham in *Great Expectations*, but she does not die for it. Male characters turn autobiographical, as John Harmon does in *Our Mutual Friend*. The shift is most marked in two first-person narratives that directly confront the self-delusion at work in long-standing resentment: Miss Wade's "The History of a Self-Tormentor" in *Little Dorrit* and the 1868 story "George Silverman's Explanation." Both stories are imagined as self-contained written narratives composed by isolated characters who write in the hope of justifying their lives. The two pieces were written many years apart, and reveal quite different pathologies of deprivation, but they share a tonelessness that is unusual in Dickens's work. They read as if he were trying to create voices of sheer loneliness, stripped of every charm, humorous fancy, satirical exaggeration, or syntactical energy that made his work "Dickensian." Yet their cases present different sides of a very Dickensian coin.

Miss Wade turns the shame of the illegitimate orphan into a proud distrust, reading every human kindness as a self-serving pretense. Although she represents herself as a passionate person, her intense jealousy comes through as an instrument for the cold torture of her "love" objects. The engines of her resentment reduce every person she encounters to an instance of the self-interested hypocrisy she expects to discover. It is not impossible that Dickens recognized in this stripped-down portrait a secret and lonely part of himself. Forster, at least, recognized in him at times "a stern and even cold isolation of self-reliance side by side with a susceptivity almost feminine and the most eager craving for sympathy" that, he speculated, arose from "a sudden hard and inexorable sense of what fate had dealt to him in those early years" (Forster 39).

"George Silverman's Explanation" spooked even its author. He wanted to disavow it; as he wrote to W. H. Wills, "I feel as if I had read something (by somebody else) which I should never get out of my mind!!!" The story came from the part of his mind that was planning *The Mystery of Edwin Drood*, in which the murderer John Jasper was to tell his own story as if it were someone else's: "The main idea of the narrator's position towards the other people, was the idea I *had* for my next novel in A. Y. R." (11.385). Indeed "George Silverman's Explanation" opens as if the narrator were attempting to overcome his reluctance to make a particular confession; the first two abandoned chapters begin "IT happened in this wise," but the reader is never to discover just what the IT is. Instead we get a fictional autobiography that might have been written by one of Dickens's "savage children," had he been allowed to grow up, sit for a Cambridge degree, and take orders. Born and then orphaned in a Preston cellar, Silverman describes himself as a wild child who sometimes resembles the Jo of *Bleak House* assailed by the rhetoric of hypocritical Chadband-like preachers. His problem lies in a secret terror of his own "worldliness," which has been instilled in him by his mother's epithet, "worldly little devil," and deepened by the pious exhortations of his so-called benefactors. His life unfolds as a long and fruitless attempt to prove that he is not worldly or mercenary, ending with his dismissal by an employer who accuses him of precisely those faults. His "explanation" is an effort to prove that his motives, always generous and self-denying, were persistently misread by others.

Just as Miss Wade's narrative turns the spotlight on a neurotic response to childhood shame, this story displays George Silverman's misreading of himself. His continuing obsession with punishing himself for the "worldliness" of having essential needs for food, warmth, recognition, and love turns him into an isolated being whose secretive ways give rise to rejection and distrust in others. This is the story of an abused and neglected child who cannot grow out of the mental condition engendered by his early deprivation, in part because he cannot bring himself to speak directly to other human beings, and in part because he is overly devoted to cherishing a beneficent image of himself. Although it has been read as an instance of Dickens's self-pity, it is, I think, just the reverse: the story critiques what Dickens called in his letter to Wills "the narrator's position toward other people." When Dickens said that the tale struck him as if it were the work of another, he may have meant that the story felt like an exposure of his own propensity to nurture and capitalize on the resentment of feeling misunderstood.

The monotonous and severely limited voice of George Silverman, so different from the rich and various tonalities of the autobiographical fragment, is a late last comment on the self-deceptive possibilities in the autobiographical impulse. Over the course of his life, Dickens had written himself into the knowledge that his Shadow would never leave his side. He had learned to stop trying to erase it, deny it, or mask it with nostalgia. He had learned that its effects, including tendencies to secrecy and self-pity, could distort adult perceptions. "George Silverman's Explanation" worries the same old material as *Oliver Twist*, but Dickens had come a long way to get at its unromantic depths.

❧ CHAPTER 4

Another Man

"Another Man" shows up regularly in Dickens's fiction. He often plays the role of a romantic rival, but he is more than likely to double as part of the self. Dickens took great delight in the idea of "t'other one," and rarely missed an opportunity to play it out in different keys. Augustus Moddle sounds the note of comic pathos as he flees from marriage with Charity Pecksniff: "I love another. She is anothers. Everything appears to be somebody else's" (*MC* 54). Years later, in *Our Mutual Friend*, multiple doublings and triplings of male figures structure the whole novel, and rivalries among men can turn murderous. Rogue Riderhood's designation for Eugene Wrayburn, "t'other governor" has to be supplemented by "t'otherest governor" when he meets Bradley Headstone, while John Harmon appears as "Another Man" in a series of different guises.

Dickens also loved to turn himself into "another man" onstage in amateur theatricals. Sometimes he used the phrase when he imagined himself in two parts, the observing self split off from the acting one. From his first Italian sojourn he wrote to Forster about rediscovering his own acting talents: "I assure you, when I was on the stage at Montreal (not having played for years) I was as much astonished at the reality and ease, to myself, of what I did as if I had been another man" (4.244). In an 1857 letter to Miss Coutts's companion Mrs. Brown, he returns to the theme of distanced self-observation in a more meditative vein: "The vague unhappiness which tracks a life of constant aim and ever impels to some new aim in which it may be lost, is so curious to consider, that I observe it in myself sometimes, with as much curiosity as if I were another man" (8.422). By the 1860s Dickens was renting houses for Ellen Ternan under false names, and visiting her in the guise of another man. Threads linking Dickens's actual friendships with his written renditions of "the other man" suggest his fascination with intense relations among men, in which identification and rivalry are intimately linked.

The blurring of boundaries between another man and the self is apparent in Dickens's fiction as early as chapter two of *The Pickwick Papers*, which stages a slapstick mixup of identities in the mistaken duel between Mr. Winkle and Dr. Slammer. The novel as a whole features repeated scenes between male characters whose acquaintance begins in jealousy and ends in vows of everlasting brotherhood. From *Pickwick* through *Martin Chuzzlewit*, Dickens created overwhelmingly male scenarios in which women most often function as occasions for rivalry among men, as comically denigrated figures—the shrew, the hysteric—or as sentimental heroines endangered by male aggression. In the two-year interval between completing *Chuzzlewit* (1844) and beginning *Dombey and Son* (1846), Dickens began to remake himself as a Victorian writer more seriously concerned with the complexity of family emotions. At the same time, his representations of male friendship and rivalry deepened into studies of fascination, in which connections between male characters are eroticized by anxiety about class status, power, and masculinity. From the beginning, however, questions of identity and knowledge are raised when two male figures are linked in the gaze of fascination. From Oliver Twist's vision of Fagin at the window, "with his eyes peering into the room and meeting his" (*OT* 34), through the murderous rivalry of Eugene Wrayburn and Bradley Headstone, fascinated looking is the conduit of secret half-conscious knowledge between men.

🐾 Dickens and His Friends

Dickens himself lived primarily in a world of men. His career began in the eminently male domain of cheap newspaper publication and competitive reporting. His higher literary tastes were formed by the masculine worlds of the eighteenth-century novelists Fielding, Sterne, Smollet, and Goldsmith, as well as essayists like Johnson, Addison, and Steele. Both his professional and his leisure hours were centered on friendships or working relationships with other men. It is not altogether surprising that relationships between men in his fiction are more fully charged with erotic energy and conflict than those between men and women. In life and in writing, relations among men allowed for expressions of affection, aggressive energy, rivalry, competition, and class anxiety that were, at least until the later novels, less evident in the realm of heterosexual romance.

While Dickens's romantic and sexual life was directed toward women, it took conventional Victorian forms. His idealizations of virginal young girls, as well as his fascination with fallen women, formed a structure of feeling shared by many of his contemporaries. His assumption that wives were meant to serve husbands, bring up children, and oversee the social life of the household was in tune with the general expectations of his culture. When he mentioned his marriage to Catherine Hogarth in response to a request for biographical information, Dickens described her only as "the eldest daughter of Mr Hogarth of Edinburgh, a gentleman who has published two well-known Works on Music, and was a great friend and companion of Sir Walter Scott's" (1.424); he repeated the formula eighteen years later in a biographical sketch written for Wilkie Collins (8.131). It is clear that he wanted to imagine his marriage as a guarantee of the genteel status that always seemed to elude him, and as a connection to an aristocracy of male writers in which he was always trying to enlist himself.

A reader of Dickens's letters readily sees that his most genial affective life was engaged with his friends. Men are his confidants, his companions in play and in travel, his ways of measuring himself. When he is away from London it is his male friends who receive passionate declarations of friendship and urgent invitations to join Dickens and his family wherever they are. The presence of a Hogarth sister—first Mary, later Georgina—in the Dickens household may well have been initiated as a way of providing Catherine with female companionship while Dickens spent many of his leisure hours with friends.

The larger part of the correspondence of a Victorian literary man would normally have been addressed to other men, but the exceptions are quite easy to summarize in Dickens's case. Many family letters, as well as the letters to Ellen Ternan, are lost to us; but apart from the modest group of extant letters to his wife, daughters, and sister-in-law Georgina Hogarth, Dickens's major female correspondent was the wealthy philanthropist Angela Burdett-Coutts. He was the active partner in their social reform efforts as well as the recipient of her help in educating two of his sons, and he took pains to present himself in ways that would retain her good opinion. He also wrote to Lavinia (the Hon. Mrs. Richard) Watson at Rockingham Castle, whom he met in the English circle at Lausanne in 1846, and to Annie Fields, the wife of his Boston publisher James Fields; both women became fond of

Dickens and welcomed the intense charm of his epistolary attentions. He had known women like Mary (Mrs. Charles Cowden) Clarke and Mrs. Watson's cousin Mary Boyle as fellow-actors in his amateur theatricals; with the spirited Mary Boyle in particular he felt free to write mock (or not so mock) love letters in the guise of their stage characters, and, later in life, to confide his sorrows. Of the women writers who contributed to *Household Words* and *All the Year Round,* Dickens's correspondence with Elizabeth Gaskell is the most substantial and reveals a good deal about his editorial styles of management. Only rarely in these letters to women did Dickens exhibit the imaginative energy that he poured into letters to his male friends, though it is possible to glimpse in his letters home to Catherine and Georgina a man less fully on display as a writer.

Between the beginning of their friendship in 1837 and the late 1850s, when their relations became more strained, John Forster was of course Dickens's primary friend and correspondent. The two men were the same age; they shared strong opinions, high energy levels, and a commitment to raise the status of literature in their time. They also suffered comparable sensitivities about their class origins; Forster was the son of a Newcastle butcher and resented any allusion to that fact. He had received a better formal education than Dickens's, and he had already formed friendships with prominent literary men in London, but he, too, was making his way up through the world as the drama critic (and later editor) of the *Examiner,* a Sunday weekly founded by Leigh Hunt. On 2 July 1837, Dickens wrote to Forster thanking him for his review of *Pickwick.* He calls the review a "beautiful notice" in which "I feel your rich, deep appreciation of my intent and meaning....You know I have ever done so, for it was your feeling for me and mine for you that first brought us together, and I hope will keep us so, till death do us part" (1.280–81). Dickens was fifteen months into his marriage with Catherine; his grief for Mary Hogarth, who had died in May, was still fresh. The "marriage" he invokes with Forster is powered both by his sense of lost companionship and by Forster's own intense rhetoric of friendship. It is underlined the following month in a note of thanks for a present sent to him and Catherine, "coupled with an expression of our most selfish hope that our friendship may be lasting as sincere. Believe that if I meant less, I should say a great deal more, and that I am My Dear Forster, Ever faithfully yours, Charles Dickens" (1.297). Late in March 1838, despite Catherine's illness at the time, Dickens invited Forster to begin what became a twenty-year tradition of celebrating Forster's birthday and the Dickenses' wedding anniversary on the second of April.

The vows, so to speak, were renewed early in 1845, after the sudden death of Forster's older brother. Dickens wrote from Italy: "I feel the distance between us now, indeed. I would to Heaven, my dearest friend, that I could remind you in a manner more lively and affectionate than this dull sheet of paper can put on, that you have a Brother left. One bound to you by ties as strong as ever Nature forged. By ties never to be broken, weakened, changed in any way—but to be knotted tighter up, if that be possible, until the same end comes to them as has come to these" (4.246–47). In the fervor often generated by distance, Dickens not only puts himself into the place of the dead brother, but competes for the stronger position in Forster's affections. The almost familial connection did last their lifetimes, though its nature was altered when Forster married Eliza Colburn in 1856. By that time Dickens had begun his friendship with the younger Wilkie Collins, and was internally moving toward a break with his wife.

From many points of view Dickens made a good choice in his professional alliance with Forster. Although Forster could be pompous, argumentative, and overbearing in social gatherings, he made Dickens's career possible in ways that extended far beyond his role as first reader and literary adviser. Forster introduced Dickens to the other men who became his intimate associates; he tried to tone down the exaggeration and melodrama in his writing; he worked hard, though often unsuccessfully, to protect Dickens from his own worst impulses on any number of occasions. He interposed his good offices as a negotiator between Dickens and trouble, whether the trouble was personal or one of the many conflicts between Dickens and his publishers. In 1845–46, Dickens made plans to edit the *Daily News* over Forster's misgivings; he resigned two-and-a-half weeks after the publication of the first issue. Forster took over the editorship until a permanent director could be found.

The relationship was hardly an exclusive one. Forster, who had trained as a barrister, made it his business to involve himself in editing the work and managing the financial affairs of a number of men in his circle. The connection with Dickens was, in retrospect, the most significant of these entanglements, both because Dickens was in special need of "Forstering," and because in 1848 he invited Forster to be his official biographer. By that time Forster had become the primary witness and consultant in Dickens's artistic struggles and triumphs. Dickens trusted him with his dark and restless feelings, with the unsteady state of his health, and even with the secret history of the blacking factory that he withheld from others. For many years Forster was Dickens's most important audience: the recipient of the wonderful letters from abroad as well as the external conscience before whose bar Dickens argued out his plans and intentions, and justified himself in the face of his friend's reservations.

When Dickens traveled in Italy in 1844, he wanted Forster to know and admire his growing facility in Italian: "I wish you could see me without my knowing it, walking about alone here. I am now as bold as a lion in the streets" (4.194). His wish to be watched by an invisible paternal or godlike figure suggests that Forster's attention had become central to his sense of self. He also wanted Forster to know how he suffered in his writing: "Since I conceived... what must happen in the third [quarter of *The Chimes*], I have undergone as much sorrow and agitation as if the thing were real; and have wakened up with it at night" (4.207). Dickens wanted his friend with him the day he lost his father. Just two weeks later (14 April 1851), Forster had what he called a "very difficult" part to play when he was informed just half an hour before Dickens was to deliver a speech for the General Theatrical Fund that Dickens's infant daughter Dora had died. Forster decided to let the speech go on, and listened with "anguish" as Dickens spoke about how we "hide our hearts in carrying on this fight of life." When it was over he and Mark Lemon told Dickens, and Lemon stayed with Dickens while Forster went to Malvern to deliver the ailing Catherine home to London (Forster 539–40). This episode may be the most poignant, though not the most difficult, of the many services Forster performed for his friend.

Dickens maintained long correspondences with several other artist-friends whom he met in the 1830s and '40s: the Shakespearian actor William Charles Macready, the painter Daniel Maclise, the playwright and editor of *Punch* Mark Lemon, the marine painter Clarkson Stanfield, and the novelist Edward Bulwer-Lytton. Each of these friendships developed a story of its own, and they flourished at different periods, often depending on who was participating in one of Dickens's theatrical schemes. The friendships with Maclise and Macready are special instances of connection with men whose backgrounds echoed parts of Dickens's own life. Macready, nineteen years older than Dickens, was the son of an Irish actor and manager who had been imprisoned for debt while his son was preparing for an academic career at Rugby. The young Macready gave up his aspirations, took over the management of his father's theater, and began a provincial acting career under his father's auspices. His diaries, which repeatedly record his rage at having to spend his talents among uneducated players and ignorant theater critics, show that he never recovered from that social disappointment. Maclise, just six years older than Dickens, also came from a humble Irish background and had, like Dickens, risen to very early fame, in his case as a Royal Academy painter. After the youthful years of their friendship, Maclise became increasingly solitary and devoted to his work. Dickens's letters display many pressing invitations to his friend, as well as his growing acknowledgment of Maclise's tendency to withdraw from social life. Both men elicited letters of particular warmth from Dickens, who often attempted to cheer them up with teasing humor and affection when they fell into melancholy moods.

In 1840 Maclise replaced William Ainsworth in a friendship triad with Dickens and Forster. Ackroyd mentions an "unstated rivalry between Maclise and Forster for the closest friendship with Dickens" (386), but the possibilities for playful rivalry and minor jealousies are more likely to have played out in all of the possible combinations. In November 1840 we find Dickens criticizing Forster to Maclise, for Forster's excessive emotion at the death of Macready's beloved daughter Joan. "I vow to God that if you had seen Forster last night, you would have supposed our Dear Friend was dead himself—in such an amazing display of grief did he indulge, and into such a very gloomy gulf was he sunk up to the chin" (2.158–59). Hardly immune himself to excessive grief at the loss of young girls, Dickens was the one indulging himself in this case; he may have turned to Maclise in protective irony at a moment when Forster's sympathy was especially dear to Macready. Maclise, tall, handsome, and attractive to women, seems to have been Dickens's companion for his anti-domestic moods; they took to low-life scenes and pursuits unnamed in Dickens's notes of invitation. Many of these early notes to Maclise are invitations to some outing or escape from home, should he feel "vagabondishly disposed" (2.60).

When Queen Victoria married Prince Albert in 1840, Dickens and Maclise amused themselves by pretending to be hopelessly in love with her. Dickens wrote several notes declaiming his passion: "Maclise and I are raving with love for the Queen—with a hopeless passion whose extent no tongue can tell, nor mind of man conceive." Forster was cast in the role of the one who pretends but "*does not love her*" (2.25). Dickens had a lot of fun with these letters of mock-despairing love, which allowed him to fantasize an escape from domesticity and deadlines. As he wrote to Forster, "I saw the Responsibilities [his children] this morning, and burst into tears. The presence of my wife aggravates me. I loathe my parents. I detest my house. I begin to have thoughts of the Serpentine, of the regent's-canal, of the razors upstairs, of the chemist's down the street, of poisoning myself at Mrs. ——'s table, of hanging myself upon the pear-tree in the garden"—the list of possible suicides extends down the page, ending "of turning Chartist, of heading some bloody assault upon the palace and saving Her by my single hand—of being anything but what I have been, and doing anything but what I have done" (2.24). Elaborated versions of the fantasy were sent at the same time to Maclise and another friend (2.25–29). In all of them the comedy of coming unhinged rests on a fantasy of male rivalry for an impossible love-object, and ends in an escape from the thralls of domesticity.

Maclise painted the great romantic portrait of Dickens at his writing desk in 1839, and a lovely portrait of Catherine Dickens in 1842. He gave Dickens other sketches and paintings as well; to circumvent his generosity Dickens once enlisted the services of his old friend Thomas Beard to buy a Maclise painting for him, through the "pious fraud" of representing an out-of-town buyer (3.396). When Maclise discovered the "device," he sent the check back to Dickens, who returned it again, insisting that he was "willing to be your debtor for anything else in the whole wide range of your art" (3.418). The little scuffle over payment suggests that Dickens was more comfortable on the patron's side of the friendship, especially when the man in question was as successful as he was in his own art.

The same tendency is almost embarrassingly apparent in an article he wrote on Maclise's behalf for *Douglas Jerrold's Shilling Magazine* in August 1845. Maclise had been invited by the Royal Commission of Fine Arts, chaired by Prince Albert, to submit a cartoon for a fresco designed for the rebuilt House of Lords. Representing "the Spirit of Chivalry," Maclise's cartoon was eventually chosen, but not before it had been criticized for its crowded design and simplified by the artist. In the interim, Dickens went to bat for his friend's work as if it were a part of himself that had been criticized, praising it in such high and exaggerated terms that the article reads almost like a parody. Being Dickens, he could not separate righteous indignation from an attack on some authority, so the royal commissioners come in for their share of contempt, while the prince receives an urgent appeal to forgo his German taste: "But there is Justice to be done! The object of this competition was encouragement and exaltation of English art; and in this work, albeit done on paper which soon rots, the Art of England will survive, assert itself, and triumph, when the stronger seeming bones and sinews of your royal Highness and the rest, shall be but so much Dust" (Dent 2.79–80). Perhaps Maclise got a good laugh from this rhetorical conquest of their former "rival," but he sensibly urged Forster to persuade Dickens to cut the references to Prince Albert and his commissioners, and Dickens complied. It is easy to see in this brief deleted passage how fervently Dickens believed that he and his friends were destined to shape "the Art of England" for the near and far future.

Dickens could make fun of his friends in private, and he would sometimes parody one friend in a letter to another. In an 1851 letter from his vacation spot at Broadstairs, Dickens wrote to his old friend Thomas Beard about various visitors the family had entertained: "Here has Forster been and gone, after patronizing with suavity the whole population of Broadstairs, and impressing Tom Collin with a profound conviction that he (F) did the Ocean a favor when he bathed" (6.506). He and Catherine had their private jokes as well. In the summer of 1850, as he was writing *David Copperfield*, Dickens invited Maclise to join him for two weeks in Paris, on one of their "vagabond" adventures. Writing home to Catherine, he complained about Maclise's dress: "I don't know what he may have, in a portmanteau like a Bible; but he certainly don't put it on, whatever it is. His shirt in front is very like a pillow-case; and I expect him, at the trois freres presently, to be the terror and consternation of the assembled guests" (6.117). Having dragged Maclise to the Paris Morgue, he described his friend's reaction to "a body horribly mutilated...It made him so sick, that to my infinite disconcertment, he sat down on a doorstep in the street, for about ten minutes, resting his cheek (like Juliet) on his hand" (6.120). In matters of fastidiousness and manliness, he could assure his wife that he was the better man.

The friendship with the older actor Macready was negotiated in more sentimental terms and elicited some of Dickens's most sympathetic letters. As a masterly Shakespearian actor, Macready was what Dickens had once aspired to be. Ackroyd tells us that Macready's acting style was the kind Dickens admired: "he was a master of pathos, remorse, the more bravura aspects of melodrama" (210). Like Dickens, Macready was tremendously class-conscious: he resented his chosen profession because it was not gentlemanly enough, and he was intent on raising the theater from the state of degradation into which it had fallen. Dickens responded warmly to Macready's sense of professionalism and to his earnest—and tortured—dedication to his art.

Unlike Forster or Maclise, Macready was also a family man, married to another Catherine, with whom he had ten children. When Dickens and Catherine traveled to the United States in 1842, Macready, who had already been there, advised them not to take their four children and persuaded the reluctant Catherine by promising to look after them in their parents' absence. Dickens later reminded Catherine of this debt when he appealed to her and Georgina to suppress their irritation with Mrs. Macready's sister, who was visiting the Dickens family in Italy. "I should never forgive myself or you," he threatened, "if the smallest drop of coldness or misunderstanding were created between me and Macready, by means so monstrously absurd" (4.215). By 1844 Catherine would have had plenty of time to realize that she was expected to support and defer to her husband's friendships, and Dickens was clearly annoyed at her failure to learn this lesson. Macready's own Catherine, who appears in his diaries as a deeply cherished domestic partner, died in 1852. After eight lonely years, Macready was happily remarried at sixty-seven to a woman of twenty-three, with whom he had two more sons. He was in all these ways the friend who "went before," marking both professional and personal paths that Dickens followed with great interest and identification.

On board a steamer during his American travels, Dickens wrote an extraordinary letter of care when he learned that Macready was suffering from critical reviews as the new manager of Drury Lane. "I have been thinking all day, as we have been skimming down this beautiful Ohio, its wooded heights all radiant in the sunlight, how can a man like Macready fret, and fume, and chafe himself for such lice of literature as these!...I have wondered a hundred times how things so mean and small—so wholly unconnected with your image, and utterly separated from the exercise of your genius, in its effects on all men—can, for an instant, disturb you." No one knew better, of course, how such things could disturb him, than Dickens in America; in his postscript he writes—ostensibly about his responses to America—"I speak to you, as I would to myself."

Two long paragraphs of the letter are devoted to chiding Macready about careless eating habits: "Old Parr [their icon of longevity] never dined off chops, or in his dressing room." Dickens prescribes sherry with an egg beaten in, the very formula that was later to sustain him during his reading tours. He begs Macready to let him know that "you have left off eating with your fingers on week days, and have taken to knives and forks again. *Do* say that you are better, and healthfully disposed—but not unless you really are so" (3.173–76). Dickens's practical and bossy voice, applied to a state of depression he knew quite well from the inside, suggests the tone he took with himself—as well as his sudden recognition that he might lose Macready's confidence if he were to push that voice too far. By the time Macready resigned from Drury Lane in June 1843, Dickens was trying out the tragic-comic routine: pretending to be the Ordinary (the chaplain) of a prison, he wrote to prepare Macready for "the scaffold" and exhorted him, to "throw the weight from off your conscience and make a clean breast" in his resignation speech (3.513). Finding a way to cheer up his friend required ingenious work, even for Dickens.

Macready gave his final performance early in 1851 after two "farewell seasons" in London, a pattern Dickens was to repeat as he approached the end of his own reading tours in the late 1860s. On the occasion Dickens wrote up an appreciation that mixed nostalgia with an appeal to his inexpressible feelings of gratitude and affection. As soon as Macready decided to retire, however, Dickens became fascinated by the prospect of his friend's aging. They had a long-standing joke about Macready's anxieties about his age; Dickens liked to pretend that it was he who was old, not Macready, or to tease him about how "tremendously old" he was, or to taunt him about being "so fearfully conceited in those pretences of growing old when you know better" (5.486; 8.77; 10.39). But he thought seriously about Macready's choices in relation to his own. In 1856, after Macready had visited him during his residence in Paris, Dickens mused about those choices in a letter to Forster:

> It fills me with pity to think of him away in that lonely Sherborne place. I have always felt of myself that I must, please God, die in harness, but I have never felt it more strongly than in looking at, and thinking of, him. However strange it is to be never at rest, and never satisfied, and ever trying after something that is never reached, and to be always laden with plot and plan and care and worry, how clear it is that it must be, and that one is driven by an irresistible might until the journey is worked out! It is much better to go on and fret, than to stop and fret. (8.89)

By this time Dickens, at forty-four, had entered the period of explosive restlessness that was to end in the separation from Catherine and the establishment of a new, equally driven life. He had begun to understand that he would never hold the "something" he was always reaching for, but he knew he would go on trying.

By 1866, when Dickens was looking older than his age, he still teased the seventy-three-year-old Macready, but privately emphasized his dismay, in a letter to Georgina Hogarth, that Macready—now remarried with young children—was *"greatly aged"* (11.175). In 1869 Dickens reported him "extraordinarily old" (12.280), "distressingly infirm and unintelligible at table" (12.282). Macready was not the only friend who elicited this fear. In 1868 Dickens described Forster to Macready in the same terms he had used to describe Macready to Forster: "I cannot but feel that he has gotten *into an old way* which is not wholesome. He has lost interest in the larger circle of tastes and occupations that used to girdle his life, and yet has a morbid sort of dissatisfaction in having subsided into an almost private personage" (12.258). In a letter congratulating Macready on his seventy-seventh birthday, Dickens seemed unable to help sounding the note again, in a postscript about the wife of Stanfield, "looking well, but curiously old" (12.484). The repetition of the theme is striking, coming from a man in his fifties, and suggests that Dickens was fearful about what he saw in his friends' faces and bodies. As it turned out, he died in harness at fifty-eight—the age Macready had been when he retired from the stage. The old actor outlived Dickens by three years. The deliberateness with which Dickens pushed himself in the face of his own bad health may have had something to do with what he thought he saw mirrored in his friends.

Dickens's letters reveal a man who prided himself on the loyalty and affection that were indeed strong forces in his friendships. They also show a strong tendency to rivalry and an instinct for triangulation, whether the triangles included an actual woman or not. Rivalry sits very close to identification in his consciousness: those beloved friends have a tendency to turn into rejected parts of himself when he writes to them, or to a third party about them. René Girard's notion of triangular desire can help to suggest the potential volatility in such situations: Girard emphasizes that desire for an object (which may or may not be a person) is generated by envious identification with a mediator who is also experienced as a rival (Girard 7, 10). Dickens's zest for such situations comes through in his relationship with the de la Rue couple, when he became obsessed by his mesmeric relationship with the wife, all the while earnestly reporting the results of their sessions to the husband. In the months before he left England for the Italian journey on which he would meet the de la Rues, he had played out another set of relationships in which the roles of mediator and rival were almost indistinguishable.

✄ The Christiana Weller Affair

In February 1844, when Dickens had just turned thirty-two, he traveled north to deliver speeches at the Liverpool Mechanics' Institution and the Birmingham Polytechnic. The occasion is notable to begin with because it introduced him to the thrill of speaking to huge, wildly enthusiastic audiences. It is more deeply predictive because in the flush of fame and publicity, Dickens was suddenly infatuated with an eighteen-year-old girl who was also a performer. Christiana Weller, a child prodigy pianist, had been concertizing with her sister since the age of nine. A year before Dickens's appearance in Liverpool, her father had made contact with the creator of the *Pickwick* Wellers, trading on the coincidence of the name and requesting an autograph for his daughter, who was by then an acclaimed concert pianist on the northern provincial circuit. Thus, Christiana's name was not entirely unknown to Dickens when she played a solo on the program after his speech. He was instantly smitten, met the father, and invited himself to lunch the next day, along with his Yorkshire friend Thomas James Thompson. After the lunch Dickens sent Christiana "a bit of doggerel" that plays further with the Weller name, ending "I find to my cost, that *One Weller* I lost./ Cruel Destiny so to arrange it!/ I love her dear name which has won me some fame/ But Great Heaven how gladly I'd change it!" (4.54 and n.). It is a tricky little ditty, which relies on the girl's understanding that he flirted as befit the status of the great author Charles Dickens. When he returned to London, however, he wrote to her father, T. E. Weller, enclosing a copy of Tennyson's poems that he had promised to Christiana. It was not just any edition, but Dickens's own, a gift, he said, from the poet himself. Nor could Dickens keep himself from telling the father how he felt. Writing, again, as the great novelist, he pontificated to Weller about the "numerous figures" he encountered, most of them raising little care or concern. "But I read such high and such unusual matter in every look and gesture of the spiritual creature...that she started out alone from the whole crowd the instant I saw her, and will remain there always in my sight" (4.58). The girl-child's figure in the crowd recalls the description of Little Nell; Dickens's response may have been affected as much by his fictional creation as by anything emanating from Christiana herself.

Christiana fell instantly into a ready-made position in Dickens's sentimental imagination; he wrote to Thompson from Birmingham that Christiana was "too good" to joke about and that she was destined for an early death (4.55). She—and Nell—are generally linked with Dickens's regressive love for the dead Mary Hogarth. But there was a difference. Like Dickens's older sister Fanny Burnett, Christiana was an accomplished pianist and a performer, not a household angel. Dickens had never forgotten the day, twenty years earlier, when he sat in the audience as a working drudge, while fourteen-year-old Fanny played a prize concert at the Royal Academy of Music. When he later referred to the occasion in the autobiographical fragment, he wrote, "The tears ran down my face. I felt as if my heart were rent....I had never suffered so much before. There was no envy in this" (Forster 34). When Dickens denied a feeling, there is good reason to believe that he felt it deeply, and disapproved of it as deeply. In Liverpool he was onstage as the great celebrity, and the young woman played in celebration of his own success. His sister Fanny, who lived nearby in Manchester, had been visiting with him before the speech, and was now a member of his audience. Dickens may have been aware of the great reversal; the outpouring of emotion for Christiana Weller might have included a kind of release from the tangle of pride and resentment he had felt about Fanny's special status during the miserable period of their youth. More than just an echo of the lost Mary Hogarth, then, Christiana was the prototype for Dickens's attraction to the equally young actress Ellen Ternan. They too shared a stage—with Ellen in a minor supporting role—at another moment, fourteen years later, when Dickens was again away from home in the northern city of Manchester and wildly excited by the reception of his acting in *The Frozen Deep*.

The Weller situation took its peculiar turn when Thomas James Thompson also fell in love with Christiana and confided his feeling to Dickens.

Thompson, a man of Dickens's age, had been a family friend since sometime in the 1830s. He was a gentleman of leisure living on his grandfather's fortune, a widower with two children who were under the care of his sister. He had been waiting to greet Dickens when he arrived in Liverpool and took part in all of the festivities there. When Dickens opened Thompson's letter, he claimed in his reply, "I felt the blood go from my face to I don't know where, and my very lips turn white. I never in my life was so surprised, or had the whole current of my life so stopped, for the instant, as when I felt, at a glance, what your letter said." Allowing for the usual exaggerations, Dickens claims to have had the knowledge before Thompson could tell it to him, as though he were specially tuned into Thompson's frame of mind. Dickens admits that he thought Thompson temperamentally incapable of such a feeling as he, Dickens, could cherish: "although I knew that the impression she had made on me was a true, deep, honest, pure-spirited thing, I thought my nature might have been prepared to receive it, and to exaggerate it unconsciously, and to keep it green long after such a fancy as I deemed it probable you might have conceived had withered" (4.69–70). This bizarre sentence mixes a competitive assertion of emotional superiority with some accuracy in self-analysis. Dickens seems to sense that the young girl's image has taken hold through unconscious processes, but he prides himself on the ability to "keep it green" longer than any other man could.

Thompson had no impediment that would prevent an actual courtship, so Dickens's fantasy of winning at a chaste competition of adoration was set at naught. The result of that recognition was that he poured himself into a courtship by proxy: his language soars into sentimental rhetoric as he tells Thompson what he would do in his place. As his imagination takes wing, Dickens begins to argue as if he were talking directly with Mr. Weller, urging the marriage as if it were the only way to save a threatened girl from early death at the hands of a father who had forced her into a fatal apprenticeship to her piano. Like Master Humphrey in the *Old Curiosity Shop*, Dickens imagines himself pleading for the girl's life against the father's willful inattention to her needs. It would take a Dickens, he implies, to effect such a change of heart in the father. And so, fighting on behalf of one man against another for the possession of an eighteen-year-old girl, Dickens entered the quadrangle of the Thompson-Weller marriage negotiations.

He was quite out of control. He fantasizes that Thompson will marry Christiana and all three of them will then enjoy a "quiet happiness" abroad, "in some delicious nook, where we should make merry over all this" (4.70). He hints to his rival that Christiana would have given her heart to Dickens himself had he been free (4.72–73). He becomes violently interested in everything about Thompson's affairs. Meanwhile Dickens is carrying on with Mr. Weller, who is trying to use his acquaintance with Dickens as an entrée to a London debut for his talented daughter. Dickens gives advice, promises to bring her together with his father-in-law the music critic, and hosts the Wellers while she performs for George Hogarth. Christiana makes a successful debut in June, and Dickens writes to congratulate her: "I felt a pride in you which I cannot express" (4.148). By that time she and Thompson are engaged, and Dickens cannot prevent himself from reminding Thompson that he "Dick, the energetic Dick, devised the visit!" to the Wellers that morning in Liverpool. He writes as if he is an indispensable part of the couple: "Shall we ever cease to have a huge and infinite delight in talking about the whole Romance from end to end!" (4.89). Then the plot thickens; the course of romance does not run smooth; it appears that Christiana loves Another—"a prior attachment—kept secret by her," Dickens notes to Catherine on 6 April. Two days later, he writes a long letter to the girl herself, pleading Thompson's case in a fairy-tale-like narrative that is really a love letter in not-very-good disguise (4.98–100).

The affair rested, from Dickens's point of view, during his year in Italy, where he moved with his family at the beginning of July in order to economize in the face of financial stress. (It is not impossible that his attraction to Christiana had been the final straw in coming to that decision.) When he returned, he reconnected with Thompson and his ongoing courtship, inviting further confidences, and offering him the role of Wellbred in his amateur production of *Every Man in His Humour*. What Thompson thought about Dickens's interventions may be surmised from a letter to Christiana about the play, which Thompson hated; he felt he was "sacrificing myself to the vanity of others" (4.345n.). Nevertheless both Dickens and Catherine seem to have been part of what Christiana's diary called the "fatal discussion at Dickens'" which laid the last-minute objections of Mr. Weller to rest (4.398n.). The Thompson marriage finally took place on 21 October 1845. Dickens was in attendance, wearing a waistcoat especially designed after the vivid pattern of one Macready had worn onstage, and intended—as he raved to Macready—to "*Eclipse* the Bridegroom!" (4.406).

Dickens's involvement in his friend's romance received its own punishment when a mirroring sub-plot developed: his younger brother Frederick fell in love with Christiana's younger sister Anna, and insisted on marrying her over Dickens's strong objections. With his irresponsible younger brother on course to grasp what the great man could not, Dickens had no more use for the Weller family. He informed Fred that their style of life would not support domestic tranquility: "They are very amiable, but especially uncomfortable. They are feverish, restless, flighty, excitable, uncontrollable, wrong-headed; under no sort of wholesome self-restraint; and bred to think the absence of it a very intellectual and brilliant thing" (4.400). In flight from his own feverish excitement, he stepped right into Mr. Weller's role as the heavy father and maintained it throughout Fred's marriage, which ended, unhappy and impoverished, in a separation.

Christiana, too, came in for her share of reassessment. When Dickens saw the married pair in 1846, he reported to Madame de la Rue that "Mrs. Thompson disappoints me very much. She is a mere spoiled child, I think, and doesn't turn out half as well as I expected" (4.604). With his oldest friend Thomas Mitton, he was more snide: "She seems (between ourselves) to have a devil of a whimpering, pouting temper—but she is large in the family way, and that may have something to do with it" (4.615). The next year he found the Thompsons "not happy . . . he screws and pinches her (I don't mean with his fingers) villainously, I am told, in respect of common comforts" (5.42–43). Despite Dickens's self-consoling critiques, the pair seems to have carried on somehow, producing, in the second of their daughters, the future Alice Meynell. The families met occasionally in later years; no doubt it would have consoled Dickens further had he known that Thompson's little girl was later to publish an essay defending the dignity and felicity of his literary style against the dismissive contempt of many Victorian critics.

While most biographers have understood the Christiana Weller episode as a revival of the Mary Hogarth fantasy or as an instance of an arrested sexual instinct revealed in Dickens's attraction to young girls, it becomes even more interesting as a set of triangulated desires and rivalries among men. In turns, Dickens both patronized and identified with three different men: Thompson, Mr. Weller, and his brother Frederick. He plays all possible roles except that of the legitimate lover, although he manages to slip in a good deal of seductive talk under cover of his role as mediator. His intense identification with Thompson's courtship suggests a desire to control him much as a ventriloquist would a dummy. And his inability to stay out of these entanglements—none of which demanded his participation—makes it clear that he was compelled to play out imaginary scenarios at which we can only guess.

❧ Fascination and Knowledge

In Dickens's novels, prolonged mutual eyeing between characters frequently places them in relationships of fascinated, unspoken exchange. Fascination has long been associated with the power of the eye. In "Fascination, Skin, and the Screen," Steven Connor offers a brief history of changes in the meaning of the term. Through the nineteenth century, he argues, fascination had "presented itself as a transitive phenomenon... exercised by one subject upon another... The idea of fascination is inseparable from the conception of the evil eye" (9). For a time, theories about physical fluids unleashed by the powers of the eye were revived to explain the phenomenon of mesmerism, through which Dickens tested the powers of his own eye to elicit internal distress hidden within others. The notion of fascination as power wielded by one agent over another gradually changed, Connor writes, "from a transitive to an intransitive condition." In the twentieth century, the ability to become fascinated has emerged as the more compelling aspect of the phenomenon. Consolidating a good deal of modern theoretical speculation, Connor calls it "a heightened rather than distorted form of relation between inner and outer. Fascination thus becomes associated with a particular kind of narcissism, characterized by the fluid interchange between self and not-self, in which the subject and object of fascination become harder to distinguish" (12). Dickens's representations of fascination play in the space between the "evil eye" theory and the more modern sense of subject-object interchange.

Fascination is also a response to enigma or mystery. Ackbar Abbas calls it "a willingness to be drawn to phenomena that attract our attention yet do not submit entirely to our understanding" (qtd. Harris 10). If one figure gazes fascinated at another, it is because the other seems to conceal some knowledge about the self that is not quite available to consciousness or language. Such "excessive identifications," as Oliver Harris calls them, show us that "at the heart of fascination there is no thing, no single and static material object, but a complex and mobile *relation*" (Harris 11). As he explores the term in connection with his study of William Burroughs, Harris also foregrounds an important point: that fascination is often "perverse, a call to *internally* divided reactions," in particular the "contrary forces simultaneously at work in fascination: seduction and shame, attraction and repulsion" (17, 15). For Dickens, who often used variants of the phrase "the attraction of repulsion," the scenario of fascination involves a compelling visual bond with an external figure who seems to conceal some secret knowledge that might illuminate the internal conflicts of the gazer.

In letters, Dickens uses the word "fascination" in various moods: it can refer to the lure of nostalgia as well as to more sinister forms of attraction. A carefully worded argument against capital punishment that he sent to the editor of the *Edinburgh Review* in 1845 shows that Dickens thought deeply about the dangerous fascination allied with the mystery of death. "The Punishment of Death," he writes, has "a horrible fascination for many of those persons who render themselves liable to it, impelling them onward to the acquisition of a frightful notoriety." But the "strange fascination" is equally observable in "tens of thousands of decent, virtuous, well-conducted people, who are quite unable to resist" anything to do with "the bloodiest and most unnatural scoundrel with the Gallows before him. I observe that this strange interest does not prevail to anything like the same degree, where Death is not the Penalty. Therefore I connect it with the Dread and Mystery surrounding Death in any shape, but especially in the avenging form." He concludes that, through its power to fascinate, the death penalty "produces crime in the criminally disposed" and "a diseased sympathy—morbid and bad, but natural and often irresistible" in the non-criminal mind (4.340). Dickens's understanding that fascination depends on "Dread and Mystery" was based on intimate experience—and not only on his own well-known fascination with hangings and corpses displayed in morgues. Through characters of the same sex who are paired in the gaze of fascination, Dickens suggested the dread and mystery that reside in hidden parts of the unarticulated mind.

Prolonged face-to-face staring contests in the earlier novels invoke primarily the evil eye, wielded by a villain and confronted or resisted by the fascinated gazer. Such scenes can range from the melodramatic to the comic. When Nicholas Nickleby meets his wicked uncle Ralph, they "looked at each other for some seconds without speaking"; this mute confrontation is enough to stir in Ralph a deep competitive hatred of his nephew (*NN* 3). The internal violence generated by such gazing takes a comic turn in *The Old Curiosity Shop* when Dick Swiveller meets the ogre-lady Sally Brass across the desk they share. Unable to keep his eyes from her, Dick begins to develop "horrible desires to annihilate this Sally Brass," until he calms himself down by waving his ruler around like a sword (*OCS* 33). In the same novel the vicious Quilp makes up for his dwarfish stature through the power of his gaze, which enforces submission on his targets. In *Barnaby Rudge*, Dickens treats the face-to-face encounter more consistently as an image of suspected but secret knowledge of identity or paternity: Barnaby is always entranced, fixated, and fascinated by the appearance of the man he does not know to be his father, while Mr. Chester and his son, unknown to each other, play out a game of dominance and fascinated submission that includes another long staring scene. Long gazes always point to secrets, intuited but inaccessible; in the early novels the secrets tend to be actions, past or plotted crimes against others.

The power of the eye begins to enter a more psychological realm in the middle novels *Dombey and Son* and *David Copperfield*, where knowledge of others' secrets figures as a tool of power in relationships of resentment and rivalry. Mr. Carker the Manager, marked as a villain of melodrama by his white teeth and his red hair, is actually empowered by the keenness of his eye to wreak revenge on his unconscious employer Mr. Dombey. Because he has seen the revengeful passion within Edith, Carker—employed by Dombey in the role of mediator—insinuates himself into the couple and breaks it apart. At the same time Carker retains a more primitive evil eye, which he exercises on Rob the Grinder. When Carker hires him as a spy, Rob "was fascinated by Mr Carker, and never took his round eyes off him for an instant." Fixated by his own resentment against Dombey, Rob's eyes cannot leave his sadistic employer; they are "nailed upon him as if he had won the boy by a charm, body and soul" (DS 22).

The oppressed child whose internalized resentment takes form as fascination reappears in David Copperfield. Although the narrative displays David's determination to represent himself as free from anger or resentment, and to forgive those who have betrayed his love, it can be very suggestive about David's attractions to powerful, punitive men. The sado-masochistic attraction to Mr. Creakle is expressed quite directly: "I don't watch his eye in idleness, but because I am morbidly attracted to it, in a dread desire to know what he will do next, and whether it will be my turn to suffer, or somebody else's." David's perverse fascination with his schoolmaster's power extends beyond physical eyeing to prolonged fantasy: "Here I am in the playground, with my eye still fascinated by him, though I can't see him. The window at a little distance from which I know he is having his dinner, stands for him, and I eye that instead. If he shows his face near it, mine assumes an imploring and submissive expression" (DC 7). Brilliantly entangling the "I" with what the "eye" is drawn to, the passage reveals that David (like Rob the Grinder) is deeply implicated in the worship of power; that (like Uriah Heep), he is personally privy to the false humility of the resentful victim. There is nothing innocent about this child's eye in its fascination with that empty window.

David's most intimate rival is, of course, Uriah Heep, who resents David's genteel status and divines the secrets David wants to evade: his shaming childhood employment, and his unconscious love for Agnes Wickfield. Like Carker, Uriah derives his power from his desire to revenge himself on those who have humiliated him, and from his knowledge of the silences and verbal pieties that sustain a middle-class life. David is immediately fascinated by Uriah's watchful repulsiveness. Describing his red-brown, eyelashless eyes, "so unsheltered and unshaded, that I remember wondering how he went to sleep," David watches Uriah watching him for full minutes at a time as he pretends to be working at his law books:

Though his face was towards me, I thought, for some time, the writing being between us, that he could not see me; but looking that way more attentively, it made me uncomfortable to observe that, every now and then, his sleepless eyes would come below the writing, like two red suns, and stealthily stare at me for I daresay a whole minute at a time, during which his pen went, or pretended to go, as cleverly as ever. (*DC* 15)

Throughout the novel Uriah's eyes can read "below the writing" David does about himself, discerning there the closeted skeletons of David's class shame and desire.

When Uriah entraps David into a silent collusion with his own design to destroy Mr. Wickfield and marry Agnes (a plot that plays deliberately on David's unarticulated love), Uriah turns into an uncanny rival who elicits David's murderous but still unconscious sexual jealousy:

I believe I had a delirious idea of seizing the red-hot poker out of the fire, and running him through with it . . . the image of Agnes, outraged by so much as a thought of this red-headed animal's, remained in my mind when I looked at him. . . . He seemed to swell and grow before my eyes; the room seemed full of the echoes of his voice; and the strange feeling (to which no one, perhaps, is quite a stranger) that all this had occurred before, at some indefinite time, and that I knew what he was going to say next, took possession of me. (*DC* 25)

The déjà vu feeling marks the action of the unconscious in the scene, pointing to Dickens's knowledge of just what he is doing with those highly sexual images. It also works to blur the psychic boundaries between the two characters, in ways that are only underlined as the scene proceeds. David instantly discerns Uriah's motives for confessing his ambitions and making David a party to them: "I fathomed the depth of the rascal's whole scheme, and understood why he laid it bare." He sees all too well how Uriah's mind works; much as he hates it, he knows his man. When Uriah borrows David's nightcap and sleeps next to his fire, the unconscious identification between the two men is sealed. It should come as no surprise that, in the very next chapter, David falls in love with his boss's daughter and goes after her with an active aggression that is distinguished from Uriah's only through its noble steadiness of purpose and the sentimentality of its diction.

The contest of dark knowledge between David and Uriah develops further when Uriah exposes David's secret suspicion that Annie Strong has betrayed her husband's love. David is furious at having his hidden doubts displayed in public. As the two male figures "stood, front to front," David breaks out of politeness and into violence for the first and only time in his story. When he slaps Uriah's face, Uriah "caught the hand in his, and we stood, in that connexion, looking at each other. We stood so, a long time; long enough for me to see the white marks of my fingers die out of the deep red of his cheek, and leave it a deeper red." The physical violence forges the most prolonged and intimate bodily link between the two; it also allows Uriah to parody David's usual strategies by "turning the other cheek" and forgiving him. "He knew me better than I knew myself," David says, as if to underline the recognition that Uriah is a figure of self-knowledge, who acts out the suspicious, hostile, and resentful underside of his self-representation (DC 42).

The worship of power in a more idealized form suffuses the novel's other erotically charged relationship, between David and James Steerforth. Like the antagonism with Uriah, this friendship begins in a fascination engendered by the friction of unequal class status and later acquires the dimension of rivalry over a love object; in this case Steerforth acts out David's disavowed attraction to the working-class Little Emily. As a schoolboy, David allows Steerforth to exploit and feminize him in return for the feeling of protection he offers; as a young man, David puts Emily in position to be more literally seduced and abandoned by his erstwhile hero. Once again, David's mistake is a mistake in processing knowledge: he is unable to see, in Steerforth or in himself, the blatant class condescension and contempt that shape Steerforth's responses to the Peggotty ménage. Being in love with Steerforth means being in love with a reckless and pre-Victorian kind of privileged masculinity that attracts David, even as he argues for the earnest, disciplined, and hard-working model of manhood he means to espouse. It seems to attract Dickens as well: the Steerforth plot remains more melodramatic, less fully scrutinized, than are the currents of secret knowledge between David and Uriah Heep. Both relationships, however, make it clear that the venture into first-person narration had revealed new possibilities for Dickens's interest in fascination between men. If a staring contest in *Barnaby Rudge* meant that there was an unknown but vital connection between the fascinated parties, it now came to mean that the fascinated hero was seeing through another man those aspects of the self that he had attempted to bury or place beyond the range of self-knowledge.

🍂 Collaboration and Rivalry: Dickens and Wilkie Collins

After *Copperfield* was complete, Dickens's life took several important turns: he began editing *Household Words*, he moved his family from Devonshire Terrace to Tavistock Square, he shifted constantly between residence in England and France, and he devoted more of his time to managing and acting in amateur theatricals. Acting, he found, was a less isolating way than writing to become "another man." As he prepared Bulwer-Lytton's *Not So Bad as We Seem* for performance in June 1855, he invited an acquaintance with this explanation: "The real Theatre is so bad, that I have always a delight in setting up a sham one—besides deriving a pleasure from feigning to be somebody else which is akin to the pleasure of inventing—with the addition of the odd novelty that this sort of invention is executed in company" (7.641). The creative link between literary and personal forms of invention makes it clear that Dickens thought of writing as acting in private. Dickens liked the formula and repeated it in letters of 1857: "I derive a strange feeling out of it, like writing a book in company... which has to me a conviction of its being actual Truth without its pain" (8.256). Clearly the sheer toil of working himself up to write had become more burdensome; as he wrote to Maclise, acting "enables me, as it were, *to write a book in company* instead of in my own solitary room, and to feel its effect coming freshly back upon me from the reader" (8.367). In the event, acting proved to have the more profound effect of turning Dickens into another kind of man than the one he imagined himself to be in 1850.

One indicator of the change in direction was Dickens's new friendship with Wilkie Collins. He met the younger novelist in 1851, after inviting him to play the role of a valet in *Not So Bad as We Seem*. By 1853 they were close enough that Dickens invited Collins and a mutual friend, the painter Augustus Egg, on a nine-week tour of Switzerland and Italy. In this new trio Dickens was the older man and the guide; he revisited many of the old haunts, writing home to Catherine and Georgina about places they had lived and people they had known. To the home audience he claimed that the three travelers "are all the best friends, and have never had the least difference." At the same time he satirized the younger men's attempts to imitate him by growing mustaches, and made fun of Collins's learned diatribes about art and music. Perhaps Dickens did not want his women to know quite how much he enjoyed being in younger male company (7.204–5).

The good-tempered Collins was twelve years younger, unattached, and happy to eat, drink, and womanize without remorse. His imagination, like Dickens's, was drawn to the macabre, the irrational, and the melodramatic—interests Forster tended to view with skepticism. Collins was also willing, for a time, to profit from the mentorship of the older novelist, who took great pains to teach Collins what he knew about the writing business. In the face of disapproval from Forster and probably from Catherine, Dickens found comradeship in the new friend who shared his propensity to spend the night hours exploring the darker haunts of London or Paris. He wrote to Collins from Boulogne in July 1854, inviting him out to play in London: "The interval I propose to pass in a career of amiable dissipation and unbounded license in the metropolis. If you will come and breakfast with me about midnight—anywhere—any day—and go to bed no more until we fly to these pastoral retreats—I shall be delighted to have so vicious an associate" (7.366). Clearly Collins's reputation as a sybarite was an affectionate joke between them. The year after Dickens separated from Catherine, Collins moved out of his mother's house and began living with his mistress, Mrs. Caroline Graves. Dickens wrote to Esther Nash in 1861, reporting on Collins's handsome rooms in Harley Street, "We never speak of the (female) skeleton in that house.... I hope [Collins's mind] does not run in any matrimonial groove.... I can *not* imagine any good coming of such an end in this instance" (9.388–89). He did not mention that his own life was very much like Collins's at that time.

Changes in John Forster's life may well have influenced Dickens's turn to a younger and wilder man who offered more easy-going company as well as the opportunity for professional patronage on Dickens's part. On 11 March 1856, Dickens learned that Forster was to be married. He wrote to Georgy that day: "Tell Catherine that I have the most prodigious, overwhelming, crushing, astounding, blinding, deafening, pulverising, scarifying secret of which Forster is the hero, imaginable by the united efforts of the whole British population" (8.70). Making play with his wife's interest in gossip, Dickens's exaggerations also manage to suggest that he felt Forster's news as a major disorientation. Other references during the period before the marriage are brief and rather facetious; he was clearly determined to write as if he did not care. In fact Forster had already left Dickens behind in the literary trenches. At the end of 1855 he accepted a position as Secretary to the Lunacy Commission that offered a higher salary than he had previously been able to muster. He resigned as editor of the *Examiner* and left the paper entirely when he married Eliza Colburn, a widow with 35,000 pounds, in September 1856. With no children to support, Forster was now a wealthy man. Dickens, still scrambling to support his large family and (after 1858) the Ternans as well, suspected that his friend's new security lay behind his severe opposition to Dickens's idea of doing public readings for money. He still felt that he had to convince Forster that he was right to begin the reading tours, but he wrote to Collins in March 1858, as the decision was pressing on him, "Forster seems to be extraordinarily irrational about it. (I have a misgiving sometimes, that his money must have got into his head)" (8.534–36). Throughout the years of public readings, Dickens regularly sent Forster bulletins about how well they had gone and how much money he had made. Although they were not as close as they had once been, Dickens continued to appeal to Forster as his bar of conscience and respectability, providing him with letters that recorded his thoughts and experiences for posterity.

Dickens also wanted to persuade Forster of Collins's virtues. In a letter describing Collins's response to the new portrait of Dickens by the Parisian artist Ary Scheffer, Dickens wrote, "Scheffer finished yesterday; and Collins, who has a good eye for pictures, says there is no man living who could do the painting about the eyes." Dickens, however, could not see himself in the portrait. "And so I come to the conclusion that I never *do* see myself" (8.66). This was his typical response to portraits or photographs; he had already complained to Forster that the Scheffer portrait "does not look to me at all like, nor does it strike me that if I saw it in a gallery I should suppose myself to be the original" (8.9). By 1861 he had made a rule of it: to Richard Lane, who had engraved a Dickens photograph, he wrote, "I do not pretend to know my own face. I *do* pretend to know the faces of my friends and fellow creatures, but not my own" (9.523). Apparently proud of his inability to "see" his own face, Dickens may have been expressing resistance to the notion that he could be captured in stasis, when he was capable of becoming so many different kinds of men. Collins's remark, that representing Dickens's eyes would be beyond the skill of any painter, would have been a welcome mirroring, in Collins's "good eye," of Dickens's own wishes. But Dickens's comments also reveal an awareness that his way of gathering knowledge, including knowledge of the self, was to look outward into the faces of others.

In letters to Collins Dickens could be informal and honest about his less-than-respectable feelings, his night wanderings, and his curiosity about figures he saw in the streets. As the friendship moved toward literary collaboration, the two writers dramatized the differences in their characters as part of their inventive process. Dickens was "the Genius of Order"; Collins "the Genius of Disorder" (8.161); Dickens the fanatical worker, Collins the dreamy idler. From 1854 until 1861, when his own career took off after the publication of *A Woman in White*, Collins contributed to the multi-authored stories that made up the extra Christmas numbers of *Household Words*. In 1856 Dickens took Collins onto the permanent salaried staff of the magazine and ran a long story of his with a byline, a distinction usually reserved for Dickens himself. Recuperating from an illness in 1861, Dickens asked Collins to substitute for him as the main speaker at a Benevolent Society dinner, writing of it as good training for public life (9.419). When Collins fell ill the next year, he offered to help complete Collins's novel *No Name* in a manner "so like you as that no one should find out the difference" (10.142), as if he could readily transform himself into a Collins clone. By that time the two men had collaborated in drama as well as fiction. Dickens produced Collins's play *The Lighthouse* at Tavistock House in June 1855. In the summer of 1856 they were at work together on the script of *The Frozen Deep,* the play that was to jump-start a radical change in Dickens's life and a shift in his representations of male identification and rivalry.

The Frozen Deep was a second stage in Dickens's response to the disappearance of Sir John Franklin's Arctic exploration party and to the speculation, voiced by Dr. John Rae, that the party had resorted to cannibalism. Dickens had pronounced on the impossibility of such degradation in a long *Household Words* article, "The Lost Arctic Voyagers" (December 1854; Dent 3.254–69). Early in 1856 he received from Franklin's widow a laudatory memoir of Franklin written by Sir John Richardson, who had accompanied Franklin on two earlier Arctic expeditions. What moved Dickens in the memoir was its testimony to male friendship. He wrote to Forster (no doubt recalling Forster's role as his own biographer), "I think Richardson's manly friendship, and love of Franklin, one of the noblest things I ever knew in my life. It makes one's heart beat high, with a sort of sacred joy" (8.66). A month later he announced to his sub-editor W. H. Wills that "Collins and I have a mighty original notion (mine in the beginning) for another play at Tavistock House" (8.81). The "original notion" was a play praising British self-control in the setting of a socked-in Arctic exploring party. His determination that Collins was to be the principal author of the play—when in fact Dickens altered the draft scripts to his own liking—may have been part of his plan to bring Collins into the public eye, to "make" Collins into a writer known as Dickens's protégé. Or perhaps he did not want to admit to having authored a play that was so clearly a vehicle for his own passionate self-dramatization.

The Frozen Deep featured Dickens in the role of Richard Wardour, a fiercely masculine Arctic explorer with a longstanding passion for Clara, who has rejected his fearsome advances and, in his absence, become engaged to the gentle and effeminate Frank Aldersley (played by Collins). Although Wardour does not know who his rival is, both men turn out to be officers in the same Arctic exploration party, whose remaining members are stranded, ill and starving, at some furthest outpost of the icy world. In a last attempt to get help, a rescue party is sent out, its members chosen by lot. Wardour discovers by chance that Aldersley is his hated rival, and arranges at the last minute to join him in the rescue party. At the end of the second act, the tension of the play lies entirely within Wardour's character: will he give in to his jealousy and murder Aldersley? Act Three builds that tension as the women wait for the rescued explorers to show up in Newfoundland: in the final scene

Wardour enters carrying the failing Aldersley in his arms, gives him back to his betrothed, and then dies in noble self-sacrifice at Clara's feet.

The play makes a clean division between male and female worlds. Act One shows us only the anxious waiting women, while Act Two is set entirely among the men of the party. When Wardour enters, his first words are that he likes the Arctic "because there are no women here" (Brannon 126). The most successful scene in the play involves a triangle of men that effectively replaces the conventional love triangle. Wardour's old and admiring friend Crayford, to whom he had once confessed his disappointed and misogynist feelings, now hears him say that he lives only for "the time when I and that man shall meet, face to face…it is written on my heart now, that we two shall meet, and know each other." Twice more Wardour repeats his mantra: that he lives "for the coming of one day—for the meeting with one man" (Brannon 134). Crayford watches in growing horror as Frank's identity is revealed and Wardour schemes to leave with him. The three men scuffle; violence threatens; Crayford tries to protect one man from the other. The drama hangs on Crayford's anxiety as the other two exit: can the man he has idealized decline into a murderer? As the "third man," Crayford plays a part that interested Dickens: he witnesses the rivalry and attempts unsuccessfully to intervene in its uncontrollable passions. Male pairs that turn into trios may remind us of mediated situations among Dickens's own friendships; they also emphasize the split between actor and observer that was so central in Dickens's relation to himself.

Wardour-Dickens becomes a one-man Franklin expedition, whose test lies before him. Dying, he explains that his murderous frozen deep was melted by Frank's childlike trust: "I set him his place to sleep in apart; but he crept between the Devil and me, and nestled his head on *my* breast, and slept *here*" (Brannon 159). As the play ends, the two men's intimacy is rendered as an interchange of qualities. Wardour calls on Clara to "love him, for helping *me!*" while Frank cries, "He has given all his strength to my weakness; and now, see how strong *I* am, and how weak *he* is!" The confrontational "face to face" meeting turns out to be an exchange in which each man infuses the other with the strength he had lacked. For Dickens, who could showcase both a violent, long-brewing sense of injustice and its transmutation into noble self-sacrifice, the play was a perfect vehicle. He played his part with a realistic passion that stunned and frightened his audiences and led one reviewer to rave that Dickens "has all the technical knowledge and resources of a professed actor; but these, the dry bones of acting, are kindled by that soul of vitality which can only be put into them by the man of genius and the interpreter of the affections" (qtd. 8.254n.).

In August Dickens took *The Frozen Deep* to Manchester, with the purpose of raising money for Douglas Jerrold's family after Jerrold's sudden death. Because the Dickens women could not be displayed in the large and very public setting of Manchester's Free Trade Hall, he hired the professional actress Mrs. Frances Ternan and two of her three actress daughters to play the female parts. On that stage, famously, Dickens met and fell in love with eighteen-year-old Ellen Ternan. When he returned from Manchester, Dickens began to dismantle his troubled marriage, along with some friendships and partnerships put under strain by the separation. His new life as a "vagabond" began almost immediately as a restless two-week trip with Collins in pursuit of the Ternans, who were now on tour at Doncaster. Their excuse was copy for *Household Words*: as they traveled, the two writers collaborated on a description of their experiences that came out during October 1857 as "The Lazy Tour of Two Idle Apprentices." Just after returning from Manchester, Dickens had written Collins of "the grim despair and restlessness of this subsidence from excitement" that led him to propose the journey. "I want to escape from myself. For, when I *do* start up and stare myself seedily in the face . . . my blankness is inconceivable—indescribable—my misery, amazing" (8.423). He did not want to let go of Richard Wardour; his face was empty without him. A year later, he still missed the role; as he told Collins while he was away on a reading tour, "I miss Richard Wardour's dress. And always want to put it on. I would rather, by a great deal, act" (8.624). He seems to have felt more emotional range disguised as Wardour than he did in his staged impersonation of the famous author Charles Dickens.

"The Lazy Tour of Two Idle Apprentices" managed to go on dramatizing Dickens through tensions between two very different men. As the title suggests, it picked up on a contrast between fanatical action and sleepy idleness that had figured briefly in *The Frozen Deep*. Even the traveling plans of Dickens and Collins were uncharacteristically vague; while they planned to stay in Doncaster for the second week, they were unclear about the first. "Conglomeration prevailing in the maps—and our minds—to an alarming extent, I have the faintest idea of our trip," Dickens wrote to W. H. Wills as they set out (8.438). But he did have a secret plan in mind: to ascend Carrock Fell, a 1,500-foot mountain in Cumberland he had read about in a guidebook. The plan, like most of Dickens's plans, was carried out despite the fact that they discovered on arrival that "nobody goes up. Guides have forgotten it." Using the comic-telegraphic style, Dickens described the ascent to Forster: "Rain terrific, black mists, darkness of night." With Dickens in the lead and their inn-keeper guide "done up in no time," the three men reached the top and had no idea how to get back down. As they spiraled around the mountain in the dark, they reached a "Watercourse, thundering and roaring." Dickens insisted they follow it down, "subject to all gymnastic hazards." After two hours of that, Collins fell and sprained his ankle badly. He was somehow brought down, and Dickens crowed: "C. D. carrying C. melo-dramatically (Wardour to the life!) everywhere; into and out of carriages; up and down stairs; to bed every step" (8.440). To Georgina Hogarth, who now received letters to the family that did not mention Catherine, Dickens repeated his obvious pleasure in having "enacted Wardour over again." He expressed no remorse about having subjected Collins to an ordeal he had sensibly resisted in the first place. A few days later, Dickens reported, Collins was walking "with two thick sticks, like an admiral in a farce"; he managed the rest of the tour with very little choice but to stay at their inns and write (8.444).

In his letters, Dickens played his usual role as the comedian of disaster. The charm of "The Lazy Tour" is quite different: its most amusing sections are dialogues or contrasts between the two "idlers," called, after William Hogarth's 1747 engravings "Industry and Idleness," Mr. Thomas Idle and Mr. Francis Goodchild. In his portion of the first chapter, Dickens claims that "there was not a moral pin to choose between them, and they were both idle in the last degree." But there are distinctions to be made: "Goodchild was laboriously idle, and would take upon himself any amount of pains and labour to assure himself that he was idle; in short, had no better idea of idleness than that it was useless industry." Thomas Idle, however, is "an idler of the unmixed Irish or Neapolitan type, a passive idler, a born-and-bred idler, a consistent idler, who practiced what he would have preached if he had not been too idle to preach; a one entire and perfect chysolite of idleness" (Dent 3.422). The national stereotypes betray the actual moral difference between the two in Dickens's mind; yet, as he wrote, he went on worrying the difference as if it offered a genuine attempt to see himself through the eyes of another.

As Thomas Idle sings "Annie Laurie," Goodchild revolts against the notion that a man would "lay him doon and dee" for a woman—better to "get up, and punch somebody's head." For him—Wardour again—love and violence go hand in hand. For Idle, it's not worth the trouble to fall in love, and Goodchild would be better off keeping out of it. "Mr Goodchild, who is always in love with somebody, and not unfrequently with several objects at once, made no reply" (Dent 3.423). The unusually autobiographical back-and-forth of such dialogues creates the freshness of a work otherwise filled with travel journalism and Gothic dream stories. As chapter four opens, Goodchild returns to the lame Idle after a day exploring the country and visiting a lunatic asylum (perhaps an in-joke about Forster's new position or Dickens's new state of mind). Idle goes on a long rant about Goodchild's wrong idea of play: "Here is a man goes systematically tearing himself to pieces, and putting himself through an incessant course of training, as if he were always under articles to fight a match for the champion's belt, and he calls it Play!" Goodchild smiles amiably—and why shouldn't he? Idle is advertising his strong suit. Idle talks on, calling Goodchild "an absolutely terrible fellow," a "fearful man" who can "do nothing like another man. Where another fellow would fall into a footbath of action or emotion, you fall into a mine. Where any other fellow would be a painted butterfly, you are a fiery dragon" (Dent 3.448). Goodchild remains unfazed and unrepentant, while Dickens pleases himself by imagining himself seen by another man as an extremity of manhood. Imagining himself from another's point of view was not so bad, after all. Still, the fact that the erstwhile champion of earnest work plays with such matters is important. All the effort that had kept his career and his family life going had come to look like a great deal of trouble that had failed to set him at ease. He knew, now, that death was the only way out of the turbulence of being Dickens.

🐛 Doubles and Triples

The new association of male pairs and trios with issues of work, idleness, and death shaped both *A Tale of Two Cities* and *Our Mutual Friend*. The idea for *A Tale* seems to have come to Dickens as he lay onstage as Richard Wardour, pretending to die while the tears of Maria Ternan fell on his face and beard. Its plot, in which Sydney Carton sacrifices his life so that Charles Darnay/ Evrémonde can enjoy his happiness with the woman they both love, puts some novelistic meat on the bare bones of the play. The relation between the look-alike doubles is minimally fleshed out, however. They meet at Darnay's English trial, during which Carton watches Lucy Manette's eyes on Darnay, and invents a strategy—based on his own resemblance to Darnay—that helps win Darnay's acquittal. After the trial the two meet face to face over dinner at a tavern, where Carton forces Darnay to toast Lucy, and announces drunkenly that he doesn't like his double. Once Darnay has left, Carton looks at his own face in a mirror and addresses himself with scorn: "A good reason for taking to a man, that he shows you what you have fallen away from and what you might have been! Change places with him, and would you have been looked at by those blue eyes as he was, and commiserated by that agitated face as he was? Come on, have it out in plain words! You hate the fellow" (*TTC* 4). With that shift to alienation and rivalry accomplished, the pair is never seen together again until Sydney Carton changes clothes with prisoner Evrémonde and dies by guillotine in his place. As in Wardour's death, the act proclaims his self-sacrificial nobility while advertising for time and eternity his superiority to the living rival.

Dickens turned from melodrama to realism when he dramatized scenes between Carton and the successful attorney Stryver, which allowed him to play further variations on the themes of work and idleness. Stryver, "already shouldering his way to a large and lucrative practice," employs Carton, "idlest and most unpromising of men," to boil down his cases to their "pith and marrow." The men drink steadily through the night, while Carton wraps cold towels around his head (shades of Collins nursing his sprained ankle) and does Stryver's work for him. When Stryver attempts to lecture Carton on his failure of "energy and purpose," Carton tells him, "You were always driving and riving and shouldering and pressing, to that restless degree that I had no chance for my life but in rust and repose" (*TTC* 2.5). Sympathy goes to the Collins figure in these scenes: he does the real work, while Stryver gets the credit and the big name; Carton understands Lucy's nature, while Stryver pompously decides that he will condescend to propose to her.

Once again the doubling of men turns into a triad, with Darnay, Carton, and Stryver (not to mention most of the older men) clustered in desire around the female figure Carton aptly—if disingenuously—calls "a golden-haired doll" (*TTC* 2.5). Among the male characters Dickens mixes and matches aspects of himself, Forster, and Collins. Carton, whose restless, depressive wanderings and sacrificial death mark him as a Wardour-Dickens figure, is explicitly stripped of the fanatical energy that characterizes Mr. Francis Goodchild in "The Lazy Tour of Two Idle Apprentices," but his role as a brilliant behind-the-scenes professional combines aspects of both Forster and Collins. It is as if Dickens were, like Sydney Carton, yearning to change places and become another man—perhaps a man less like his "striving" self and more like Wilkie Collins. When, some years later, Dickens came to write *Our Mutual Friend*, he explored such pairings and exchanges of male energy in a more detailed and satisfying way.

"It is questionable whether any man quite relishes being mistaken for any other man," the narrator remarks early in *Our Mutual Friend*, but the novel is all about men who are and men who arrange to be mistaken for others (*OMF* 1.2). John Harmon and his look-alike double George Radfoot meet because each has been mistaken for the other. The "horrible old Lady Tippins" carries her title only because her late husband was "knighted in mistake for somebody else by His Majesty George the Third" (*OMF* 1.10). In fact, claims the narrator, the wrong ideas of the present time are "generally some form of tribute to Somebody for something that was never done, or, if ever done, that was done by Somebody Else" (*OMF* 2.11). Bradley Headstone "in his own schoolmaster clothes... usually looked as if they were the clothes of some other man," but dressed to imitate Rogue Riderhood "he now looked, in the clothes of some other man or men, as if they were his own" (*OMF* 4.1). Taking on the role of Somebody Else has become essential to the exploration of manhood.

Partnerships abound in the novel, most of them operating as intimate alliances of distrust, in which suspicion of the partner is hardly different from suspicion of the self. The alliances are for the most part betrayed when one partner makes a secret alliance with another man. The young male figures—Eugene Wrayburn, Mortimer Lightwood, Bradley Headstone, John Harmon—are all doubled and redoubled in ways that display the splits in their inner worlds. The novel is full of eyes and looks that signify knowledge, or the absence of knowledge, between two parties. So systematic and forthright a focus on the connection between the depths of the self and "another man" is proof that Dickens was consciously and deliberately playing as many variations on the theme as he possibly could. Even the nickname given to that most unfascinating of characters, "Fascination Fledgby," represents an act of projection onto another man. After Mrs. Lammle accuses her husband of exercising his "dangerous fascinations" upon Georgiana Podsnap, the two schemers confer that "honorary title" on Fledgby while Mr. Lammle courts Georgiana Podsnap as Fledgby's proxy (*OMF* 2.4).

Dickens clearly wanted the word "Fascination" to circulate in his narrative, preferably in a free-floating and preposterous way. The title, *Our Mutual Friend*, has its own floating meanings, some of which look back to the Christiana Weller affair. Apologizing to Clarkson Stanfield about missing an engagement because of a crisis in the Weller-Thompson marriage, Dickens had described Thompson as one who, "on the very eve of his marriage with a very beautiful girl—the ring purchased, wedding dresses made, and so forth—finds the whole contract shattered like Glass, in an instant, under the most inexplicable circumstances that ever distracted the head of 'a mutual friend'" (4.397–98). The ironies of rivalry and mediation are in full play when Dickens uses that conventional phrase, both in the letter and in the title of his novel.

The man who exists in violent intimacy with another man sits at the heart of the tale, in the rivalry of Eugene Wrayburn and Bradley Headstone. Bradley Headstone is given Richard Wardour's energy, his obsessive unrequited love, and the murderous, jealous rage that is inseparable from his love for Lizzie Hexam. Eugene Wrayburn is given Sydney Carton's indifference, his inability to strive for his own advancement, and the opportunity of self-redemption through love. In this last great novel, however, Dickens allowed himself to uncover a great deal more about the story. Headstone is a version of Dickens (minus the genius, of course): he has a low past that he prefers to have forgotten, he works under strict self-discipline to maintain his respectability, and he has achieved a certain success which he is trying to pass on to his young pupil-teacher Charley Hexam. Meeting Lizzie (his Ellen Ternan) undoes Headstone in a way that is all the more painful because he is fully aware of how completely his life has escaped his grip. Unlike Wardour or Carton, Headstone is given no miraculous self-sacrificial change of heart, only a gradual degradation into death.

Eugene Wrayburn's case is humanized through his loving partnership with Mortimer Lightwood, his schoolmate, fellow-barrister, roommate, and confidant. As the two set up house together in a bachelor cottage, Eugene wishes they were keeping a lighthouse together far from the inanity of social forms. The in-joke reference to Wilkie Collins's *The Lighthouse* suggests that the intimate, playful, wry wit that sweetens their dialogues may be a more innocent version of the Dickens-Collins friendship. Once Wrayburn becomes obsessed with Headstone, Lightwood becomes the required third man, voicing concerns of conscience and sanity that go unheard in the tussle of fascinated rivalry.

The contest between the rivals Wrayburn and Headstone is charged with hostility from the moment of meeting; Dickens manages to keep the alternating current crackling in their scenes together. When they meet, they regard each other with cruel looks; Eugene's is cruel "in its cold disdain of him, as a creature of no worth"; Bradley's "had a raging jealousy and fiery wrath in it." The scene evolves as Dickens's greatest staring contest: "those two, no matter who spoke, or whom was addressed, looked at each other. There was some secret, sure perception between them, which set them against one another in all ways" (*OMF* 2.6). The greatness of the dialogue lies in its fairness to the worst aspects of both participants. It reads as an intensely uncomfortable humiliation of a lower-middle-class man by an upper-class man; it also reads as an offensive intrusion of paranoid and self-humiliating suspicion on Headstone's part. There is little to choose between them; each releases the other's hidden resources of aggression. The "sure" knowledge between them is of sexual rivalry and class antagonism, wedded firmly together.

Over and over Schoolmaster Headstone plays into Lawyer Wrayburn's hands by delivering lines that Wrayburn mocks, twists, and returns, like a series of poisoned darts. Wrayburn manages to penetrate Headstone's motives, negate Headstone's identity, and reveal nothing himself. He can do so only because he is a man who occupies a ground identical to Headstone's; both men are drawn toward the corpse-robber's daughter as if she were a lifeline thrown out to succor failing souls. For Headstone, who suffers deeply from class resentment, the loving of Lizzie Hexam and the hating of Eugene Wrayburn are inextricable. But, although he cannot conceal that resentment, he is quite capable of condemning Wrayburn's clever moves and insisting on the seriousness of his threats. One has the class assurance, the other the emotional drive, that the other lacks, and they recognize each other; each conveys to the other, "I see who you are and what you're doing."

The wordless nocturnal cat-and-mouse chases around London dramatize this same dynamic in dumb show. Eugene, the goader, leads Bradley hither and yon, only to turn suddenly and pass him. As Eugene narrates to the horrified Mortimer Lightwood, "Then we face one another, and I pass him as though unaware of his existence, and he undergoes grinding torments" (*OMF* 3.10). Both men seem equally compelled to rehearse and defer the moment when they might turn and meet each other "face to face." Eugene knows that tormenting Bradley is a way of projecting onto him the emotional situation that they share. He tells Lightwood, "I own to the weakness of objecting to occupy a ludicrous position, and therefore I transfer the position to the scouts [Headstone and Charley Hexam]." When he takes Lightwood on the chase with him one night, Lightwood feels "astonishment that so careless a man could be so wary, and that so idle a man could take so much trouble." Eugene has come alive in his courtship of the danger suppressed within his lethargic idleness. It is Lightwood who cannot sleep that night; he "cannot lose sight of that fellow's face" (*OMF* 3.10).

Wrayburn's crisis comes in his face-to-face encounter with his would-be murderer. As the narrator tells it, the murder attempt is an intimate encounter in which the bodies of the two men are fused in an embrace of assault and dependence. When they fall on the riverbank together, it is not entirely clear who has gone into the river: "After dragging at the assailant, he fell on the bank with him, and then there was another great crash, and then a splash, and all was done" (*OMF* 4.6). Through this near-fatal identity exchange, Eugene gets what he needs: enough of Bradley's primal energy to survive, and a blurring of class status that allows him to do what Bradley would have done: to marry Lizzie. As in *The Frozen Deep*, the power flowing from one man to another is eroticized but not specifically homosexual. The sheer energy of released desire—whether it's a renewed desire to live or an active embrace of death—is the product in Dickens's fantasies of male fusion.

Bradley Headstone continues the chain of self-projection down the social scale when he doubles with the pure aggression of Rogue Riderhood, hoping to throw suspicion on Riderhood for his own assault on Wrayburn. In another of the novel's great scenes, Riderhood figures out his game and enters his classroom, where he plays elegantly with Headstone's two identities as murderer and schoolmaster in front of his pupils. When he sees that Riderhood has fished up the clothes in which Headstone meant to impersonate him, the schoolmaster turns and slowly wipes his "respectable" name off the blackboard. His only remaining job is to kill the murderous part of himself in another intimate embrace, this time with Riderhood. Their face-to-face double drowning, Riderhood "girdled still with Bradley's iron ring" (*OMF* 4.15), renders Headstone's death a permanent return to the willed self-mastery of the life he had intended to lead.

In the John Harmon—Julius Handford—John Rokesmith story, the themes I have been sounding are gathered together within the boundaries of a single body. In this character, otherness becomes the explicit condition of identity. On his return to England, Harmon takes up with his sailor double George Radfoot, in a plot to spy on Bella Wilfer and defer his father's injunction to marry her. Like Wrayburn and Headstone, Harmon evades the predictable marriage plot by mediating his desires through another man. As he reconstructs his story, he recalls himself drugged and placed in a room full of men. "I saw a figure like myself lying dressed in my clothes on a bed. What might have been, for anything I knew, a silence of days, weeks, months, years, was broken by a violent wrestling of men all over the room. The figure like myself was assailed, and my valise was in its hand." It is unclear whether he or George Radfoot is the figure on the bed; we learn only later that Radfoot has secretly plotted to steal Harmon's fortune and destroy him, but that others have intervened to attack them both. As Harmon tells it, his sense of identity was destroyed: "There was no such thing as I, within my knowledge." When both he and Radfoot are dumped into the Thames, Harmon's return to his own name is figured as the falling away of a "heavy horrid unintelligible something": the part of himself that falls away as Radfoot dies and he comes back to self and survival (*OMF* 2.13). When he tells his retrospective story, however, Harmon speaks as if he were another man, interrogating himself. He is not yet finished with self-division.

When he decides to "kill" his identity as John Harmon and appear in the world as John Rokesmith, he splits himself between the desiring Harmon and the bland Secretary Rokesmith. Rokesmith is identified with self-sacrifice and duty: he must stay away from Bella, clear Gaffer Hexam's name, and clean up the other moral messes his deceit has created. John Harmon is identified with the man whose life force resisted drowning, the aggressive and sexual desire that has to be crushed under piles and mounds of figurative earth.

The masculine force of John Harmon only emerges when he becomes an unnamed "man," dressed up in George Radfoot's coat and carrying Radfoot's knife to scare Riderhood until he signs a retraction of his accusation that Gaffer Hexam was John Harmon's murderer. After this burst of aggressive manhood, he returns to his impersonation as Secretary and agent of another, re-choosing a death-in-life that is comparable to Bradley Headstone's school-master self. The difference is that Harmon-Rokesmith gets to cast himself in both parts and to control the staging. So the two Dickens figures split between them the controlled impersonation of acting "another man" and the uncontrollable self-destruction of a man relentlessly drawn toward an inner underworld he has labored all his life to escape.

Dickens's plan for the ending of *The Mystery of Edwin Drood* brought the theme of murderous rivalry to its highest focus. As Forster summarized it, *Drood* was to be the story "of the murder of a nephew by his uncle; the originality of which was to consist in the review of the murderer's career by himself at the close, when its temptations were to be dwelt upon as if, not he the culprit, but some other man, were the tempted. The last chap-ters were to be written in the condemned cell, to which his wickedness, all elaborately elicited from him as if told of another, had brought him" (Forster 808). The plan brings Dickens's journalistic interest in the cool demeanor of guilty murderers together with his personal interest in the dissociated self. Stimulated by opium, John Jasper alternates between different states of being that allow him to discuss himself as if he were somebody else. At the same time the bonds of male rivalry are tightened by the blood connection between uncle and nephew—a connection that allows Jasper to act out a passionate and loving identification with his victim Edwin Drood while he toys with Drood's fiancée Rosa Bud. The difference in generation suggests a move into new personal territory: the older man's envious attachment to the young. Even in its unfinished form the novel reveals the intensity of its concentration by producing, chapter after chapter, instances of triangulated desire among its array of characters. In *Drood* Dickens used elements of the sensation novel he had learned from Wilkie Collins, but his primary quarry lay in his long, richly elaborated obsession with "another man."

It might be argued of *Our Mutual Friend*, as it has been argued of *David Copperfield*, that its emotionally compelling male friendships and rivalries are succeeded in the plot by conventionally heterosexual marriages. I would sug-gest that in Dickens's imagination the internal energies stirred up by desire for an elusive object are redirected as identification and aggression aimed at other men. The erotic charge of fascination is not so much an indicator of sexual attraction or repulsion as it is a kind of internal shift in the fantasy of the self. Fascination does not end or get diverted to other channels; it floats, in a perpetual state of knowing and testing the limits of the self through the other. Dickens's fascinated men are enthralled with—and by—the men they might have been but for their pride, their shame, their age, their class position, or their need for respectability. They are, to put it another way, in love with their own transformational possibilities, the potential, yearned-for multiplicity of themselves.

CHAPTER 5

Manager of the House

Shortly after Dickens's twenty-seventh birthday, he tried to put his parents away in a cottage. John Dickens, whose debts had been accumulating for some years, was headed for bankruptcy again; his Holborn landlord had given him notice and bill collectors were at his door. Midway through *Nicholas Nickleby* and relatively secure in his prospects, Dickens decided to settle the matter of his embarrassing parents once and for all. After completing the monthly number for March 1839, he would find them a cottage far from London, pay the rent, give them an allowance, and get his father out of the vicinity of his publishers Chapman and Hall, from whom John Dickens had been regularly begging. Speed was essential: he wanted his parents to disappear the day their lodging expired, before their creditors could be notified. He would have to pay the bills, but might, he thought, be able to get away without paying in full if John Dickens were "non est inventus," not to be found (1.515). The town of Exeter in Devon was chosen, far enough from London on the southwestern coast, and Dickens booked himself a place in a coach for Monday, 4 March, leaving his lawyer Thomas Mitton and his friend John Forster to carry out the London details of the business. The move was to take place on the following Saturday.

The "toilsome journey" he anticipated in a letter to Forster (1.515) became, in his letters home, a triumphant success story. On Tuesday morning he "walked out to look about me," and immediately found Mile End cottage just a mile out of Exeter. "Something guided me to it," he wrote to Catherine, "for I went on without turning right or left, and was no more surprised when I came upon it and saw the bill up, than if I had passed it every day for years." Everything about it was perfect, from its landlady to its "excellent parlor," its "noble garden," its numerous cellars, meat-safes, and coalholes, and its exquisite neatness and cleanliness. The rent was low, only twenty pounds a year. He took it immediately (1.517).

In the long and detailed letters he wrote from Exeter to Catherine, Forster, and Mitton, Dickens's sense of competence and dispatch is on full display. He is charmed by his ability to charm the landlady, the upholsterer's daughter, and everyone else he encounters. He enumerates for Catherine just what furniture he has chosen for each room, down to "the crockery and glass, the stair-carpet, and the floorcloth"; he assures Mitton of the beauty and interest of the spot (1.522–24); he regales Forster with comic accounts of the rural characters he has met, rehearsing them for future fictional roles (1.518–21). He arranges for precise sums of money to be given to his parents for their coach journeys. Every detail of the ignominious retreat is—as he tells it—under his control. The anger, disappointment, and sense of interruption that fueled his decision to banish his parents from London were transformed, or bound, by the excitement of making a house into which they would safely fit—for the rest of their lives, he trusted. John Dickens, at fifty-three, was willing and able to work, but that inconvenient fact was swept under the rugs that Dickens had chosen for the cottage's two sitting rooms.

The exile was tolerated for about four years; by the end of 1842 the John Dickenses were back in the outer boroughs of London. Their complaints had begun as early as four months after the move, making Dickens "sick at heart" after all he had done in his whirlwind reorganization of their lives (1.560). Putting intractable human material into magically appearing cottage retreats was not turning out as well as it did in his fiction. Nonetheless, the business of making houses to contain family scenes and family secrets, as well as other kinds of humanly unmanageable experience, was to become increasingly important to Dickens, both in his life and in his narratives. His way of writing novels in monthly numbers, requiring the regular production of a precise number of chapters and pages within a ritualized time frame, was just one example of a characteristic negotiation between highly ordered frames and their potentially explosive contents. This tendency came to its fullest expression during the busiest decade of Dickens's life, from the late 1840s to the late 1850s, when his managerial talents and obsessions were engaged in a variety of ways: running the Home for Homeless Women at Urania Cottage, managing elaborate amateur theatricals, creating and editing *Household*

Words, acquiring and furnishing houses for his own family and others, and enforcing household disciplines on his wife and children.

Houses—as distinguished from the inns and lodgings of the early fiction—came into greater prominence in the fictions of this decade, beginning with *Dombey and Son*, and continuing through *David Copperfield*, *Bleak House*, and *Little Dorrit*. In the 1850s Dickens also began experimenting with collaborative forms of storytelling in the Christmas numbers of *Household Words*, for which he would create frame stories—narrative houses, so to speak—and ask other writers to furnish individual rooms with their own inventions. All of these enterprises reveal variants of the pattern or rhythm that showed itself in the matter of Mile End cottage: Dickens takes detailed control over the practical housing of a complex human situation, and discovers that, in one way or another, his willed order fails to contain either his own emotional conflicts or those of others.

The almost automatic association of Dickens with the celebration of hearth and home went unquestioned for many decades after his death; he was, after all, its first promoter. Whether critics participated in that celebration or criticized Dickens for indoctrinating his readers with Victorian domestic ideology, Dickens and the sentiments of Home seemed virtually inseparable. Recent studies of the concept of home and the representation of family in Dickens have pushed beyond the mythic quality of that association to study the many ways in which Dickens's fiction flies in the face of such idealizing concepts, even when they continue to hover in the wings as lost paradises or futures just off the page. Focusing on the house itself rather than the home or the family allows for some new perspective on the necessarily intertwined themes of house, home, and family life.

Dickens experienced the house as a site for the exercise of managerial control and as a neat and pretty world he could make; he found it both a burdensome locus of family responsibility and a proud setting for scenes of family hospitality. In his fiction, houses are sometimes allegorically or metaphorically expressive of the lives of their inhabitants; like all inanimate objects in Dickens they are injected with living qualities by the pressure of his narrative voice. In this chapter, however, I will be most interested in the interplay between Dickens's experiences of acquiring, furnishing, and running three large family houses and his shifting representations of fictional houses. As he moved from Doughty Street to Devonshire Terrace to Tavistock House to Gad's Hill Place, changes in his emotional apprehension of the family he housed, as well as his social experiment in housing homeless women, brought about developments in his fictional depictions of what houses meant. Recurring concerns include the space of the writer who works at home in relation to the space of the larger house, the tension between the house as a safely grounded place and as an imprisoning container, the house haunted by lingering family secrets, and the insistence on good housekeeping that arises not just from Dickens's fantasy of the ideal Victorian woman, but from the extraordinarily neat and tidy housekeeper he was himself.

🐌 Devonshire Terrace, 1839–1851

In the young writer of 1839, the obsessive tinges that were to color the hyperactive decade of his forties were not yet so apparent. Once *Nickleby* was completed on 20 September 1839, Dickens turned his attention to the project of moving his own family from 48 Doughty Street to a larger London house more fully in keeping with the status he had so rapidly earned. His third child, Kate Macready Dickens, was born at Doughty Street on 29 October; by 1 November Dickens was immersed in house hunting, apparently hoping to settle the move as rapidly as he had set up the Devon dollhouse for his parents and youngest brother. Although his mother had returned to London to help with both the new baby and the house hunting, Dickens quickly began to "droop and despair" after Macready warned him that a desirable house in Kent Terrace was subject to "the stench from the stables at certain periods of the wind" (1.597). Three days later he was in "ecstatic restlessness" while Mitton negotiated for the remaining eleven years on the lease of One Devonshire Terrace, near the York Gate at Regents Park, which was to serve as the family residence until 1851 (1.598). His references to the furnishing and moving process during the month before taking possession in early December express efficiency and impatience to have it over. Always conscious of his own expenses, he is eager to sell to his landlord the made-to-order fixtures he had had installed at Doughty Street, and writes persuasively of the advantages he is offering by leaving the house empty while he continues to pay the rent for the remaining months on the three-year agreement. We also learn from this letter that smelly drains have contributed to the family discomfort at Doughty Street: despite many visits from plumbers, "we have not been able to make them last our time without often receiving strong notice of their being in the neighborhood" (1.600). Less delicately phrased struggles with drains were to recur in each of his future houses, offering small glimpses of the sewage and disposal problems that Londoners had to tolerate on an individual as well as a city-wide scale.

Devonshire Terrace was newly furnished, carpeted, and draped in respectable style; the years of household improvisation were at an end. Yet the young

Dickens seems to have maintained his perspective; a healthy irony is evident in his announcement to Forster that a "house of great promise (and great premium), 'undeniable' situation, and excessive splendour, is in view" (1.598). His letters complain briefly about the trials of moving and his impatience with legal processes: "I am in the agonies of house-letting, house-taking, title proving and disproving, premium paying, fixture valuing, and other ills to numerous to mention," he wrote to an acquaintance. "If you have the heart of anything milder than a monster, you will pity me" (1.603). Only the brevity and sparseness of the extant letters suggest his absorption in the details of the process.

Like all of Dickens's family houses, One Devonshire Terrace was often left behind; his impatience to set a house in order was matched only by his desire to be somewhere else. The house was rented to others during the Dickenses' six-month tour of the United States in 1842 and during their year's residence in Italy, 1844–45. Anticipating their return in the summer of 1845, Dickens wrote to Mitton in April with requests for redecoration. He wanted "a nice, bright cheerful green" paint on the garden doors and railings and for the indoor hall and staircase, but later bowed to the combined advice of Catherine and Mitton, who deplored the notion of green walls. As an Italianate surprise for Catherine, he wanted an estimate for repapering the drawing room in purple or blue and gold with gold molding around the paper, the ceiling painted with "a faint pink blush in it," and a wreath of flowers painted around the lamp: "I should wish it to be cheerful and gay" (4.297–98; 4.312). It is the first time we see direct evidence of "the kind of interest in a house which is commonly confined to women" that his eldest daughter Mary (called Mamie) described in *My Father as I Recall Him* (M. Dickens 12).

The estimate for the drawing room proved to be "what Mr. Swiveller calls, a Staggerer," Dickens discovered, but he leaned toward doing the work, "for as it is, it is very poor and mean in comparison with the house—and I had been 'going' to do it these five years" (4.312). He also asked Mitton to set in motion all the tradespeople Dickens regularly hired to do thorough yearly cleanings of the house and its fixtures, hoping to return to a pristine dwelling. Apparently his elated return was shadowed by disappointment on that score: "Once more in my own house!" he announced to Count D'Orsay on 5 July 1845, "If that can be called mine, which is such a heap of hideous confusion, and chaos of boxes" (4.325). Even a temporarily messy, disorderly house was anathema to his temperament.

Just eleven months after the return from Italy, the Devonshire Terrace house was rented again and the family moved to Switzerland, then Paris, while Dickens struggled to write *Dombey and Son*. By this time there were six Dickens children; Catherine and her younger sister Georgina, who had joined the household in 1842, had a great deal to organize at each move. Except for a two-year break between the birth of the fourth child, Walter Landor, in February 1841 and a new pregnancy, with Francis Jeffrey, in March 1843, Catherine had become pregnant again six to twelve months after the birth of each child; the pattern was to continue until the tenth, Edward Bulwer Lytton (called Plorn), was born in March 1852. (Catherine's mother, Georgina Thomson Hogarth, had borne ten children herself; Catherine may well have felt it normal to follow in this tradition.) Sydney Haldiman, the seventh Dickens child, was born in April 1847 in a house on Chester Place that Dickens took when the family returned to London before the Devonshire Terrace rental contract was up at the end of June. Whatever household charms Dickens may have lavished on his young wife and small children, providing a continuity of residence for pregnancy, childbirth, and infancy was not among them.

Wherever the family was at home, there was the problem of managing a large household that also served as a writer's workplace. "When at work my father was almost always alone," Mamie Dickens recalls, "so that, with rare exceptions, save as we could see the effect of the adventures of his characters upon him in his daily moods, we knew but little of his manner of work. Absolute quiet under these circumstances was essential, the slightest sound making an interruption fatal to the success of his labours." She does not elaborate on what was required to keep a brood of children quiet for five hours a day, mentioning only that the study at Devonshire Terrace was "a pretty room, with steps leading directly into the garden from it, and with an extra baize door to keep out all sounds and noise." The children's conversation at the lunch table "did not seem to disturb him, though any sudden sound, as the dropping of a spoon, or the clinking of a glass, would send a spasm of pain across his face" (M. Dickens 46, 49, 65). Mamie's lifelong adoration of Dickens pervades her reminiscences; she remembers lovingly his extreme tidiness and punctuality, as well as his praise for her childish housekeeping duties: "A prettily decorated table was his special pleasure, and from my earliest girlhood the care of this devolved upon me" (M. Dickens 37). The reader is left to wonder about the inner life of a child so attentive to the faces and moods of her father.

When he wrote *Dombey and Son*, Dickens seems to have been wondering about it too, in his own transformative way. When he is ensconced in his own suite of ground-floor rooms, Mr. Dombey's absent presence dominates his household. Dombey, who represents what Dickens consciously abhors,

sins most egregiously in his dismissal of daughters. When Dickens's grandly
named fourth son, Alfred D'Orsay Tennyson Dickens, was born on 28 October 1845, he announced the birth with a caveat: "I care for nothing but girls
by the bye; but never mind me." "I am partial to girls, and had set my heart
on one—but never mind me," was the way he put it to Clarkson Stanfield
(4.418; 4.419). When Stanfield's wife produced a new son the following
year, Dickens—with three more sons in his own future—grumbled, "I suppose you are (like me) past all congratulations on that score" (4.527). The
preferred daughters Mamie and Katie were eight and nearly seven years old
as Dickens began to work out the story of Dombey, Florence, and the house
that was not a home.

Dombey's house is located "on the shady side of a tall, dark, dreadfully
genteel street in the region between Portland-place and Bryanstone-square"
(*DS* 3)—that is, in the immediate neighborhood of Devonshire Terrace. Dickens smothers the house in a number of paragraphs mythily evocative of decay
and death, but its most chilling feature is that each inhabitant is confined
to a separate zone within it, and incurs penalties for violating the boundaries between zones. This way of imagining the house is the more powerful
because it is not directly addressed in the narration. Dombey's three rooms
on the ground floor (placed, like Dickens's studies, facing the garden) form
a self-contained male unit in which library, study, dressing room, and dining
room are combined. When Dombey wants to see his infant son Paul, he
orders the nurse to walk with the baby in the third glassed-in room, while he
sits in one of the others looking at his son as if through a distant window. To
Nurse Richards, Dombey looks like "a lone prisoner in a cell, or a strange
apparition that was not to be accosted or understood" (*DS* 3). It is not impossible that Dickens imagined himself in similar terms while he was engrossed
with his work in his study; it is certainly clear in Mamie's account that a
father "not to be accosted or understood" was the father often presented to
the Dickens children.

Florence's ever-hopeless attempts to find a home in her father's affection
are expressed in her efforts to enter these rooms. After Paul dies she sneaks
downstairs in the middle of the night to crouch at Dombey's door, which
never opens; "Perhaps he did not even know that she was in the house."
One night the door is ajar and she enters, only to be rejected and ejected.
Her father redraws the zone boundaries as he lights her up the stairs: "The
whole house is yours above there...You are its mistress now" (*DS* 18). When
Dombey leaves town, Florence performs secret rituals of housekeeping in
the forbidden territory, nestling in her father's chair, putting things in order,
"binding little nosegays for his table, changing them as one by one they

withered," and dreaming up cozy devices for his use; she hides the evidence before he returns (*DS* 23). At the novel's climactic moment Dombey emerges from his room and strikes his daughter as she tries to express her pity for him; her rush from his house only literalizes the emotional homelessness she has suffered in all her years of living there. Florence's nearly endless capacity to appeal to her father's affection by attempting to care for his needs and prettify his house represents on Dickens's part a fantasy that his daughter Mamie was quite willing to absorb.

Dickens's pathos is not entirely reserved for the abandoned child in the half-empty house, though that image appears in so many guises throughout his work. Edith's sumptuous apartments diminish and eject Dombey as effectively as his own rooms eject Florence. After the collapse of the firm, the house is invaded, the furniture is auctioned off, and the house carries a To Let sign, but Dombey continues to hide in his rooms while loyal female caretakers remain in obscure corners, leaving plates of food for him to eat when no one is near. His internal collapse takes the form of being unable to leave the house; tied to it in remorse, he goes on midnight trips to the upper rooms—he doesn't know which was Florence's—where his children had lived. Florence rescues him from suicide and makes him part of her family, but the house is left behind, still badged with To Let notices. The figure of a character bound to a house because he or she is trapped in unspeakable guilt, resentment, rage, or remorse becomes a repeated motif in Dickens's work. So does the house To Let, which always evokes failure and shame made visible to the street and vulnerable to the depredations of neighborhood boys.

Dombey's house is, of course, the antithesis of Devonshire Terrace with its involved, home-loving father, its colorful furnishings, its careful maintenance, its frequent dinner parties, and its family fun. Yet the story of a man who hides out in his own house while others lurk in upper regions or creep around in silence has its own spectral qualities for a preoccupied novelist working at home. The empathic attention given to both Dombey and Florence raises the probability that Dickens knew a guilty underside of emotional distance from the children he courted with charm during his intervals of accessibility. He joked about it in a letter to Lavinia Watson about six months after the final number of *Dombey* was published, as he was beginning *The Haunted Man*: he was "falling into a state of inaccessibility and irascibility which utterly confounds and scares the House. The young family peep at me through the bannisters as I go along the hall; and Kate and Georgina quail (almost) when I stalk by them" (5.419). The habit of imagining his life as if it were a part of a recent novel shows itself here, but so does the consciousness that imagined the separate zones of Dombey's house. The alternative household in *Dombey and Son*, Sol Gill's shop-home in the City, is ship-shape, snug, and ready to create a safe nest for Florence when she is astray in the London streets. Its obsolescence marks it with a kind of nostalgia—perhaps for the days of bachelor improvisation in small spaces, before the "dreadfully genteel" years at Devonshire Terrace had come upon the ever-expanding Dickens family. Like the flights to the Continent that produced it, *Dombey* has something to say about Dickens's reluctance to get stuck in a house.

Well before *Dombey* came to its end in March 1848, however, Dickens had recommitted himself to a life in London marked by engagements with new projects that connected him with wider circles of English life and allowed him to exercise his managerial talents outside his own home. His amateur theatrical company coalesced in a production of Ben Jonson's *Every Man in His Humour* that Dickens stage-managed in 1845. In 1847–48, after his return from Switzerland and Paris, the play was revived and performed on tour in a number of northern cities. Dickens reveled in his double roles as mastermind manager and as the bombastic swaggerer Bobadil, dressed in bright red breeches and wide boots designed to meet his standards of perfect historical accuracy in costume. Between 1850 and 1854 the amateur players became part of a more grandiose scheme, the Guild of Literature and Art, proposed by Dickens and Edward Bulwer-Lytton and intended to dignify the profession and to support artists who found themselves in financial need. It was characteristic of this time in his life that Dickens should attempt to justify his own delight in the theater by assigning to it a philanthropic social purpose and a dream of systemic reach. A set of cottages meant to solve the problems of indigent retired artists was planned, though never executed; Dickens was not confronted with the actual difficulties of running this pet housing project because the Guild failed to garner widespread support.

Meanwhile, Dickens planned and founded his weekly magazine *Household Words*, employing William Henry Wills as his reliable sub-editor. The magazine began its run in 1850, and connected Dickens with fiction-writers, poets, and journalists throughout the country. In this case his very directive editorial management proved a workable if controversial procedure; Dickens's hand could be felt in every piece, but he was a good, meticulous editor who spoke from the center of his expertise. As early as 1851 Wills had become the anchor of the *Household Words* office, steadily and intelligently keeping the magazine going while Dickens came and went, sending in editorial decisions and orders from wherever he was staying. Wills was soon a Dickens agent for other matters than the magazine; he clearly had a rare capacity to subordinate himself to his boss's formidable will while retaining his own judgment and sense of integrity. Dickens gradually came to recognize the value of a man he tended to disparage early on with comments about his sharp nose and his unimaginative nature; eventually he would recommend Wills's acumen in business by referring to him as "my other self" (9.34). Agents who carried out his desires to the letter without complaint, whether W. H. Wills at the office or Georgina Hogarth at home, were becoming essential to his way of life.

🎞 Urania Cottage

The third new project of the decade was the Home for Homeless Women, which involved the creation, organization, and maintenance of a literal house. Urania Cottage, as it was sometimes called, was the most substantial product of Dickens's friendship with the wealthy but shy heiress Angela Burdett-Coutts. After her parents' deaths early in 1844, Miss Coutts began to seek fit objects for philanthropy, and Dickens became one of her chief consultants. The relationship was delicate, not least because the Dickens family was one of her first charities: Miss Coutts funded the education and training of Dickens's elder sons Charley and Walter. Her annual gifts of Twelfth Night cakes to celebrate Charley's birthday are elaborately acknowledged in Dickens's engaging and deferential letters to her. Between May 1846, when he responded to her desire to set up an asylum for the reform of prostitutes, and 1858, when their friendship cooled in the wake of his separation from Catherine, Dickens became the worldly agent of Miss Coutts's efforts at social reform. He planned and managed Urania Cottage, vetted and recommended people who deserved individual charity, and researched London sites that might be appropriate for the housing projects she planned in 1852–53. In the process he attempted to educate her in the ways of the lower classes, and to counter what he considered the overly religious and conservative aspects of her social attitudes.

Both of the collaborators were peripatetic, and Dickens's letters often record the failure of his attempts to find or reach her. The "Spell," as he called it, became a standing joke; "we are always like the gentleman and lady in the weather-glass" (5.201; 7.442). His penchant for immediate, willful action was disturbing to her; more than once Dickens commented, as he did in 1850, "I am always for the promptest measures—and I suppose I made you laugh by my ferocity" (6.86). Responding to a note of praise from her in 1855, he explains, "You think me impetuous, because I sometimes speak of things I have long thought about, with a suddenness that brings me only to the conclusion I have come at, and does not shew the road by which

I arrived there. But it is a broad highway notwithstanding, and I have trod it slowly and patiently" (7.617). Miss Coutts served as lady patroness in many ways; among them, she was a figure for whom Dickens could project his best representations of himself.

As they appear in his writing about Urania Cottage, those self-representations are singularly free of conflict or anxiety about the authoritarian nature of his management practices. The Home, as its inmates were taught to call it, essentially served as a halfway house between prison or prostitution and emigration to Australia or the South African Cape. Most of the young women (there was room for thirteen when the house opened in November 1847) stayed there for about a year, during which they were supposed to tame their natures and to become adept at a range of household tasks that would enable them to become servants, or wives and mothers, in the colonies. The daily routine was completely ritualized; every hour was accounted for, and the girls were subject to surveillance at all times. They did not leave the cottage except to attend church in groups on Sundays, or to exercise and tend little gardens on the premises. Incoming and outgoing mail was read by one of the matrons. There was neither privacy nor ownership; the women made and wore clothes they did not own, from materials chosen—at least initially—by Dickens in four different colors, to avoid the stigma of uniforms. If they ran away wearing these clothes—which were kept under lock and key—they were subject to arrest for theft. Those who rebelliously insisted on leaving were, Dickens decided, to be threatened with a common, ugly, coarse (but of course clean) dress acquired for the purpose of making them think twice about an impetuous and resentful departure (6.804).

In effect, the house was run on principles Dickens had—rather imaginatively—adapted from studying prisons and other institutions that attempted to effect reformations of female character. His strategies must therefore be read against the background of punitive discipline and religious reclamation that prevailed across this Victorian enterprise in general. "These unfortunate creatures are to be *tempted* to virtue," he insisted to Miss Coutts when she wanted clergymen on the scene. "They cannot be dragged, driven, or frightened." Everything about their treatment was to be subject to two guiding principles: *"first to consider how best to get them there, and how best to keep them there* (5.183). Clergymen might present obstacles: "the almost insupportable extent to which they carry the words and forms of religion" in other refuges and asylums "is known to no order of people as well as to these women," who retain "an exaggerated dread of it" (5.182). Clearly Dickens's battle against cant was a driving force in his enthusiasm for creating Urania Cottage.

Finding and interviewing appropriate inmates was one of Dickens's primary tasks; not many women would commit themselves to enforced domesticity and emigration (which they sometimes quite naturally confused with penal transportation) as conditions of their acceptance, nor did many meet his standards of truthfulness and deference. Developing reliable sources of potential candidates was always an issue. When the Home opened, nearly all the inmates came directly from serving light sentences in prisons, on the recommendation of Augustus Tracey, Governor of Cold Bath Fields, Bridewell, or G. L. Chesterton, Governor of the Middlesex House of Correction. By the spring of 1850 Dickens was responding to Miss Coutts's desire to widen their nets; he tried "the Ragged School class of objects" (6.160), and suggested that he write an article in the newly formed *Household Words* that might attract recommendations. (It was not until 1853 that Miss Coutts could be convinced to approve such an article.) Gradually the range of sources expanded to include local magistrates of police courts, other institutions like the Magdalen hospitals, and individual social workers.

Dickens wrote brief reports of each woman he recommended for Miss Coutts's approval; as the admissions process became routine, he increasingly decided on his own. In addition to selecting inmates, Dickens helped to interview and train the two matrons or superintendents who kept the daily life of the cottage going. His management of these managers was fraught with distrust, doubtless on both sides, until in 1849 Miss Coutts produced a Mrs. Morson, a matron he thoroughly approved. Her powers, like those of all Dickens's agents, had their limits; he was the person who intervened and laid down the law during the numerous crises of conflict, insubordination, theft, and escape that erupted regularly in the life of the Home. He also organized and ran the weekly meetings of the oversight Committee, tried to find well-regulated ships that would not tempt emigrants to fall back into their old ways during the voyage out, and organized major and minor repairs to the cottage with the same vigilance he demonstrated in his own houses.

Critical accounts of Urania Cottage have recently concentrated on Dickens's insistence on separating the young women from the stories of their pasts. As each inmate entered the Home, Dickens would interview her alone under a promise of confidentiality, eliciting a history that often included parental abandonment or abuse, dubious associates, failed attempts to make livings, homelessness, petty crime, or seduction and prostitution. He would record the story in his Case Book, and forbid the woman to tell the story again, to anyone; from that point on she was to make herself into someone who bore a good character, and she was to be protected from anyone who had knowledge of her past. Miss Coutts had access to the volume, but

Dickens told the matrons of the Home only as much as he felt necessary for them to know. This practice, sometimes read as a kind of co-optation or dubious identification, was in Dickens's view a cornerstone of the project. In his first outline of plans for the Home (to Miss Coutts, 26 May 1846), he wants to represent the past life of a fallen woman not as a social disgrace but as "destructive to *herself*, and that there is no hope in it, or in her, as long as she pursues it" (4.553).

As the Home opened its doors Dickens wrote "An Appeal to Fallen Women," a pamphlet directly addressed to women in prisons, intended to interest them in the Home. Carefully avoiding the rhetoric of redemption, he asked his reader to imagine her future life if she were to continue in her present course—or rather, he imagined her life for her, in images and cadences that only Dickens could invent. The Home, he promised, would substitute for these horrors "an active, cheerful, healthy life" where women would be "entirely removed from all who have any knowledge of their past career, will begin life afresh, and be able to win a good name and character" (5.698–99). The policy was defended again in a letter to Miss Coutts of 28 March 1849: Dickens claimed that the prison governors Chesterton and Tracey had strongly recommended the measure, and pointed to "the promise of confidence under which they [the women] have yielded up their secrets" (5.516).

He was not, of course, doing to the women anything he had not done for himself. His own autobiographical confession was written during the first year of the Home's existence, and, locked in Forster's drawer, was subject to a similar embargo. He wanted genuinely to believe that a sealed confession could "put away" a shameful past and allow for a changed future. He was also quite alert to the meaning of "a good character" in the sense that it was used by servants seeking employment; the interval at the Home was meant to allow such a "character" to be attested to in a letter of reference. Nor were the cases grist for his fiction mill in any direct way. As Philip Collins points out, the idealized and conventional portraits of fallen women in the novels have little connection with the stories of misdoings at the Home with which Dickens regaled Miss Coutts (Collins 1962, 112–16). The Case Book provided material for selected success stories, identified only by case number, that Dickens presented in "Home for Homeless Women," the article he wrote for *Household Words* in April 1853 (Dent 3.127–41); if Dickens had had other plans for the book, they never came to fruition.

There is little doubt that Dickens took special pride and pleasure in his role as sole confessor. In his reports to Miss Coutts he assessed each case for truthfulness, and seemed to be quite sure that he knew when a girl was lying; if she acted up later on, he would claim that he had had doubts about her from the first. Truthfulness was his first principle, the symptom that guaranteed internal reform; in the "Appeal to Fallen Women" he called on prospective inmates to "be truthful in every word you speak. Do this, and all the rest is easy" (5.699). In his adaptation of Alexander Machonochie's Marks System, a system of incentives for good conduct developed for prisoners on Norfolk Island, Dickens created nine categories in which inmates could receive daily good or bad marks; the first was "Truthfulness." How, exactly, a woman was to be assessed in this category was not explained in *Household Words*. Dickens did, however, explain how he got truthful histories in his interviews: "nothing is so likely to elicit truth as a perfectly imperturbable face, and an avoidance of any leading question or expression of opinion. Give the narrator the least idea what tone will make her an object of interest, and she will take it directly. Give her none, and she will be driven on the truth, and in most cases will tell it" (Dent 3.134).

That arguably good advice contains a measure of the self-imposed blindness in Dickens's assessment of his role at Urania Cottage. He was exquisitely aware that his "cases" were savvy about the right language to put on when appealing to reformers or agents of the law. He did not, however, want to know that he produced his own reforming rhetoric, or that the inmates of Urania Cottage learned to conform to it. In place of religion, he preached the doctrine of Home—which for Dickens meant order, punctuality, neatness, and good housekeeping. Persuading the religious Miss Coutts of his plan, Dickens managed to slide neatly from religion as "the basis for the whole system" to "a system of training" that is "steady and firm" as well as "cheerful and hopeful": it was to consist of "order, punctuality, cleanliness, the whole routine of household duties—as washing, mending, cooking" (4.554). Once he had found the house in Shepherd's Bush that was to serve their purpose, he furnished and arranged it in every detail before allowing Miss Coutts to see it; in anticipation of her concerns he had framed and put up in the living room inscriptions from Jeremy Taylor, Isaac Barrow, and Jesus, as well as "a little inscription of my own, referring to the advantages of order, punctuality, and good temper" (5.185–86).

After "Truthfulness," Dickens's categories for daily marks were "Industry, Temper, Propriety of Conduct and Conversation, Temperance, Order, Punctuality, Economy, Cleanliness" (Dent 3.132). He reported in "Home for Homeless Women" that the names of the girls responsible for the neatness and work for each room were hung there, "framed and glazed," on each Monday morning; this "was found to inspire them with a greater pride in good housewifery, and a greater sense of shame in the reverse." Similarly—and despite the fact that they did not own their clothes—"They have a great pride in the state of their clothes, and the neatness of their persons" (Dent 3.130, 132). He could not let go of this theme: if new inmates struggle to learn self-control, "Patience, and the strictest attention to order and punctuality, will in most cases overcome these discouragements" (Dent 3.135). Like the occupants of his own houses, the residents of Urania Cottage were enjoined to conform to the needs of Dickens's own temperament.

It did not seem to occur to him that his own neatness and punctuality were not universally acknowledged forms of virtue, or that even the most sincere young women had figured out how to get good marks and the small monetary rewards that came with them. Nor did he seem to make a clear distinction between what he wanted to hear and truthfulness. He reported that during the inmates' private weekly meetings with the Committee, they are "under no restraint in anything they wish to say. A complaint from any of them is exceedingly uncommon" (Dent 3.130). No doubt he had a good ear for cant, but his insistence that he knew when a woman was lying took a comic turn in 1857, when he lectured Miss Coutts about giving the inmates colorful clothes instead of the drab working-dress material she had bought for them. Apparently the women had reported their satisfaction to Miss Coutts, but Dickens knew better how to assess their remarks: "I do not believe them to be true, and I have a very great misgiving that they were written against nature, under the impression that they would have a moral aspect." Dickens, of course, thought the love of colorful dress was natural, and helped to create "a buoyant, hopeful, genial character"; it followed that the girls must have been lying when they approved the drab material (8.310–11).

Dickens counseled Miss Coutts wisely and often about limiting their expectations of success, but in practice he was angered by any form of insubordination. His letters tell vivid stories about bad apples who had to be expelled, leading some critics to applaud his empathy and pleasure in those escapades. Dickens was almost always keen to give the inmates a second chance if they broke rules, consorted with men over the garden fence, or threatened to leave, but his role in these stories is invariably that of the hero and detective, the lone male in a covey of women who drops into a crisis, sorts it out, thinks of an ingenious solution, and disappears. When Jemima Hiscock and Mary Joynes got "dead drunk" after forcing open a small beer cellar in 1850, Dickens was furious; he suspected them of getting spirits over the wall from outside and of plotting to leave after robbing the house of clean linen. Jemima was dismissed immediately; both were put down as liars with "pious pretences" (6.84–85). Later that year, Dickens was "in a mighty state of indignation" when two girls stole some money from a matron and absconded; in full detective mode, he invented an elaborate explanation of how they had managed to get hold of a key to the wardrobe (6.207). When a girl secreted some clothes in which to escape, Dickens announced to the Home that she was to be discharged the next day; when she robbed and escaped early in the morning a policeman was in the lane to apprehend her. Dickens, who found the example instructive to the others, made sure she was taken into custody and convicted summarily (6.540–41). In 1854 Dickens dismissed Frances Cranstone as an evil-doer who had corrupted the whole house, and took firm measures with another girl who claimed to be her friend, in order to "crush the bad spirit summarily" (7.316). As the years passed, he increasingly regretted decisions in which leniency had triumphed over suspicion. Once again, it appeared that it was easy to put destitute people into well-regulated cottages, but not so easy to keep them there. As for the success stories—by Dickens's count about half the cases they accepted—they were promptly dispatched overseas once they had performed to standard.

David Copperfield, written during the height of the Home's brief history, may be more deeply related to Urania Cottage through its emphasis on housekeeping than in its sentimentally stylized portraits of the fallen women Martha and Emily. Dickens had displayed his penchant for erotic domesticity through Ruth Pinch's pie making in Martin Chuzzlewit, but Copperfield is the first of his novels to make a sustained connection between good housekeeping and good character. Agnes Wickfield's perfect but unobtrusive housekeeping serves to shore up her father's respectability (and later her husband's), while Dora Spenlow Copperfield's domestic ineptitude is a kiss of death, the sign of her inability to grow from a girl into a woman. The tightly packed Peggoty boat/house, complete with ship-shape fittings, follows in the wake of Sol Gills's shop as a fantasy of neat bachelor improvisation. No married couples or biological parents and children live there. Sexual love destroys it, as it corrupts or threatens so many of the novel's other houses: the Copperfields', the Wickfields', the Steerforths', the Strongs'. The substitution of housekeeping for sexuality, as well as the expression of acceptable sexuality through housekeeping, is a peculiarity of Dickens's imagination whose origins can only be guessed at.

Along with such familiar fantasies, however, David Copperfield suggests a kind of knowledge that does not appear in his letters about the Home for Homeless Women. Betsey Trotwood's neat-as-a-pin cottage in Dover is the house that saves young David from his life as an abandoned working boy; its extreme order, like that of Urania Cottage, is a welcome haven from the shame of his immediate past. Yet Betsey's housekeeping is obsessive;

shooing donkeys from the tiny lawn speaks of all the human disorder she works to keep out of her little domain, while the periodic returns of her rejected husband make it clear that the project is impossible. In that portrait Dickens understands the self-defensive nature of orderliness; in David's frustrated efforts to domesticate Dora he recognizes the implicit violence of the attempt to impose it on others. However, Dickens/David cannot sustain the tension between the desire for domestic dominion and the moral imperative of letting others be themselves: Dora dies, and David marries the perfect housekeeper. Just after writing the number narrating Dora's death, Dickens referred to Georgina as "my little housekeeper, Miss Hogarth" (6.158). Catherine, enduring her usual postpartum suffering, was busy nursing the newborn Dora Annie Dickens, who had just eight months to live.

🐌 Tavistock House, 1851–1860

When *David Copperfield* was complete, Dickens turned his attention to house hunting; the lease of One Devonshire Terrace had run its course. It was a disruption he had been dreading since September 1847, when he was dismayed to learn from Mitton that the lease was two years shorter than he had thought. He was quick to worry about compensation for the new gas fixtures he had just installed: "I am paid for them when my time is up; am I not?" (5.162). That time was also on his mind as he responded to his brother-in-law Henry Austin's move in March 1849: "I suppose you have been washing in a cheese-plate this morning, and breakfasting out of a clothes-basket. Those agonies of moving, though two years off, afflict me already" (5.516). The rapid transfer of the move from Doughty Street to Devonshire Terrace was not to be repeated; instead the process of resettlement stretched through most of 1851, accompanied by periods of acute distress and an anxious sense of houselessness.

Houses were on Dickens's mind after he returned to London from a January theatrical performance for his friends the Watsons at Rockingham Castle; as usual he suffered from leaving the little world of theater behind: "What a thing it is," he moaned to Mrs. Watson, "that we can't be always innocently merry, and happy with those we like best, without looking out at the back windows of life! Well—one day perhaps—after a long night—the blinds on that side of the house will be down for ever, and nothing left but the bright prospect in front" (6.266). As 1851 rolled on, allegorical houses gave way to the realities of bricks, doors, and drainage, while Dickens engaged in prolonged brooding over a new novel, *Bleak House*, in which concrete images of household disorder—like washing in cheese-plates and breakfasting from laundry baskets—would take a prominent place.

Henry Austin, an architect and secretary to the Board of Health, was on demand to assess potential houses for their structural and sanitary soundness. But things did not go smoothly or rapidly. Dickens made two offers that were not accepted, and looked at several other houses before considering Tavistock House in Tavistock Square, the residence of his artist friend Frank Stone. The eighteen-room house was in dirty, dilapidated condition and would require extensive repair, but it was prudently inexpensive for its size and location. The decision to take the house was long in coming. Dickens was preoccupied in the early months of 1851 with the amateur players' performance before the queen at the duke of Devonshire's estate, which required the rigorous drilling of his not-always-disciplined troops as well as the construction of an elaborate movable stage set. The infant Dora was seriously ill in January and February. In the midst of Dickens's theatrical frenzy, his father had his sudden bladder operation and died on 31 March. Catherine, suffering from a nervous illness Dickens could not quite name, was sent for a hydropathic cure to Malvern. Dickens stayed there with her much of the time between mid-March and mid-April, while the children, including the apparently recovered seven-month-old Dora, stayed at Devonshire Terrace. On 14 April Dora died as Dickens was presiding over the annual meeting of the General Theatrical Fund. The performance before the queen at Devonshire House had to be delayed until mid-May, while the family recovered from the successive shocks of bereavement. Dickens took Catherine to see Tavistock House days after Dora's death: "I am anxious to direct Kate's attention to our removal, and to keep it engaged," he wrote to Stone (6.357). But Catherine was ill, and it was no time for decisions. Dickens let Devonshire Terrace until September and engaged a favorite vacation house at Broadstairs from mid-May through October. He set up a "gipsy tent," as he called it, in the back rooms of the *Household Words* office in Wellington Street, where he stayed when he came into London on business (6.393). It was not as yet clear where the family would be when they returned.

It was not until 14 July that Dickens asked Henry Austin to look at Tavistock House for him; the decision to make a definite offer came six days later. Austin now moved into position as Dickens's London agent for remodeling and repair, serving as a crucial mediator between Dickens's careful planning and Dickens's uncontrollable impatience to have the work completed. Frank Stone, on Dickens's suggestion, moved his household temporarily into One Devonshire Terrace when the tenant departed, leaving Tavistock House free for repairs beginning early in September. By 7 September Dickens was already writing to Austin from Broadstairs: "NO WORKMEN ON THE PREMISES along of my not hearing from you!! I have torn all my hair off, and constantly beat my unoffending family." The letter, often quoted as evidence of his frantic state, goes on in this half-comedic vein; then it modulates into Dickens's other house voice, which coolly describes a change in his plan of renovation. The next day the cool voice is in charge: Dickens has heard from Austin, who has suggested a builder and arranged for a meeting at the house (6.478–79). On 11 September the meeting takes place, and Dickens writes happily to Catherine about how well the house looks once the dirty blinds are down. He wants her to come to London with him and decide on the allocation of bedrooms and the wallpapers. Catherine is still treated as a partner in the household business, and he counts on her to sympathize with his account of the Stones' hapless housekeeping: "Think of all the broken birdcages in the world, sticking in all the broken chairs, with their legs uppermost—and you will have a faint idea of their 'moving'—not including the dust" (6.482).

Frank Stone's son Marcus, who became a Dickens protégé and illustrated *Our Mutual Friend*, remembered the contrast he observed while staying at Devonshire Terrace: "The presiding influence of the master was visible all over the house, his love of order and fitness, his aversion to any neglect of attention, even in details which are frequently not considered at all. There was a place for everything and everything in its place, deterioration was not permitted." Nor did Dickens allow dust, or even a "lumber room or glory hole" to hold the leftover or abandoned things that most households put away out of sight. "If he was something of a martinet he certainly spared himself less than anybody," Marcus Stone observed. "A Napoleonic commander-in-chief, he found able and active allies in his sister in law and eldest daughter who were geniuses in carrying out his ideas" (Collins 1981, 184–85). Although Stone may have been recalling the years at Gad's Hill after the marriage ended, his exclusion of Catherine is notable.

Henry Austin offered the builder a month for the Tavistock repairs, and promised Dickens that the repairs would be complete "within a week of that time" (6.481), but of course they dragged on, and the family did not move in until mid-November. Dickens and Austin seem to have come to the strategic agreement that Dickens was to come into town only at long intervals to view the progress on the house, and Dickens tried his best: "Calm in my great confidence in you—sedate—even cheerful—I shall remain here, until summoned to behold the Works" (6.489). Letters to Austin during that period continue to alternate between detailed practical planning and comic reminders of the writer's impatience: "Phantom lime attends me all day long. I dream that I am a carpenter, and can't partition off the hall" (6.485); "I dream

of the workmen every night. They make faces at me, and won't do anything"
(6.495). His inability to make the workmen work faster also expressed itself
in the exaggerated despair of letters to other friends, especially during October, when Dickens felt ready to begin *Bleak House* and had no study to write
in. "I *can not* work at my new book—" he complained to Miss Coutts on
9 October, "having all my notions of order turned completely topsy-turvy."
He hopes that when she returns she "will find us settled, and me hard at
work—and will approve, both the tangible house and the less substantial Edifice" (6.513). The same day he vented his hostility about invading workmen
to another correspondent, describing "how low this makes the undersigned,
who is accustomed to keep everything belonging to him in a place of its
own, and to sit in the midst of a system of Order" (6.514). As comic relief,
Dickens amused himself by inventing silly titles for the fake book-backs
that were to adorn shelves on a sliding door connecting his study with the
drawing room: "Five Minutes in China. 3 vols."; "Bowwowdom. A Poem";
"Growler's Gruffology, with Appendix. 4 vols." and the like (6.851). He was
quite pleased when these were skillfully executed by the strangely named
bookbinder Mr. Eeles.

The Tavistock House letters show Dickens mediating a rebuilding of garden walls shared by all three adjacent houses (the Stones rented one of them),
insisting that the cold shower bath, an essential part of his daily regimen, be
curtained off from the W.C., and worrying that hard dancing in the schoolroom would bring down the kitchen ceiling beneath it. The study–drawing-
room door, which spoke to his negotiations between writing and family life,
was the most elaborate of his innovations. Planning for that door, designed
both to create and to conceal a passage between the all-important study and
the large drawing room, occupied a number of Dickens's letters during September. He was willing to go to some extra expense—though he worried over
it—in order to get both a sense of seclusion and access to house space. "When
the rooms were thrown together," Mamie remembered, "they gave my father
a promenade of considerable length for the constant indoor walking which
formed a favorite recreation for him after a hard day's writing" (M. Dickens
51). Arranging the door to balance the design of both rooms grew into a
rather complex negotiation with Henry Austin and the carpenters: a large
mirror taken from Devonshire Terrace was reframed and installed in a recess
of the door-bookcase directly opposite the study window, while other mirrors
were installed in three recesses on the drawing-room side. The mirror on the
study side was probably the one in which Mamie, convalescing from an illness
on the sofa in Dickens's study, once saw him making "extraordinary facial
contortions" while in the throes of creating a character (M. Dickens 49–50).

Dickens's love of household mirrors was not an uncommon Victorian preference, but he seems to have had a special investment in expanding the imaginary space of a room by hanging mirrors opposite windows, or placing them where they would magnify the scale of social occasions. The actor Henry Compton remembered that Dickens's dining tables were "purposely made very narrow, to facilitate opposite guests talking with one another. Sometimes the end of the table touched a mirror, which reflected the whole scene, and increased the brilliance of its appearance" (Collins 1981, 191). Dickens himself revealed the distancing, stagy aspects of his dining-room mirrors in *Our Mutual Friend* when he described the Veneering dinner guests only as they appear reflected in the mirror as static, one-dimensional caricatures. Despite his reputation as a perfect host who brought out the best in his guests, a quiet part of him was observing those guests without having to look directly at them. Early in 1865, his actor friend Charles Fechter presented Dickens with a miniature Swiss chalet that Dickens used as a writing room on the grounds of Gad's Hill. He put five mirrors in it; as he wrote to Annie Fields in 1868, "they reflect and refract in all kinds of ways the leaves that are quivering at the windows, and the great fields of waving corn" (12.119). Mirrors were the decorative equivalents of Dickens's imaginative ability to expand, heighten, or double everything he looked at.

Three weeks after moving into the Tavistock study, Dickens had completed most of the first number of *Bleak House*. With "the tangible house" in place, "the less substantial Edifice" grew into a remarkable feat of engineering, the most intricate fictional mansion Dickens ever built. Fresh from a year of immersion in the details of theatrical production and house moving, he invented a narrative that lures the reader into a detective-like attentiveness: we sense from the start that any detail tells or foretells. The design of the interlocking stories justifies that sensation; each separate piece takes its proper place in a remarkably resonant whole, as though Dickens were taking a kind of artistic revenge over the delays and distractions of practical life by subduing them firmly to his systematizing imagination. Esther's narrative gives full play to the precision of Dickens's own housekeeping eye, while the novelist sits at last "in the midst of a system of Order" that revels in the representation of disorder.

Esther, we are told, has trained for six years at the Greenleaf boarding school, where she has led only a somewhat less carceral existence than the women of Urania Cottage. "Nothing could be more precise, exact, and orderly, than Greenleaf," she writes approvingly. "There was a time for everything, all round the dial of the clock, and everything was done in its appointed moment" (*BH* 3). Rather like Urania Cottage, Greenleaf is designed to cover up the shame and humiliation of her early experience, and to give her a place in the world authorized by her ability to serve in the houses of others. Esther with her bunch of household keys is an emblem of feminine housekeeping that frequently makes Dickens a target for feminist impatience; yet the early sources of Esther's need for order, as well as her observant eye for household detail, are as intimately linked with Dickens himself as with a simple Victorian ideology of womanhood.

Dickens could hardly wait to describe the Jellyby household, which appears in the first number he wrote at Tavistock House. Mrs. Jellyby's messes are beyond Esther's capacity to tidy, but her orderly eye allows Dickens to elaborate on the comedic potential in household articles that are misplaced, misused, or badly improvised. Mrs. Jellyby's dress fails to meet at the back, and is "railed across with a lattice-work of stay-lace—like a summer house"; Esther finds that "the curtain to my window was fastened up by a fork"; the doors do not close, "for my lock, with no knob on it, looked as if it wanted to be wound up; and though the handles of Ada's went round and round with the greatest smoothness, it was attended with no effect whatever on the door." Richard "had washed his hands in a pie-dish," and "they had found the kettle on his dressing-table"; the dish of potatoes is "mislaid in the coal skuttle," while "the handle of the corkscrew" comes off and strikes the servant on the chin. When Caddy visits Esther late at night, she carries a broken candlestick and an egg-cup filled with vinegar in which to wash her inky middle finger (*BH* 4).

Dickens had never written quite like this before; the clash of his careful habits with the prolonged disruptions of the move and the dirty, dilapidated state in which Stone had left Tavistock House had added a new note of humorous specificity. Once the Jellyby house has advertised its shame with a To Let sign, and the Jellybys have been relocated in a furnished lodging in Hatton Garden, Dickens returns to the game of category mixing as Esther lists what tumbles out of Mrs. Jellyby's closets. The list includes such brilliant touches as "damp sugar in odds and ends of paper bags," "books with butter sticking to the binding," "guttered candle-ends put out by being turned upside down in broken candlesticks," and "heads and tails of shrimps" (*BH* 30). The human costs to the physical and mental health of Mr. Jellyby and the Jellyby children are of course the novel's overt thematic concern, but Dickens's ability to evoke disgust at the way disorderly housekeeping turns everything to garbage makes its own powerful effect.

Esther's eye is also employed to register the chaos of Krook's shop, in thoroughly Dickensian style: "Everything seemed to be bought, and nothing to be sold there." Krook's inability to part with the accumulated litter of the legal system or to endure any "sweeping, nor scouring, nor cleaning, nor repairing going on about me" is the central image of social disorder on which the novel is built (*BH* 5). Like Mrs. Jellyby's household, the shop is dangerous to humans because anything might show up there in the wrong place: old love letters, for example, that might destroy the present life of their writer. Esther articulates a central image here, but she also shares with the omniscient narrator the habit of noticing out-of-the-way details of maintenance: the way "an old tub was put to catch the droppings of rain-water from a roof" at the brickmaker's cottage (*BH* 8), or the way one of lawyer Vholes's "dull cracked windows" is occasionally "coerced" to open by "having a bundle of firewood thrust between its jaws in hot weather" (*BH* 39).

Just about every character in the novel's enormous cast is judged through his or her style of household management. Mrs. Bagnet, a perfect manager who runs a house that "contains nothing superfluous, and has not a visible speck of dirt or dust in it," is doubly virtuous because she endures the agonies of watching her children prepare her birthday dinner without interference (*BH* 27, 49). Mrs. Bayham Badger's drawing room is narcissistically decorated with objects meant to display her many types of artistic dabbling. Guppy's down-and-out friend Mr. Jobling (alias Weevle) turns surprisingly sympathetic when we see him redecorate the dismal room in which Captain Hawdon died: "Weevle, who is a handy good-for-nothing kind of young fellow, borrows a needle and thread of Miss Flite, and a hammer of his landlord, and goes to work devising apologies for window-curtains, and knocking up apologies for shelves, and hanging up his two teacups, milkpot, and crockery sundries on a pennyworth of little hooks, like a shipwrecked sailor making the best of it" (*BH* 20). Other bachelor establishments, like Boythorn's house and George's Shooting Gallery, attest further to the motif of ingenious male housekeeping. The "wonderfully neat" Mrs. Rouncewell is the ideal servant at Chesney Wold, where "the whole house reposes, on her mind" as she sits in her ground-floor room (*BH* 7).

Bleak House itself presents more ambiguity about the meanings that accrue to houses and housekeeping. Like Chesney Wold, it comes with a historical curse, though one of more recent and middle-class origin than the legend of the Ghost's Walk. John Jarndyce tells Esther that the house received its name from his great uncle Tom Jarndyce, who allowed the place to decay and rot as he ruined and then killed himself in Chancery. The inheriting John Jarndyce has restored the house to order and charm, but he has not changed its name; moreover, the house has a double, a property in London "which is much at this day what Bleak House was then" (*BH* 8). Esther's apparently rapturous description of the intricate maze of rooms, stairs, and passageways in Bleak House has engendered a range of critical readings so various as to suggest some interesting instability in the text. The layout of Bleak House evades interpretation: "you come upon more rooms when you think you have seen all there are"; Esther's room "had more corners in it than I ever counted afterwards"; if you take "crooked steps that branched off in an unexpected manner from the stairs, you lost yourself in passages, with mangles in them, and three-cornered tables, and a Native-Hindoo chair, which was also a sofa, a box, and a bedstead, and looked, in every form, something between a bamboo skeleton and a great bird-cage, and had been brought from India nobody knew by whom or when." This collection of oddities does not sound like anything Dickens would have allowed in a house of his own. Every room "had at least two doors," and the sentences themselves get the reader successfully lost as Esther works to set in narrative order a situation that defies straight lines or architecturally plausible floor levels (*BH* 6).

Allegorical readings come to mind: Bleak House is like *Bleak House*, a very surprising and intricately related set of plots and passages. Or, Bleak House is an image of Esther's story, clogged by obscure remnants of other lives, never to be fully sorted out or brought to the light of day. Less allegorically, it seems that something is wrong with Esther's initial rapture. In her eagerness to take her place as the little housekeeper, she praises the perfect order of the household and its organized system of drawers, but does not quite register the potential connection between forgotten objects in odd passageways and the grotesque disorder of Krook's shop. Bleak House has been brought back to life, but Jarndyce has not thrown out either the "exposed sound" of its name or remnants of its history (*BH* 6). Nor has Dickens forgotten Frank Stone's birdcage-like broken furniture, or the deceptive door he made in Tavistock House.

Like Dickens, and like Dombey, Jarndyce occupies "male" spaces that set him apart from the rest of the house. His bedroom is a "plain room" that suggests Dickens's own health regimes: he sleeps with his window open on a "bedstead without any furniture standing in the middle of the room for more air, and his cold bath gaping for him in a smaller room adjoining" (*BH* 6). The Growlery adjoining the bedchamber is another mix of study, library, and dressing room to which Jarndyce repairs when he is "deceived or disappointed" by the objects of his charity, and where he is willing to talk or think about things he will not otherwise mention (*BH* 8). Though Dickens relied on a split between his writing space and the positive role he tried to project in his family life, his representation of Jarndyce critiques the effort of walled-off negative feeling. Jarndyce is apparently the "good philanthropist" of the novel: his hatred of being thanked and his close-to-home good works mark him as the antithesis of self-advertising do-gooders like Mrs. Jellyby and Mrs. Pardiggle. But his guilty dismay when a recipient like Richard Carstone or Harold Skimpole fails in gratitude or proves undeserving makes it impossible for him to withdraw support. Esther sees the harm that ensues: Skimpole is allowed to damage Richard, Richard damages Ada's life, and Jarndyce himself is stuck in his conflict between generosity and unacknowledged suspicion. He is, perhaps, a version of Miss Coutts without a hardheaded Dickens to vet the begging letters, or to banish the schemers from Urania Cottage.

Jarndyce's relations with Esther begin in that strange Dickensian crossover zone where good housekeeping takes the place of romantic love. Jarndyce does not ask Esther to marry him; he asks her "would I be the mistress of Bleak House" in a letter "that was not a love letter though it expressed so much love" (*BH* 44). The words "husband," "wife," "proposal" and "marriage" are never sounded in connection with this apparent engagement; they remain ambiguously subsumed under the euphemism "mistress of Bleak House." Under cover of the same phrase Jarndyce re-places Esther in a new Bleak House furnished with the younger man she actually loves, and decorated to reproduce "in the arrangement of all the pretty objects, *my* little tastes and fancies, *my* little methods and inventions which they used to laugh at while they praised them." Announcing that he is now her father, Jarndyce gives her away to Allan Woodcourt in a move that reinstates romantic love within a generational and familial fiction.

The new Bleak House is not, however, a copy of the old. It is "a cottage— quite a rustic cottage of doll's rooms" set far away in the Yorkshire countryside. The winding passages and impossible staircases are gone; painful memories are put away, and Esther is granted the old pastoral fantasy of a new beginning. Guppy is brought into the same chapter to emphasize that point, as well as to parody Jarndyce's generosity: he offers Esther a renewed suit, bolstered by "a ouse" in Lambeth, a "six-roomer, exclusive of kitchens" that is "in the opinion of my friends, a commodious tenement" which the happy couple will share with Jobling and Guppy's mother. Saved from that all-too-realistic fate, Esther lives happily with Allan and their children in the doll's cottage, eventually "throwing out a little Growlery expressly for my guardian" when he comes to visit (*BH* 64). His moods and memories are, as before, confined to an annex.

The writing of this marriage plot during the spring of 1853 coincided with Dickens's ambivalence about the future of his "little housekeeper" Georgina Hogarth, who had joined the family at the age of fifteen, turning twenty-five in 1852. Sometime that year Dickens's artist friend Augustus

Egg had proposed to her and been refused, whether because Georgy had decided to dedicate her life to her brother-in-law's household or because she was not interested in Egg. "Georgina is not yet married," Dickens wrote to his Swiss friend William de Cerjat, "and not in the least likely to be. She seems unaccountably hard to please" (6.671). "Unaccountably" may have been disingenuous, but Dickens was determined to see himself as a neutral factor. "I took no other part in the matter than urging her to be quite sure that she knew her own mind," he assured Miss Coutts, but the sentence that follows might tell a different story: "He is very far her inferior intellectually; but five men would be out of six, for she has one of the most remarkable capacities I have ever known" (7.172). How could Georgy have failed to know that Dickens himself was a sixth man?

Nevertheless her choice was a topic for family concern. When Dickens, Egg, and Wilkie Collins traveled together in the fall of 1853, Dickens reported back to Catherine, "A general sentiment expressed here this morning, that Georgina ought to be married. Perhaps you'll mention it to her!" (7.167). He did not yet know that Georgy would choose him rather than her sister when the Dickens marriage was dismantled a few years later, but it had been clear for a long time that she was essential, not only to the smooth running of the household, but as a sturdy walking companion and a quick study of Dickens's habits and needs. What was Dickens, fifteen years older, to his useful sister-in-law? A brother? A father? A fantasy partner whom she served as mistress of the house? The ambiguities of the relationship hover in the Esther-Jarndyce-Woodcourt plot, which Dickens may have used to assure himself that, were Georgy really to fall in love, he would be nobly willing to give her up. He was careful, however, to steer away from the explicit rivalry between sisters he had felt free to satirize a decade earlier in the Pecksniff sisters of *Martin Chuzzlewit*. In the 1850s he was beginning to experience his own version of the wider cultural anxiety that lay behind the Deceased Wife's Sister's Act of 1840, which outlawed marriage between a widower and the sister of his late wife. The dearth of employment opportunities for unmarried women created all too many reasons for a sister-in-law to become an integral, potentially competitive, part of a couple's household.

Dickens's fear of losing Georgina centered in his view that she was essential to the care and training of his children. As his agent rather than the children's mother, Georgy was quick to follow the household rules of orderliness, punctuality, and discipline that Dickens thought appropriate to impose on his offspring no less than on the women of Urania Cottage. The children were later to recall his practices in quite different ways. "We can see by the different child characters in his books what a wonderful knowledge he had of children, and what a wonderful and truly womanly sympathy he had with them in all their childish joys and griefs," writes the enchanted Mamie, perhaps not quite recognizing that she has put Dickens's imaginary children first. She is quick to retrieve: "I can remember with us, his own children, how kind, considerate and patient he always was" (M. Dickens 14). Writing at fifty-eight in her last illness, she still buys into Dickens's household management, recalling his careful attention to the room she and Katie had shared in a garret at the top of Devonshire Terrace, where they could put up any prints so long as the job was neatly done. "Even in those days," Mamie writes, "he made a point of visiting every room in the house once each morning, and if a chair was out of its place, or a blind not quite straight, or a crumb left on the floor, woe betide the offender" (16–17). In her eyes, such attentions were proof of the theme she sought to impress on her reader: "From his earliest childhood, throughout his earliest married life to the day of his death, his nature was home-loving" (11).

What we know of Katie Dickens Perrugini's last memories comes filtered through her friend Gladys Storey, whose unsystematic narrative leaves some doubt about their authenticity. According to her, Dickens inspected the insides of drawers as well as the neatness of the children's rooms. If they used language he disapproved, he would write remonstrating notes, "folded neatly and left by him on their pincushion, which they called 'pincushion notes.'" Like a number of others who left memories of Dickens, she calls his punctuality "almost painful"; even Mamie admits "And then his punctuality! It was almost frightful to an unpunctual mind!" before she goes on to justify it as a form of consideration for others (Storey 77; M. Dickens 17).

The memories of Henry Fielding Dickens, the sixth and only successful one of Dickens's sons, represent the brood of younger boys that Dickens found rather superfluous; ten years younger than Katie, Henry experienced a quite different distance from his father. In *Memories of My Father* (1929) he speaks for his brothers: "In his habits his methods of tidiness were very marked, so pronounced, indeed, as to fail to meet with the entire approval of us small boys." Dickens's rather military idea of how to treat a group of little boys emerges in the practice "which went by the name of 'Pegs, Parade, and Custos.' To each boy was appropriated a particular peg for his hat and coats: a parade was held once a week for overhauling the inevitable fresh stains on our garments; and one of us was deputed in turn to be the general custodian of the implements of the games, whose duty it was to collect them at the end of the day and put them in their appointed places." In retrospect, Henry finds these rules reasonable enough, but he admits that reason is sparse in young boys: "they were received by us with mingled feelings of dislike and resentment. It is true we gave no open utterance to our feelings of antagonism. That we dare not do. Our resentment took another form, the more insidious form of deeply whispered mutterings among ourselves on the subjects of 'slavery,' 'degradation,' and so forth." Though ineffective, they "still served as a kind of safety-valve and helped to soothe our ruffled feelings" (H. Dickens 25–26). His wry, twentieth-century voice offers some clue about the difficulties of growing up a Dickens son.

Henry was about five when Dickens's disapproval began to descend upon the carefully nurtured eldest son Charley. At seventeen, Charley was failing to live up his father's hopes: a German professor, to whom he had been sent to learn the language in preparation for training in a German commercial school, had advised Dickens that the discipline at the school would be too harsh for a child of Charley's sensitivity and inaptitude for study. Dickens duly reported to Miss Coutts, his special confidant where Charley was concerned, and added his own assessment. Charley was "gentle and affectionate" but "I think he has less fixed purpose and energy than I could have supposed possible in my son. He is not aspiring, or imaginative in his own behalf." Dickens blamed this on Catherine, from whom "he inherits an indescribable lassitude of character—a very serious thing in a man—which seems to me to express the want of a strong, compelling hand always beside him" (7.245). The complaint was the first of many about successive sons. Dickens felt that Catherine did not manage the household of children the way he wished them to be managed, and that she had failed to model a kind of temperament that would render the children as independent and resourceful as he had been. He was conveniently forgetting, or fearing to recognize, that his own family included several men—his younger brothers as well as father John—whom he had propped up for years. Nor did he consider his own precocious independence, the different economic situations of the two generations, or the fact that his tendency to take energetic charge left little room for the initiatives of others and enforced their dependency on him. Instead, he withdrew his trust from Catherine and invested it in Georgina.

🐚 Gad's Hill Place, 1855–1870

When Dickens, at thirty-nine, bought a forty-five-year lease on Tavistock House, he assumed that he had settled his final family home. In fact his years of house-taking had barely begun. His interest in room design did not diminish either, once Tavistock House was, in his word, complete. On 1 November 1854 he inspected a drawing room that Miss Coutts was refurbishing in her house on Stratton Street, and made a detailed recommendation: "The general compactness of this important part of the room is greatly marred by there being nothing in the little piers on either side of the looking glass opposite the door." He prescribed for each pier "a long tasteful piece of drapery" that would "hold the whole together, and make the rest tell for a great deal more than at present." He insisted on a table next to the bookcase, "because the bookcase as it stands, is quite insanely perched in the air, without appearing to have any root in the ground—which is always disagreeable; and secondly, because *there must be no table in the middle of the room*, or you destroy the fireside." He also recommended a new carpet "in dark chocolate or russet, with maybe a little green and red. The eye would rise from a dark warm ground, with great pleasure, to the light walls and the rich-colored damask" (7.450).

More than any other letter, this one displays the habits of interior decoration, along with the "Napoleonic commander-in-chief" style, that Marcus Stone recalled. Dickens's sense that the look of a room must create a sense of natural "grounding" may also indicate the role that houses played in stabilizing his inner world. As he grew older, the need for ritual stability became more extreme. It became necessary to rearrange the furniture of any house in which he stayed. Eliza Lynn Linton, from whom Dickens bought Gad's Hill Place, recalled that Dickens "was always fidgety about furniture, and did not stay even one night in an hotel without rearranging the chairs and tables of the sitting-room, and turning the bed—I think—north and south. He maintained that he could not sleep with it in any other position; and he backed up his objections by arguments about the earth currents and positive or negative electricity. It may have been a mere fantasy, but it was real enough to him" (Collins 1981, 213).

It was the inner world of fantasy that came into play when Dickens noticed, on a wintry forty-third birthday walk from Gravesend to Rochester, that Gad's Hill Place was for sale. "The spot and the very house are literally 'a dream of my childhood,' and I should like to look at it before I go to Paris," he wrote to Wills. "And I want you, strongly booted, to go with me!" (7.531). The dream he referred to was the famous childhood story that Dickens had apparently told to Forster whenever they passed the house on their walks. Forster retells it on the second page of his biography: "upon first seeing it as he came from Chatham with his father, and looking up at it with much admiration, he had been promised that he might himself live in it or in some such house, when he came to be a man, if he would only work hard enough" (Forster 2–3). Forster oddly attempts to "authenticate" the story by referring to a later retelling, in Dickens's *Uncommercial Traveller* essay "Travelling Abroad" (*AYR*, 7 April 1860). Whether it was true or not, the story held a central spot in Dickens's personal mythology.

For Cerjat in Switzerland, the new house was further mythologized as "Shakespeare's Gad's Hill, where Falstaff engaged in the robbery" (8.265). This identification, along with a speech of Falstaff's from *Henry 4 Part I*, was framed and placed on the first floor landing at Gad's Hill Place as soon as Dickens moved in (Forster 652). He also fabricated for Cerjat a retrospective tale of destiny, in which he and Wills see the house on a walk; the same evening Wills meets the owner, Eliza Lynn (Linton) at a dinner party, where it is revealed that she spent some childhood years in the house; Wills returns to Dickens saying, 'It is written that you were to have that house at Gad's Hill" (8.265–66).

In fact Wills looked at Gad's Hill Place while Dickens was in Paris and was unimpressed with anything but the "the view and the spot." Dickens concluded that it was not worth the money, and announced that the house "is to be thought no more about" (7.541–42). He did continue to think, of course; his other trusty agent Henry Austin was sent to look at the house in July. By mid-November 1855, Austin, Forster, and Wills were engaged in helping Dickens make an offer; by February 1856 he was calling it "my house" (8.50). Though it was the first house owned outright as a freehold in the Dickens family, it was not a house he needed or that he could really afford. He planned to "make it clean and pretty" and rent it out; "Whenever I cannot, I shall use it for myself and make it a change for Charley from Saturday to Monday," he told Miss Coutts (8.50). A few days later he told Forster that he planned to do the repairs and "keep it for myself" during the summer of 1857 (8.57). He never did rent it to anyone; in retrospect, it looks as though he was, half-consciously, preparing an escape hatch. The house also served as a writer's purchase that placed him among the gods of the British literary tradition—a position that few have denied him since.

Repairs began in February 1857, once the sitting tenant was out. Henry Austin resumed his role as Dickens's building contractor, and the house was inaugurated on Catherine's birthday, 19 May 1857, with family and a few friends. In June the family returned for the summer, though Dickens commuted frequently to London; it appeared that the country house was now to replace family summers in Boulogne, where they had gone in 1853, 1854, and 1856. (Broadstairs had been abandoned after the prolonged stay during the Tavistock repairs.) Dickens enjoyed filling "the little old-fashioned place" with his "ingenious devices"; even the lingering presence of workmen on the premises was not so disturbing when the family had a home elsewhere (8.330, 331). When he reported to Austin that the well had to be redug—they did not hit a spring for two months—or that the drains had to be redone, he put on some mock despair, but sounds more amused than anxious. Full ownership of Gad's meant that he could improve his estate without restriction, and he seems to have taken pleasure in "throwing out" additions: an extended drawing room, additional bedrooms under a raised roof, a conservatory, a servant's hall, a coach-house schoolroom and dormitory, a tunnel connecting the house with an additional piece of land across the Gravesend Road. By the late 1860s "last improvements" had become a standing joke among the Dickens children (M. Dickens 115).

Little Dorrit was composed during the period between the negotiations for Gad's Hill and the family's first summer residence there. In light of this juxtaposition, the most striking common features of the novel's London interiors are their airless stuffiness and their bad smells. Dickens conveys the impression that it is impossible to breathe in a London house; only the Meagleses' country cottage provides freshness and sweet air. His variations on the theme are characteristically ingenious, and suggest the sensitivities of an asthmatic. Mrs. Clennam's personal prison holds "a smell of black dye in the airless room, which the fire had been drawing out of the crape and stuff of the widow's dress for fifteen months, and out of the bier-like sofa for fifteen years"; the whole place is pervaded by "the musty smell of an old close house" (*LD* 1.3). Frederick Dorrit's house "was very close, and had an unwholesome smell" (*LD* 1.9). Tite Barnacle has a fancy address, but "to the sense of smell, the house was like a sort of bottle filled with a strong distillation of mews; and when the footman opened the door, he seemed to take the stopper out" (*LD* 1.10). The jars of "old rose leaves and old lavender" in the Casby house seem promising, but they have not been freshened for twenty years (*LD* 1.13). When Mr. Meagles and Arthur Clennam try to find Miss Wade, they search among "ricketty dwellings... of a capacity to hold nothing comfortable except a dismal smell" (*LD* 1.27). After Fanny Dorrit marries Mr. Sparkler they live at a most fashionable address in "a little mansion... with a perpetual smell in it of the day before yesterday's soup and coach-horses" (*LD* 2.24). Bad smells, indicative of clogged-up psyches as well as bad drainage, know no social boundaries in *Little Dorrit*. All of London is now, in Dickens's imagination, rendered as a place of stifled impulse and feeling.

From the street view, most of the houses in London are either squeezed into their spaces or literally falling down; the Clennam house, most dramatically, is "leaning on some half dozen gigantic crutches" that offer "no very sure reliance" (*LD* 1.3). The house collapses in allegorical fashion once Mrs. Clennam's choked story of self-imprisoning resentment is aired, but there is no hope of renewal—or stability—anywhere in town. Arthur Clennam goes directly from his prison room to his wedding, and the end of the novel leaves the married pair apparently houseless in the streets. For other characters, urban dwelling is a form of camping. The inhabitants of Bleeding Heart Yard live there "as Arabs of the desert pitch their tents among the fallen stones of the Pyramids" (*LD* 1.12). The pretentious Mrs. Gowan lives at Hampton Court, whose "venerable inhabitants seemed, in those times, to be encamped like a sort of civilized gipsies. There was a temporary air about their establishments, as if they were going away the moment they could get anything better" (*LD* 1.26). The peripatetic Miss Wade is discovered in "an airless room" containing odd scraps of furniture and "a disorder of trunks and travelling articles," "as she might have established herself in an Eastern caravanserai" (*LD* 1.27).

Instability and restlessness mark the inhabitants of houses of *Little Dorrit* as they marked Dickens's life in the mid- 1850s, when he was more often out of London than at home. Arthur finds the comfortably well-organized Meagles cottage a welcome alternative to London, but when Mr. Meagles greets him at the door, he describes himself as "boxed up . . . within our own home-limits, as if we were never going to expand—that is, travel—again." In Mr. Meagles's "whims to have the cottage always kept, in their absence, as if they were always coming back the day after tomorrow," Dickens describes himself (*LD* 1.16). Houses had to be perfect in their readiness, yet easily left behind. The acquisition of Gad's Hill Place assured him that there would always be a comfortable place to be—elsewhere. Still, when he invented Mrs. Plornish's fantasy of the thatch-roofed Happy Cottage, its exterior painted on a wall of her parlor in Bleeding Heart Yard, Dickens struck a comic death-blow to the pastoral solution he had employed so recently in *Bleak House*. "To Mrs. Plornish, it was still a most beautiful cottage, a most wonderful deception; and it made no difference that Mr. Plornish's eye was some inches above the level of the gable bedroom in the thatch" (*LD* 2.13). For the narrator and the reader, it is simply a most wonderful deception.

Little Dorrit is notably uninterested in housekeeping; its houses are traps for foul air and festering secret resentments. Dickens was not to return to the theme of the little housekeeper for a decade, until, near the end of *Our Mutual Friend*, he sounds a brief farewell reprise of the erotic-domestic tune in Bella Rokesmith-Harmon. In *Great Expectations* the fatally house-bound Mrs. Clennam reappears in the guise of Miss Havisham, Mrs. Joe's household efficiency is rendered as domestic terrorism, and Wemmick's heavily fortified suburban "castle" features Wemmick himself as a comical suburban Dickens, the proud genius of clever arrangement. Between the depressive *Little Dorrit* and the demythologizing *Great Expectations*, Dickens had another plot to manage: the destruction of his marriage.

Meeting Ellen Ternan, the young actress who took part in the 1857 Manchester performances of *The Frozen Deep*, was apparently the precipitating factor in the marriage crisis. Dickens had met and flirted with plenty of young actresses in his life; he liked lively performing women, and had managed to inspire a lifelong devotion in at least one, Mary Boyle, who called him "the only despot I ever tolerated" (Boyle 234). Ellen herself does not explain enough; certainly Dickens himself could not have foreseen in 1857 that his infatuation with her would lead to a twelve-year secret affair that would occupy the rest of his life. Like other Victorian men, he might have kept an actress on the side; only the terror of losing his public reputation would have prevented that course. But, for reasons that no one will ever fully understand, it became necessary for him in 1858 to exile Catherine completely, from his house and from his presence.

The title of Claire Tomalin's biography calls Ellen Ternan "the invisible woman," but it was Catherine of whom Dickens first required invisibility. His first act in the dismantling of his marriage was quite literally to wall her off. On 11 October 1857 he wrote to their faithful servant Anne Cornelius while the family was staying at Gad's Hill Place, to order new sleeping arrangements for himself and Catherine at Tavistock House. The letter never mentions this central fact; it concerns itself with the moving of furniture. The servants were to move his washing stands into the bathroom, and to "get rid altogether" of the chest of drawers in his dressing room (adjoining the marital bedroom); that item was to be brought down to Gad's Hill. The "recess of the doorway between the Dressing-Room and Mrs. Dickens's room" was to be "fitted with plain light deal shelves, and closed with a plain white deal door, painted white." He is sending a small iron bedstead with bedding, that is to stand behind the door, "its head toward the stairs, and its foot towards the window"; he wants it all done before the family returns to London at the end of October (8.465). The letter conveys the plan as if it were just another of his ingenious little household arrangements that the servants could readily implement—an odd repetition of the Tavistock House study door, or the bachelor male house spaces Dickens had been writing about for years.

Perhaps even Dickens himself did not yet know quite what he meant by it. Catherine was forty-two; he was forty-five. Their last child had been born five years earlier, in 1852. Had they prevented subsequent pregnancies through abstinence, or had Dickens lost interest in his wife? Was the story he told to himself, or to her, about his night wanderings rather than about their sexual relations? Catherine would have known and demurred when he crept out of bed in his restless anxiety; had they euphemistically agreed to protect her from these disturbances? Dickens's famous thirty-mile night walk from London to Gad's Hill took place sometime during this troubled month of October, but it is not clear whether Dickens was walking from his office digs toward Catherine at Gad's, or away from Tavistock House after their return at the end of the month; on 7 December he told Lavinia Watson that the walk had occurred "six or eight weeks ago" (8.489). It is often assumed that the walk was a result of a fight with Catherine, and that the walled-off bedroom was a definitive turning point made in response to some incident of Catherine's jealousy, but there is no hard evidence about either assumption. Nor do we know if Catherine bought into the bedroom decision, or whether it greeted her as an awful surprise on her return to Tavistock House. We do not really know anything about what happened between them.

We do, however, have access to one of Dickens's fantasies, a Gothic tale often referred to as "The Bride's Chamber," that was completed on 2 October 1857 as part of the fourth chapter of "The Lazy Tour of Two Idle Apprentices." Triggered by Dickens's and Collins's stay at the King's Arms Inn at Lancaster, where a man who murdered a wife called Ellen had recently been hanged, the tale is narrated to the traveling pair at the inn by the ghost of the hanged man (Dent 3.447). The ghost narrator is doubled with the Dickens-Goodchild figure through the gaze of fascination: "threads of fire stretch from the old man's eyes to his own, and there attach themselves" (Dent 3.452). Every critic who pays attention to the story recognizes that the tale of an older man who terrorizes his pathetic young bride until she is abject before him, and then orders her to die, expresses something about Dickens's marital feelings. It goes almost without saying that the story dramatizes a death wish that does not involve an act of actual murder: after signing away her property, the Bride dies (it takes many days and nights), simply because she can no longer hold out against the will of her husband.

In the elaboration of this fantasy, however, Dickens reveals a complex set of understandings. The wife-killer forms his victim's mind from childhood on: "The girl was formed in the fear of him, and in the conviction, that there was no escape from him"; she sees in him the embodiment of "power to coerce and power to relieve, power to bind and power to loose." As a result, she can do nothing but apologize, plead forgiveness, and promise to obey his every wish; and as a result of that, he hates her for her abjection (Dent 3.454). The portrait of sado-masochistic psychological abuse drew on intimate material that was familiar to Dickens and doubtless to Catherine; as early as 1842, in a thank-you letter to an acquaintance in New York, he signed—apparently from them both—"Bully and Meek" (3.291). Perhaps they were joking about the absoluteness of his will in those days, but in 1857 it was no longer a joke. Catherine had succumbed, and Dickens could no longer bear the sight of what he had done; he wanted her to disappear.

In the story, the wish to achieve a guilt-free liberation is punished through-out the narrator's lifetime and even beyond his death. (In this respect the fantasy is predictive if not self-fulfilling: Dickens did not experience relief or a new lightness of being even after he declared that Catherine had been wiped out of his memory.) The agent of punishment in the story is a "slen-der youth of about her age, with long light brown hair," who loves the Bride, and has watched the older man imprison her emotions and destroy her will. He displays "a tress of [her] flaxen hair, tied with a mourning ribbon," and speaks passionately of his feeling: "Murderer, I loved her!" Surely this figure of mourning is the young Dickens who had loved Catherine, arriving in the fantasy to insist on the purity of his original feelings and to damn the older man who has made such bad work of the marriage. When the older man suddenly kills him and buries him in the garden of the secluded house in which he had kept the young Bride, the young man's corpse becomes an agent of delayed revenge. The murderer's plan to escape with his ill-gotten wealth is now paralyzed; he is "chained to the house of gloom and horror, which he could not endure. Being afraid to sell it or quit it, lest discovery should be made, he was forced to live in it" (Dent 3.457–48).

Inevitably, discovery is made and he comes to be hanged—for the "real" murder of the young romantic self, though the fantastic wife-murder comes to light as well. As the fantasy begins to reincorporate the scene of confessional telling at the inn, the Dickens-Collins duo is split into two other Dickenses. One speaks of the other's readiness for any adventure, and the other replies, "Not quite so, Dick; if I am afraid of nothing else, I am afraid of myself" (Dent 3.462). The daydream narrative clarifies the rage and the attendant guilt and shame with which Dickens approached the idea of a marital disso-lution, leaving no doubt that he had a conscience. The rage is directed toward the wife figure, who is described as a "weak, credulous, incapable, helpless nothing" (Dent 3.453) and, briefly, toward the memory of the romantic youth who had loved her; guilt and shame figure in the older man's impulsive mur-der of his more innocent self, in the house-bound self-destructive paralysis of emotion that follows, and in the exposure to public infamy.

For a few months after the fantasies and events of October, Dickens may have contemplated living, chained to the corpse of a marriage, in a desolate house. In late March 1859 he wrote to Forster, "It is not, with me, a mat-ter of will, or trial, or sufferance, or good humour, or making the best of it, or making the worst of it, any longer. It is all despairingly over. Have no lingering hope of, or for, me in this association. A dismal failure has to be borne, and there an end" (8.539). According to a letter written by Catherine's aunt Helen Thomson, Dickens at one point proposed that Catherine should continue to live at Tavistock House, keeping to her own apartments but appearing on social occasions as "mistress of the house" (8.746). By early May, however, the decision to separate had been made, and the battle of rumor, accusation, and mediated negotiation began. In response to speculations that he was sexually involved with Georgina or with an actress (neither was probably true at the time), Dickens felt compelled to fabricate explanations for the consumption of his friends and for the public he wished so desperately to keep on his side. Ever since Michael Slater published his judicious account of the marriage and separation in *Dickens and Women* (1983), it has been generally accepted that Dickens invented a distorted retrospective account of a marriage troubled from its very beginnings, and of Catherine as an unfit, emotionally disturbed mother. That would, of course, have been his way of treating any situation in which he could be accused of bad feeling or wrongdoing; the pattern I have described in "Language on the Loose" came naturally to hand in the most important severance of his life.

It has become common in biographical accounts to link Dickens's choice of the "bad mother" story with anger at his own mother, and to find in the episode a regression to the feelings of the child in the blacking warehouse. It seems to me, however, that there were more immediate situations that helped to determine the particular cover story he told. Dickens tried out a version of the story for Miss Coutts on 9 May before he toned it down in the so-called "Violated Letter," written on 25 May and given to his reading tour manager Arthur Smith with the injunction to show it "to any one who may have been misled into doing me wrong" (8.568). (Smith gave a copy to the *New York Tribune*, where it was published on 16 August and reprinted in other American and British papers.) Dickens knew that Miss Coutts would disapprove of the decision, and he wrote to prepare her for the news, trying to summon the voice of his most thoughtful self for her sensitive ears (8.558–60). "You know me too well to suppose that I have the faintest thought of influencing you on either side," he said. "I merely mention a fact which may induce you to pity us both, when I tell you that she is the only person I have ever known with whom I could not get on somehow or other." He was especially concerned to ward off Miss Coutts's quite accurate perception that he was willful and impulsive: "I am patient and considerate at heart, and would have beaten out a path to a better journey's end than we have come to, if I could."

His next move was to suggest that the separation was an acknowledgment of a long-standing situation: "We have been virtually separated for a long time. We must put a wider space between us now, than can be found in one house." Now, as the appeal heats up, the children appear in the story as the prime victims, and Catherine grows ever more Gothic: "It is her misery to live in some fatal atmosphere which slays every one to whom she should be dearest"; in her aura her daughters "harden into stone figures of girls" and "have their hearts shut up in her presence as if they closed by some horrid spring." Oddly, Dickens represented the children's alleged lack of love for their mother as a fact that made the separation more rather than less difficult. Perhaps he meant, consciously or not, that it would have been easier had he simply walked away from the family altogether. Unable to tolerate that picture of himself as the abandoner, his inventive pen created instead a wife of "confused mind" harboring "miserable weaknesses and jealousies"—in short, a mad wife who had to be ejected from a sane household.

Miss Coutts knew better than to give the letter the "kind construction" Dickens pleaded for; their cordial relations began to fade. From our distant perspective, kinder constructions may be possible. Few conscientious people leave marriages without constructing temporarily oversimplified stories for themselves, though few have quite the imaginative resources of a Dickens or the need to display those stories in public. By the time he wrote the "Violated Letter" on 25 May Dickens had boiled down the bad mother fantasy to a single main clause: "the peculiarity of her character has thrown all the children on someone else." By this time his effort was to defend Georgy from scandal by highlighting her devotion "to our home and our children," and to defend himself by attributing the break to Catherine's own sense of unfitness as his wife, and her long-held wish to separate (8.740).

The evil Dickens did may lie less in the exaggerated fiction that allowed him to make the break than in the way he continued to impose it on his children. The separation agreement gave Catherine full access to them, but Dickens's disapproval clouded their rare visits to her. After what he had done, he did not want to know about Catherine's existence, and he hated to be reminded that she was in fact the mother of his children. Supported by Dickens's 600 pounds a year, Catherine took a house at 70 Gloucester Crescent near the northeast corner of Regent's Park, where she lived until her death in 1879. Not long after she was resettled, Dickens found that sending his wife out of the house was not enough; he had to get rid of the house as well. In the summer of 1860 he sold the lease on Tavistock House, moved the family permanently to Gad's Hill, and burned a lifetime of past correspondence.

Although Dickens invented a retrospective story about Catherine's character, the feelings that made the separation necessary to him did have a long history. Catherine had always appeared to him as a kind of management problem. During their engagement, Dickens was training her to be the wife he needed. His letters of 1835–36 are intimate and expressive, but they make it clear that she is not to complain when his work comes first, that she is to appear punctually at appointed times, and that she must control her feelings in the light of his sensitivities. Taken together, his later letters attest to the understandings of a deeply married couple: he writes with affection, full of detail about the physical comfort or discomfort of his travels, married gossip about their acquaintances, and references to their shared views of his own character. When Dora died during Catherine's nervous illness in April 1851, Dickens was kindly and carefully solicitous in breaking the news step by step.

Yet there is very often a strain of distrust; he is never entirely sure that Catherine will behave with the social grace or the emotional control he thinks appropriate. He was enraged at her betrayal of a perfectly natural jealousy of his mesmeric relationship with Mme. de la Rue, and at every sign of jealousy thereafter; he could not bear to see in her response that there was anything amiss in what he was doing. In the Dora letter he writes, "I cannot close it without putting the strongest entreaty and injunction upon you to come home with perfect composure." Should she hear on her arrival that Dora is dead (as Dickens already knew she was), "you are to do your duty to the rest [of the children], and to shew yourself worthy of the great trust you hold in them" (6.353). His insistence that she control even the expression of a loss that the children shared suggests his intolerance of freely demonstrated feeling, as well as his self-appointed role as the manager of household emotions.

However well he may have succeeded in bending Catherine to his will, he could not control her body or her emotional being. He kept his own body in rigorous health, but he could do nothing about the process of swelling and suffering that Catherine displayed before him for seventeen consecutive years. After the birth of Walter, the fourth child, Dickens seems to have been satisfied with the size of his family. Letters to friends after each successive birth regularly suggest, lightly enough, that Catherine had presented him with a child he did not need or want. The births themselves were anticipated with dread, because they were difficult for Catherine and threats to her health. He was solicitous for her, but he did seem to feel that he might have had a right to sexual relations without quite so many consequences. For someone of Dickens's passionate and idealistic nature methods of birth control may not have presented themselves as possibilities, but we cannot know about that; perhaps he was actually bragging about his own virility when he complained about new babies. All of this is speculation, of course, but it is meant to suggest that Catherine had by the 1850s come to represent everything, physical and emotional, in himself and in others, that Dickens could not manage to his satisfaction. She was the flaw in his imaginary system of household Order.

Anxiety about the futures of all those boys was also a factor in Dickens's state of mind during and after the marriage crisis. In 1858 the seven sons ranged in age from six to twenty-one. The two youngest, Henry and Plorn, were at home; the middle boys, Frank, Alfred, and Sydney, were at school in Boulogne and came home for holidays. Seventeen-year-old Walter was serving with the 42nd Highlanders in India, where he was to die of disease at twenty-two. Charley, the first-born child, had received more of Dickens's attention than the rest, but at twenty-one he was working at a bank, not quite living up to the hopes he had raised when Miss Coutts paid for his Eton education. At the time of the separation he put a distance between himself and Dickens by choosing to live with his mother. At twenty and eighteen, Mamie and Katie were still Dickens's favorites, Mamie because she idolized him and Katie because she had an independent temperament and did not fear him as the others did. Dickens thrilled Mamie's heart by appointing her as mistress of his house when Catherine left; her memoir suggests that she had no trouble with the idea that she could replace her mother. Katie, more divided in her feelings about her parents, married Charles Collins in 1860 and left her father's house.

The sense that daughters were easier to manage and more gratifying as companions may well have been at play when Dickens became involved with the all-female Ternan household. A family consisting of a self-reliant professional mother and three close but independent professional daughters could appear as a dreamlike alternative to his large household of dependents. When he met them in 1857, mother and daughters had all had quite successful careers on the stage since early childhood. Frances Ternan's husband had died in 1847; her daughters were in the age range of Dickens's three eldest children: Fanny was twenty-two, Maria twenty, and Ellen eighteen—the same age as Katie. Dickens first entered this hard-working but financially insecure family in the role of the fairy godfather. He used his connections to find work for the young actresses. In 1858 he sent Fanny and Mrs. Ternan to Florence so that Fanny could train as a singer. Maria and Ellen now turned up in a West End lodging near the theaters where they were employed; possibly Dickens helped pay the rent. In March 1859 Dickens put the family into a house at 2 Houghton Place near Mornington Crescent, purchased in the names of Frances and Maria Ternan, but meant for Ellen, who became its owner when she turned twenty-one.

Dickens's own "gipsy tent" at the *Household Words* office was expanded that spring into serious bachelor digs when the office moved to larger quarters a few doors down Wellington Street. In 1865 the Ternans left Houghton Place, but Ellen was to profit for the rest of her life from its rental. She had not lived there long, having spent most of the 1860s in various undisclosed houses that Dickens took for her, often under false names. After she was injured in the 1865 Stapleton railway accident, Dickens placed her in London suburbs with good rail connections to London and Gad's Hill: Elizabeth Cottage in Slough and then Windsor Lodge in Peckham. Claire Tomalin notes that Ellen, trained for the stage rather than the home, was "totally undomesticated; household management and cookery were of no interest to her at all" (Tomalin 124). His irregular, migratory love life had finally allowed Dickens to put sexual intimacy and housekeeping under different roofs.

Finding houses for Ellen was just one of the many real estate transactions that were to occupy Dickens during the 1860s. His brother Alfred Dickens died in 1860, leaving no money to support his widow Helen and their five children. Dickens found and supported London houses for Helen, and she reciprocated by caring for his mother as Elizabeth Dickens declined into senile dementia. The following year Henry Austin died, leaving Dickens to advise his sister Letitia about her housing arrangements. Letters to her during November and December 1861 show him urging her to leave her house and take furnished lodgings while she flurried about making money by keeping the house and taking in lodgers. He finally secured a government pension for her as Henry's widow; she seems to have capitulated and gone into lodgings. In addition, Dickens rented West End houses nearly every year so that Mamie could be in town during the social season. If we consider all of these houses, combined with the support of Catherine, improvements at Gad's Hill, and the expenses of launching the younger boys, it is no wonder that Dickens became obsessed with his public readings. They were not just a way to revel directly in the approval of his public, but a financial necessity.

Houses were constantly on his agenda, but he was always in motion, between the apartment in the office of *All the Year Round*, Gad's Hill, Ellen's lodgings, and the prolonged, strenuous reading tours. "I cannot regard myself as having a home anywhere," he wrote to Wilkie Collins in 1863, though Gad's "gets so pretty, that I can't help being fond of it, and I am always touching it up with something new" (10.239). The dream of being grounded in a stable domestic space was gone, but so were the nightmare visions of characters stuck for a lifetime in houses that could barely contain the emotional tensions they were intended to hide. Brief descriptions of houses continued to appear in the late novels, but the characters in *Our Mutual Friend* and *The Mystery of Edwin Drood* tend to be, like Dickens, on the move.

At the end of the managerial 1850s, however, houses became structuring images for the special Christmas issues of *Household Words* and its successor *All the Year Round*. Like previous Christmas numbers, "A House to Let" (1858) and "The Haunted House" (1859) were organized as frame stories into which the contributions of other writers could be fitted. Working closely with Dickens's idea, Wilkie Collins wrote much of "A House to Let," which is rarely discussed except as an example of their collaboration. It is important, however, that in the year of his separation from Catherine Dickens chose a title and a situation that had a longstanding internal association with failure. The "To Let" motif takes us all the way back to his 1834 sketch "Shops and Their Tenants," in which Boz observes from the street the rise and fall of a shop's fortunes. Once the To Let sign goes up he loses hope, "for that the place had no chance of succeeding now, was perfectly clear." After a few more permutations the shop turns into the Gower Street house in which Elizabeth Dickens had vainly hoped to support her family by running a school, forever symbolized for her son by the brass plate advertisement on the door of the house. Observing "these signs of poverty, which are not to be mistaken," Boz turns away, thinking that the house "had attained its lowest pitch of degradation" (Dent 1.63–64). When they show up throughout his subsequent work, To Let signs invariably suggest sad stories of decline that can only be imagined from the street. The poverty of family life inside Mr. Dombey's house is mirrored in "the dirty house to let immediately opposite," and when Florence is left alone, the neglected outside of the Dombey mansion is treated as if it too were a house both haunted and To Let: "boys chalked the railings and the pavement... and drew ghosts on the stable door" (*DS* 3.23).

"A House to Let" is narrated by an old woman who takes lodgings in London across from a house that has stood apparently empty for years; no one will take it. The frame story turns on discovering the reason and uncovering the family secret hidden behind the To Let sign. The first chapter, "Over the Way," establishes the narrator in a rather jaunty, fast-moving Collins voice, interrupted occasionally by paragraphs unmistakably written by Dickens. The description of the house opposite has all of his markers: the rusty, peeling area-railings, the broken glass and stones telling of mischievous neighborhood boys: "there were games chalked on the pavement before the house, and likenesses of ghosts chalked on the street door... the bills 'To Let,' had curled up, as if the damp air of the place had given them cramps" (*CS* 261–62). It is doubtless also Dickens who invests the old lady with a lost beloved brother called Charley, whose child she had once yearned to raise. Inset stories by Dickens ("Going into Society") and Elizabeth Gaskell ("A Manchester Marriage"), as well as a poem by Adelaide Procter ("Three Evenings in the House") fill the empty rooms of the frame story.

The secret is revealed in "Trottle's Report," written primarily by Collins, but clearly imagined by Dickens. The mysterious house conceals—how could it have been otherwise?—a bright-eyed young boy abandoned to his caretakers; a "little, lonely, wizen, strangely-clad boy, who could not at the most, have been more than five years old." He spends his days scouring the floor of his garret room with "a mangy old blacking-brush, with hardly any bristles left in it, which he was rubbing backwards and forwards on the boards, as gravely and steadily as if he had been at scouring-work for years, and had got a large family to keep by it" (*CS* 291–92). No one but Dickens could have written the sentences that reveal how the collapse of his marriage, long concealed within the beautifully ordered family home, has merged with the traumatic prison years of the Dickens parents. The child and the ceaselessly working novelist are one, both scrubbing away to clean up the shame of family failure.

"The Haunted House" (1859) was more fully in Dickens's charge; he wrote the beginning and ending frame narratives, as well as a long inset story called "The Ghost in Master B's Room," while Collins joined four others who contributed the other inset tales. Each was supposed to unmask a ghost in a particular room, though the contributors in fact went their own ways, as Dickens complained to Forster on 25 November; he could put fellow-writers into a house together, but he could not force them to decorate the rooms the way he wanted. The idea for the issue had arisen from Dickens's correspondence that year with William Howitt, a spiritualist and believer in ghosts; Dickens was now out to demonstrate that there were no haunted houses, only minds haunted by human fears and memories. His frame narrative features a Dickens-like narrator determined to make his point by renting a "haunted" country house which, like "A House to Let," has stood empty for years because of its reputation. The narrator's rational skepticism is set against the uneducated hysteria of his female servants, who catch the infection of fear disseminated by local workers; so far as he is concerned, the house suffers primarily from cheap repairs, bad maintenance, and thoughtless furnishing. His sister, even more cheerfully rational than the narrator himself, proposes that they send the servants away and invite friends to stay with them to test the house. The friends arrive, each is allotted some household duties, and they agree to say nothing until Twelfth Night, when they will meet and tell stories set off by their experiences in the rooms assigned to them. With these good companions and snug arrangements in place, the narrator "never was happier in my life" (CS 325).

The contrast between the rationalistic frame story and the wild contents of Dickens's inset tale makes a striking instance of the pattern I have been following throughout this chapter. "The Ghost in Master B's Room" may be the most chaotic, dreamlike narrative Dickens ever allowed into print. Deborah Thomas emphasizes its autobiographical visions, as well as its loose, associative organization and its lack of narrative control (Thomas 75–80). When the narrator shaves in the mirror of Master B's room, he is terrified by seeing, not his own face, but those of a boy, an adolescent, a young man, his father, and even the grandfather he never met. In this generational sequence there is, perhaps, an implicit recognition that he is after all no better than his dubious predecessors. As if returning to more comfortable territory, the piece closes with self-pitying childhood memories of family debt, the repossession of "my own little bed" in a mixed lot of family furniture, and shame at school. As in "A House to Let," Dickens's most primary association of houses with exposure, failure, and shame returns to haunt his tale. These memories allow him to end the story with the moral he intends: there has been "no other ghost" than "the ghost of my own childhood, the ghost of my own innocence, the ghost of my own airy belief" (CS 337).

Between the recognitions in the mirror and the sad songs of youth Dickens wrote some fantasies bizarre enough that Thomas does not even mention them—fantasies of forbidden male power and sexuality that suggest anything but childhood innocence. At this point in the narrative "I was marvelously changed. I was myself, yet not myself." Behind a door, to a doubled figure, the narrator confides a proposition: "The proposition was, that we should have a Seraglio." The other creature assents: "he had no notion of respectability, neither had I" (CS 331). As the narrative proceeds, it becomes clear that the participants are children at school, who spend much of their energy hiding their sexual fantasy from the schoolmistress Miss Griffin. Yet the childhood setting does not conceal the narrator's urges for power: he gets rid of the double, appoints himself Caliph, and reigns supreme among eight beautiful little girls. Rules about the Caliph's kissing rights are debated and settled. "There were difficulties in the formation of the desired institution, as there are in all combinations," says the fantasist, but it is only enhanced by the "mysterious and terrible joy" of secrecy: there was "a grim sense prevalent among us that there was a dreadful power in our knowledge of what Miss Griffiths . . . didn't know" (CS 332–34).

In this oblique way, Dickens celebrated his new life. Written some months after he had established the Ternan women at Houghton Place, the Caliph story embeds a tale of joyful, secret, guiltily empowering sexual dominion at the center of a narrative house. "A Haunted House" appeared in the first Christmas issue of the new journal that announced Dickens's break with the alliances of his past, but it epitomizes one of the organizing rhythms in his life and art: the house is rationally ordered and respectable, but the dream life of its occupant is not.

❧ CHAPTER 6

Streets

Should you want to know how to get to the coffee-house where Mr. Squeers stays when he is in London, Dickens's narrator will be glad to oblige: from that particularly steep point on Snow Hill, turn into the coachyard of the Saracen's Head Inn, noting the booking office on your left and the spire of St. Sepulchre's to your right; straight ahead "you will observe a long window with the words 'coffee-room' legibly painted above it" (*NN* 4). Or, perhaps you would prefer to get to Mrs. Jellyby's house from Lincoln's Inn: ask Mr. Guppy and he will tell you to "twist up Chancery Lane, and cut along Holborn, and there we are in four minutes' time" (*BH* 4). Fagin's first den isn't too hard to find: as you come into London through Islington, the Artful Dodger will escort you on St. John's Road, making a cut through Sadler's Wells and down through Exmouth Street and Coppice Row to Saffron Hill, conveniently located near Smithfield Market (*OT* 8). Later Sikes will drag Oliver westward from Bethnal Green on their way to the robbery, crossing Finsbury Square to Chiswick Street going toward Barbican, then into Long Lane on the way to Smithfield, then past Hyde Park Corner and into Kensington, where they pick up a ride to the western suburbs (*OT* 21).

Or, you could get lost in another part of town with Florence Dombey, if you start at Staggs's Gardens in Camden Town and take an hour-long detour to the east along City Road. Somewhere along that road Good Mrs. Brown will take you through brick-fields and tile-yards to her dingy back room, perhaps in Shoreditch, where she will strip you of your expensive clothes, put you in rags, and escort you through "a labyrinth of narrow streets and lanes" to "the roar of a great thoroughfare." If you are a lost young girl dressed like a beggar child, it will take you two hours of asking your way to the City until you find yourself at a wharf near London Bridge where you will finally be rescued (*DS* 6).

Everyone knows that Dickens rewrote and permanently transformed the literary image of London; he is rightly recognized as the first great urban novelist in English. But how did he do it? Street by street, house by house, walker by walker. The description of getting to a place is an essential part of the place itself; Dickens is not a novelist who picks up his audience and sets us down in a new scene as if travel and distance shrink to nothing in the art of fiction. As he advised an aspiring novelist in 1866, "Suppose yourself telling that affecting incident in a letter to a friend. Wouldn't you describe how you went through the life and stir of the streets and roads, to the sick-room? Wouldn't you say what kind of room it was, what time of day it was, whether it was sunlight, starlight, or moonlight?" (11.161). For Dickens, nothing could be more obvious or necessary to an effective story. Of course we cannot quite pinpoint all those houses or shops he walks us to; there is always a little gap between the description of the route and the imagined place of arrival. Real or imaginary, however, the city is seen from the point of view of a person in the street, most often coming or going by foot.

Dickens's transformation of the urban writing that had grown up with him during the Regency period depends on that walker and those streets. London is realized neither through panoramic views nor by urban spectatorship in the rebuilt West End avenues, squares, and parks sponsored by George IV during the 1820s. Instead it is a dense but known network of streets and turnings that are ways to get from here to there, or an intricate maze of little alleys in which the poor and the hunted can escape from view. Someone is always in possession of knowledge about those networks and mazes. It might be the "bad un's" like Sikes or Good Mrs. Brown or George Radfoot leading their victims on winding routes they cannot later recall. It might be the good ones like Amy Dorrit or Kate Nickleby, treading their paths from home to work with faithful regularity. It might be the followers like Nadgett or Bucket or Arthur Clennam in detective mode, contriving to hide in plain sight as urban pedestrians while they gather information about the comings and goings of their suspects. Shadowing every fictional walker is the narrator, whose knowledge of London streets had been on public display ever since the twenty-two-year-old Dickens began publishing his "Street Sketches" in the *Morning Chronicle.* As Forster writes of this London, "Its interior hidden life becomes familiar as its commonest outward forms, and we discover that we hardly knew anything of the places that we supposed we knew the best" (Forster 123).

Although Dickens's knowing voice gives the impression of vastness and complexity, the London most central to his imagination is not terribly large. Apart from the Limehouse area, it comprises perhaps three to four square miles reaching in a southeasterly band from Camden Town to the City, and across the river into Southwark—the areas north and south of the Thames between the Westminster and London bridges. This, of course, is the territory marked out by Dickens's childhood years; the autobiographical fragment details the walking routes of the twelve-year-old boy even more carefully than the novels mark out the paths of their characters. From North Gower Street, where his mother tried and failed to set up a school, to the warehouse at the Hungerford Stairs on the river; from his Chatham lodgings down Tottenham Court Road and St. Martin's Road through Covent Garden to Warren's, and then across the Blackfriars Bridge into "the Borough" where the Marshalsea, and later the child's Lant Street attic room, stood. The areas near the London Bridge, where he used to wait for the Marshalsea gates to open. The coffee-houses he frequented on Maiden Lane and St. Martin's Lane; the new Warren's warehouse nearby on Chandos Street; the Adelphi arches, equally close at hand, where he used to hang about alone during the dinner break.

Dickens never really left this central area of London: his home at Devonshire Terrace near the southeast corner of Regent's Park was as far west as he went for his years of respectability. His next residence, Tavistock House, was not far from Gower Street or the Doughty Street house where the Dickens family had spent two early years. His characters live in the same region. Mr. Dombey's house, on a "dreadfully genteel street between Portland-place and Bryanstone-square" (*DS* 3) is not far from Devonshire Terrace; Ralph Nickelby's house in Golden Square, which "is not exactly in anybody's way to or from anywhere," could easily be right on the way from the river to Hanover Square, where Dickens picked up his sister Fanny on Sunday mornings to visit the family in prison (*NN* 2). The house in the East End where Ralph Nickleby sends Mrs. Nickleby and Kate seems to be in approximately the same place off Lower Thames Street as the dismal Clennam house to which Arthur returns, walking from his lodging in Ludgate Hill past St. Paul's and "down, at a long angle, almost to the water's edge" (*LD* 1.3). It is not the same place as Warren's, which is further upriver off the Strand, but it is endowed with memories of decrepitude that belong to Warren's. Rather like the topography of *Bleak House*, with so many different households crowded within an easy walk of their source of pain at Lincoln's Inn, Dickens's London keeps his history close at hand. Perhaps more important, his history underlies the sense of mastery crucial to his creation of London as a known and yet secret landscape of particular streets, houses, churches, and shops.

Critical accounts of Dickens's London have been roughly divided between a London seen from above as a coherent system and a London created through a dispersed series of particular localities. I tend toward the latter view: views of roofs and chimneys from above street level—like the dismaying view from the room where Oliver Twist is imprisoned by Fagin—are associated with confusion, indistinctness, isolation, and the arrest of motion. The land-scape of roofs, chimneys, and masts that Arthur Clennam sees from the Iron Bridge is less a widening of vision than a jumbled "wilderness" (*LD* 1.9). Certain rather atypical set pieces like the opening of *Bleak House*, the view from Todgers's in *Martin Chuzzlewit*, and the Asmodeus passage in *Dombey and Son* ("Oh, for a good spirit who would take the house-tops off") have accumulated so much commentary over the years that they seem to stand for Dickens as an omniscient city observer. In my view such moments register most of all the impossibility of achieving a panoramic or comprehensive view of the metropolis. Perhaps they have received more than their share of critical attention exactly because of their obtrusiveness in narratives whose business as usual takes us on walks through city streets.

How can a great metropolis be apprehended or represented? Raymond Williams finds Dickens's vision of urban modernity neither in "topography" nor in "local instance," but "in the form of his novels...It does not matter which way we put it: the experience of the city is the fictional method; or the fictional method is the experience of the city." He refers to Dickens's way of presenting characters as if they were isolated entities observed in the streets, members of a crowd rushing past one another. As the novels proceed, relationships and commitments are "forced into consciousness," thus provid-ing an underlying grid of connection beneath "the sheer rush and noise and miscellaneity of this new and complex social order" (Williams 154–55). The image evoked here is a literary convention already known to the young Dickens: the city-as-crowd. As Richard Maxwell suggests in *The Mysteries of Paris and London*, the great metropolis is unknowable and must be allegorized though certain figures; his own touchstones of modernity are the labyrinth, the crowd, the panorama, and paperwork, hidden or passing from hand to hand. Michel de Certeau's essay "Walking in the City" also approaches the great metropolis as a figure of the unknowable, though it takes a more impro-visatory approach. Dismissing the illusion of omniscience offered by the panoramic view from above, de Certeau meditates on the act of walking as an articulation of city space: footsteps crossing and mingling "give their shape to spaces. They weave places together." He asks us to think of city streets as a system analogous to the system of language: particular walks taken or sentences uttered will activate certain potentials of the system and not others (de Certeau 97–98).

Although it is not difficult to find Dickens playing rhetorical variations on already recognizable images of isolation in crowds or labyrinthine mazes, such tropes are hardly central to his most engaged imagination of the metropolis. So I find de Certeau's "Walking in the City" suggestive about Dickens in special ways. He—and his characters—are extraordinary examples of the walkers de Certeau calls "the ordinary practitioners of the city" who "live 'down below,' below the thresholds at which visibility begins," and create the city through "the act itself of passing by" (de Certeau 93, 97). For all its recognizable public landmarks—Smithfield Market, the dome of St. Paul's, the walls of Newgate, Waterloo Bridge—Dickens's London is readily imaginable as a series of footsteps marking private, sometimes intersecting, paths through the streets. The analogy between walking and language is also suggestive: it has always been tempting to identify Dickens's walking with Dickens's writing, although it is difficult to stabilize the relation between the two. Before turning to Dickens's own writing about walking, I want to sketch out two lines of speculation that have become prominent in the critical conversation about Dickens the walker.

G. K. Chesterton initiated the romantic psycho-biographical approach in his 1906 study of Dickens. Borrowing a phrase from *The Pickwick Papers*, in which being locked out of lodgings for the night is ironically described as holding "the key of the street," Chesterton turns it to his own purpose: "Dickens himself had, in the most sacred and serious sense of the term, the key of the street." Chesterton turns the phrase around so that the streets themselves become a "great house locked up" that few can enter until Dickens enlightens them. "He could open the inmost door of his house—the door that leads into that secret passage which is lined with houses and roofed with stars." The interior landscape evoked by that image is not accidental; Chesterton goes on to imagine Dickens's days of "drifting" through the streets during his childhood employment, as if they had produced not an observant little walker but a dreamily unconscious absorber of the places that formed backgrounds to his silent woe. "For him ever afterwards these streets were mortally romantic; they were dipped in the purple dyes of youth and its tragedy, and rich with irrevocable sunsets. Herein is the whole secret of that eerie realism with which Dickens could always vitalize some dark or dull corner of London" (Chesterton 34–36).

Stephen Marcus vigorously contests Chesterton's theory of unconscious absorption, evoking a child who was already "exercising, in fact, his novelistic gifts. Even in his darkest days of orphanage these gifts had never ceased to serve and delight him; hurt as he was, he never stopped observing, never fully withdrew, never walked through the streets of London without being absorbed by what he saw and taking pleasure in his ability to see it." But if his powers of observation kept Dickens alive, as Marcus suggests, they did so exactly because the orphanage had been so intense: "as his writing remained his chief resource for understanding and controlling his early experience of separation and estrangement, it also continued to develop as the theater for re-enacting that experience, and he returned to those streets, it seems, to seek and recover that part of himself which had almost literally to be re-lived in order for him to write—indeed for him to live." Although Marcus celebrates the wide-awake talent that allowed the child to survive, he ends up with another kind of romantic mythology: Dickens had to re-walk those streets at night in order to write, in order to live; his writing "was mysteriously and irrevocably connected with that epoch in his life when he was literally a solitary wanderer in the city" (Marcus 279–81).

"Literally?"—the rest of his walking life was metaphorical, an attempt to recapture an awful but singular reality? The subject of Dickens's walking has a tendency to elicit a certain kind of melodrama in those who try to understand it primarily as an effect of the child's experience of the blacking days. The tone is audible again in Ned Lukacher's pages on Dickens: "Coerced as a child into an anxiety-producing cycle of over-production, Dickens the adult, once again compelled to please the crowd, once again returns to the streets that he has always identified with such feelings of crisis. He is certain of only two things: that he must write and that he must walk. . . . He was indeed caught in a vicious circle, consumed by the obsessive patterns that indissolubly joined his nightwalks and his artistic production" (Lukacher 293–94). What's interesting about such interpretations is the urgency with which Dickens's walking and writing are joined and identified with an "original" kind of walking that is situated in the suffering twelve-year-old worker.

As I have already suggested, Dickens's London was co-extensive with the region of his childhood experience, and he regularly represented fear and vulnerability in characters that are lost or threatened in city streets. When he wrote about himself, however, walking was a sign of independent competence and health. As I will argue later in this chapter, walking was less a way back to his early terror and isolation than a means of escape from his fear of reentering such a state. Even the careful accounts of the child's walking routes in the autobiographical fragment add to its verisimilitude and attest to Dickens's ongoing interest in particular streets and bridges; there is more pride than pathos in those memories. Moreover, Dickens had been drawn to the seamy neighborhoods of London even during his pre-blacking days. Forster corroborates the attraction when he says of Dickens's first two years in the family house in Camden Town: "If he could only induce whomsoever took him out to take him through Seven-dials, he was supremely happy" (Forster 11).

Forster may have derived at least part of his impression from "Gone Astray" (1853), a memory-piece Dickens published in *Household Words*. In this nostalgic essay, the narrator recalls himself as a very young child who becomes separated from his adult companion and spends the day quite happily walking and fantasizing in the City. On the remembered morning, the child and his companion set out for St. Giles Church; the child supposedly nurtures fantasies of beggars who, on Sundays, set aside their pretenses and go to church. From there they proceed to Northumberland House on the Strand "to view the celebrated lion over the gateway." There they are separated, and Dickens writes in his time-traveling way, "The child's unreasoning terror of being lost, comes as freshly on me now, as it did then" (Dent 3.156–57). It doesn't last long; soon the child is making plans to entertain himself for the day. He asks his way to the Guildhall (a substantial walk away) so he can gaze at the Giants Gog and Magog; he buys himself lunch, which is snatched from him by a friendly but self-interested dog; he wanders about the City, idealizing the grandness of its institutions; he strays into the East End and takes himself to a working-class pantomime. Only then, in the rainy dark, does he miss home and think to find a watch-house from which his father can be notified to fetch him.

The memory—if it is one—mixes the pleasure of walking, gazing, and making up stories with the apprehensions of a child afraid of being noticed by others, who pretends that there is nothing unusual about his being alone in the streets. Its blend of innocent romanticism and self-conscious play-acting captures the aura that suffuses *David Copperfield*, as well as the journalistic reminiscences that followed after it. The piece as a whole defies the vulnerabilities of the autobiographical fragment, in a way suitable for light entertainment in *Household Words*. The ending, however, registers guilt. "By daylight, I had never thought of the grief at home. I had never thought of my mother. I had never thought of anything but adapting myself to the circumstances in which I found myself, and going to seek my fortune" (Dent 3.165). Independent city walking is a flight into fantasy that forgets domestic connections. Those sentences might be read as an internal reversal: the child walker abandons and forgets the parents rather than the other way around.

Or, they might signify for the adult writer, whose fascination with the city takes him, every day, miles away from home.

Looking at Dickens's multiply inflected writing can help to loosen, if not to break, any absolute bonds that biographical speculation may forge between blacking, walking, and writing. A more recent line of criticism alters the emphasis: it has become common to identify Dickens with the figure of the *flâneur*. This has the advantage of placing Dickens in a more literary way, within a tradition of urban walking and writing featuring the detached but curious spectatorship of the city stroller. To compare *Sketches by Boz*, as Deborah Nord does, with earlier urban sketches by Pierce Egan, Charles Lamb, Thomas De Quincey, or Leigh Hunt is to appreciate the originality of Dickens's middle- and lower-middle-class terrain, the familiarity of a city that is inhabited, not just observed, by its narrator, and the way Boz gives places and people a depth of life over time (Nord 30–64). Such comparisons tend to move Dickens further from the conventional image of the *flâneur*, although the label tends to return whenever a critic finds Dickens at a classed, gendered, or unsympathetic distance from his subjects. Michael Hollington, who has done the most detailed work of attaching Dickens to the concept of the *flâneur*, also opens productive questions about Dickens's literary relations with Paris and its writers. It's important, however, to distinguish between Dickens's invocations of the urban stroller in the self-descriptions of Boz or The Uncommercial Traveller, and his personal mythologies of walking.

The *flâneur* theory has the disadvantage of coming at Dickens through a series of other figures as they are sifted through the fragmentary meditations of Walter Benjamin. In Benjamin, *flânerie* is a deeply ironized, deeply compromised series of poses that are always in the process of historical transformation. At times the *flâneur* seems to be a figure with which Benjamin identifies, especially when he imagines the city's history in the paving stones pressing against the soles of the walker's feet, or when he writes about Baudelaire's capacity for empathy with the crowd in which he feels his solitude. For the most part, however, Benjamin points to the various incarnations of *flânerie* as consolatory delusions that make urban modernity bearable, or as forms of self-commodification disguised as alienation from the marketplace. "The man of letters," he writes, "goes to the marketplace as a *flâneur*, supposedly to take a look at it, but in reality to find a buyer" (Benjamin 1973, 34). At other moments the *flâneur* morphs into the detective, the man of the crowd, the shopper, the journalist, even—"the last incarnation"—the sandwich-board man (1999, M 19.2). For the conventional image of the *flâneur* as a removed urban spectator who thinks he can read people's stories or characters through glimpses of faces on the street, Benjamin has nothing but contempt. Reading

Dickens through Benjamin points to the historical typicality of Dickens's various street poses as walker, watcher, man of the crowd, detective, and journalist. Yet Benjamin, who knew little of Dickens, does not hold the key to Dickens's street.

John Forster may not have held the key, either, but he can tell us about his friend's walking habits. Dickens was a man who had to walk, first and foremost as a form of physical exercise; as Forster puts it, he "was always passionately fond of walking." Speaking of the early fifteen-mile horseback rides he took with Dickens, Forster observes, "His notion of finding rest from mental exertion in as much bodily exertion of equal severity, continued with him to the last" (92). The experience of the young man can be glimpsed in *Nicholas Nickleby* when the hero responds to his own anxiety by taking to the streets. Worried about how to survive in London, Nicholas "resolved to banish [his worries] from his thoughts by dint of hard walking." But, though he "mingled with the crowd," trying to speculate about the people who pass him, he is unable to banish his anxieties, "walk as fast as he would" (*NN* 16). Later, worried about his sister, he repeats the strategy, and "increased his rate of walking as if in the hope of leaving his thoughts behind." He fails again; once in Hyde Park, "They crowded upon him more thickly...now there were no passing objects to attract his attention" (*NN* 32). It's a contest between anxiety and rapid motion, between inner and outer crowdedness, in which anxiety has the leading edge.

Having watched his friend push himself toward death in defiance of his illnesses, Forster recalls that seven- or eight-mile walks were sufficient in the early days, but that Dickens had later insisted on the "too great strain" of walking fifteen miles or more, often at night (Forster 92). In fact Dickens was boasting about doing fifteen- and twenty-mile night walks as early as 1843, during the composition of *A Christmas Carol*; in 1845, he reported walking twenty miles a day during his holidays at Broadstairs (4.2; 4.358). When Forster describes life at Gad's Hill in the 1860s, he emphasizes the ritual alternations of Dickens's days: "Perhaps there was never a man who changed places so much and habits so little. He was always methodical and regular; and passed his life from day to day, divided for the most part between working and walking, the same wherever he was" (Forster 656). Sticking to his principle of emphasizing his friend's discipline, Forster nevertheless manages a neat juxtaposition of Dickens's restless roaming and his need for a daily schedule of work and exercise. Although Forster touches only reluctantly on Dickens's personal disappointments and endless financial responsibilities for family members, it is grueling anger and anxiety, rather than problems of invention or composition, that lie behind an outburst like the one to Forster of September 1854: "If I couldn't walk fast and far, I should just explode and perish" (7.429). Dickens walked to write; he also walked to let off steam from the frustrations of family life.

On those rapid walks, in town or in the country, Dickens counted the miles and watched his pace as athletes do; nor could he resist climbing an interesting mountain if he was traveling in its vicinity. In these ways he has more in common with his fellow Victorian long-distance walkers than with any incarnation of the *flâneur*. He liked company on his walks, especially if his companion could keep up with his normal pace. Writing to John Leech from his holiday in Folkestone in 1855, he complained about his sister and brother-in-law the Austins "as taking crawls rather than walks"; Georgina Hogarth, on the other hand, was a frequent companion who was willing to splash cheerfully through the Paris mud with him (7.700; 8.15). His explorations of London's byways were sometimes nights on the town with a friend like Daniel Maclise or Wilkie Collins, sometimes expeditions in search of specific material, and sometimes the night roamings of an anxiety-ridden insomniac.

Walking to Write

Dickens counted pages as well as miles. His sense of the intimate relation between walking and writing can best be glimpsed through his correspondence, which attests to a strenuous interplay between the two. Throughout his life, he wrote letters excusing himself from social visits because of the pressure of work and the necessity of walking. Consistently, he represented himself as a kind of emotional machine that required careful handling. As he was courting Catherine Hogarth he instructed her about the peculiarity of his composition style: "I never can write with effect—especially in the serious way—until I have got my steam up, or in other words until I have become so excited with my subject that I cannot leave off" (1.97). "Spirits are not to be forced up to the Pickwick point, every day," he pointed out to his publishers when his monthly installments were running late (1.189). Discipline came hard in the early years, when he caged himself in with multiple deadlines. After going out with Forster "I couldn't write a line 'till three oClock, and have yet 5 slips to finish, and don't know what to put in them for I have reached the point I meant to leave off with" (1.395–96). Still working on *Nickleby*, he confesses that he had written much of the night, but had left four slips, "and as I foolishly left them 'till this morning have the steam to get up afresh" (1.425). After finishing a number, Dickens would sometimes describe himself as "breaking out," as though he had been imprisoned or enchained by his own practice of publishing in serial installments.

By 1850 he could boast that he was working at *Copperfield* "like a steam engine" (6.64), and he sounded more assured about the necessity for keeping his working and walking hours free from distraction: "at this time of the Month, I *must* get air and exercise in the evening—and think.... This is really the sort of condition on which I hold my inventive powers; and I can't get rid of it" (6.98–99). Excusing himself from a social invitation, he wrote to Miss Coutts as he was working on *Bleak House* that he was anxious to get the month's number done, "And if I let myself out of my room under such circumstances, I have lost my power over myself for the day" (6.688). By 1857, as his personal unhappiness mounted, he was referring to his restlessness as "the penalty of an imaginative life and constitution" or "the wayward and unsettled feeling which is part (I suppose) of the tenure on which one holds an imaginative life" (8.422; 8.434). His talent, as he experiences it, is a "tenure" that required both rigorous harnessing and daily bouts of physical release. He is required to hold it, but it comes with conditions and penalties that exempt him from ordinary social behaviors.

Walking was essential both to bring his books into being, and to calm the effects of his intense engagement with his characters. Repeatedly his letters mention extended periods of walking as he is working toward a new project. The activity of walking allowed him to think his way into new fictional worlds, while allaying the increased restlessness that came upon him when he was still in a state of uncertainty. As Dickens joked about this state to Miss Coutts, he evoked the emotional violence that accompanied the process: as he is "in the agonies of plotting and contriving a new book...I am accustomed to walk up and down the house, smiting my forehead dejectedly; and to be so horribly cross and surly, that the boldest fly at my approach." At such times, he claims, his publishers never visit him alone "lest I should fall upon a single invader and do murder on his intrusive body" (3.367). In the earliest stages of *Dombey*, "Vague thoughts of a new book are rife within me just now; and I go wandering about at night into the strangest places, according to my usual propensity at such a time—seeking rest, and finding none" (4.510). Half-comic images of murder show up frequently to describe both the ends of numbers and the deaths of characters: Dickens begs off a dinner "until my February work has had its throat cut: which laudable deed I shall perform with all convenient dispatch" (3.437); the death of Little Nell is a "Nellicide" (2.228).

Violent or not, endings required walking. As he was completing *Martin Chuzzlewit*, he begged off from Lady Holland because "I am obliged to walk about the fields and streets every evening... otherwise I should not be steadily enough set upon the dismissal of two of the greatest favorites [Tom and Ruth Pinch] I have ever had" (4.145). Paul Dombey "died on Friday night about 10 o'Clock; and as I had no hope of getting to sleep afterwards, I went out, and walked about Paris until breakfast-time next morning" (5.9). As he worked on *Little Dorrit* in Paris: "my head really stings with the visions of the book, and I am going, as we French say, to disembarrass it by plunging into some of the strange places I glide into of nights in these latitudes" (8.40). Forster writes that Dickens needed "an equal severity" of mental and physical exertion; he also seems to have needed a balance or interchange between the internal stimulation of his imaginative labor and the external stimulation of the streets.

Dickens came to understand his need for night streets as "quite a little mental phenomenon" during the mid-'40s, when his writing slowed down and left him restlessly moving between London and the Continent (4.622). As he geared up to write *The Chimes* in Genoa in the fall of 1844, he complained to Forster: "I want a crowded street to plunge into at night" (4.200). But that was only one side of the picture. A few weeks later, *The Chimes* complete, Dickens wrote to Thomas Mitton: "I have worn myself to Death, in the Month I have been at Work. None of my usual reliefs have been at hand; I have not been able to divest myself of the story—have suffered very much in my sleep, in consequence—and am so shaken by such work in this trying climate that I am nervous as a man who is dying of Drink: and as haggard as a Murderer" (4.211). The story he works so hard to master during the day's writing possesses him at night. Dickens's images of insomniac self-destruction—he's a drunkard or a murderer—are characteristic of his outbursts to friends, but they suggest that the imagined actions and reactions of the writing process left him subject to disturbing arousals of violent and guilty feeling. He felt something like a murderer whenever he completed a story or killed off a character that had been brought to life with such internal intensity.

The best-known letters about writing and city streets come from 1846, during Dickens's residence in Lausanne. When he arrived there he recognized that he might "want streets sometimes," and he imagined that Geneva, twenty-four miles away, might suit the purpose (4.560). The Lausanne streets were steep and uninteresting, but the country provided plenty of walking along the lake, in the hills, and along "excellent country roads," he told Forster (4.568). As he wrote the first numbers of *Dombey and Son*, he reported himself full of invention, "but the difficulty of going at what I call a rapid pace, is prodigious.... I suppose this is partly the effect of two years' ease, and partly of the absence of streets and numbers of figures. I can't express how much I want these. It seems as if they supplied something to my brain, which it cannot bear, when busy, to lose. . . . *My* figures seem disposed to stagnate without crowds about them" (4.612–13). The use of the word "figure" to describe both human shapes seen in crowds and Dickens's already invented characters suggests an intimate interchange between external and internal visualizations that Dickens recognizes as essential, but which he cannot name. This interchange is connected with a desire for rapid motion, and a corresponding fear of stagnation, of being unable to move.

Being unable to move forward in composition has its obverse side: being unable to get away from his writing. Three weeks later Dickens repeated his complaint with a different twist: "The absence of accessible streets continues to worry me . . . at night I want them beyond description. I don't seem to be able to get rid of my spectres unless I can lose them in crowds" (4.622). "My figures" have turned into "my spectres": the possessor is again possessed. Dickens's anxiety about accessible streets suggests that streets are themselves an important "figure" for him. They provide the half-lit glimpses which activate the imagination, as well as the stage against which characters may be seen as one sees, in relief, a figure who stands out against the crowd. At the same time the night streets are a place of anonymous merging, where crowds of other walkers can absorb, or reabsorb, the interior "spectres" that refuse to dissipate of themselves. The physical action of walking anonymously in a large city provides motion that might outrun the internal phantasmagoria, while the city itself provides immersion in another element: the moving visual entertainment of crowded streets. These 1846 letters get as close as Dickens ever did to formulating the relationship between streets and narratives. To my mind they convey little evidence that ties Dickens's writing process directly to memories of walking to and from the blacking warehouse. Rather, they suggest that the forward impetus of walking stimulated invention as well as release from its attendant feelings, and that walking and writing were metaphorically entwined with the tension between motion and stasis, or creation and death.

🖎 Street Sound

In the 1841 edition of *The Old Curiosity Shop*, Dickens had imagined the difference between figuration and stasis in terms of a contrast between the activity of seeing and the paralyzed passivity of hearing. The novel's original narrator, the deformed Master Humphrey, introduces himself with the sentence "Night is generally my time of walking." He explains: "it affords me greater opportunity of speculating on the characters and occupations of those who fill the streets...a glimpse of passing faces caught by the light of a street lamp or a shop window is often better for my purpose than their full revelation in the daylight." For the strolling imaginist, night is "kinder" than day, "which too often destroys an air-built castle at the moment of its completion, without the smallest ceremony or remorse." After encountering Nell in the street and leading her back to the curiosity shop, Humphrey speaks of the "visible aids" which allow his imagination to be possessed by the figure of Little Nell. The "heaps of fantastic things" in the shop "crowding upon my mind," allow Nell to be seen by the contrast that "brought her condition palpably before me." The figure of Nell emerges as a potential source of narrative—she carries Humphrey's mind along "at a great pace"—when she is outlined against a contrasting crowd of people or objects (*OCS* 1).

The chapter is remarkable, however, for the meditation that follows on the heels of Humphrey's initial description of night walking. Suddenly he is not seeing but imagining the mind of a listener confined indoors on a city street. When the observer is deprived of the organizing power of vision, the crowded city becomes an unstoppable torment. "The constant pacing to and fro, that never-ending restlessness, that incessant tread of feet wearing the rough stones smooth and glossy—is it not a wonder how the dwellers in narrow ways can bear to hear it!" Humphrey muses. He imagines a sick man forced against his will to listen to every footstep and identify the age and class of the walker, his senses unable to screen out "the hum and noise" or "the stream of life that will not stop, pouring on, on, on, through all his restless dreams, as if he were condemned to lie dead but conscious, in a noisy churchyard, and had no hope of rest for centuries to come." Figured as an auditory phenomenon, the city invades the conscious and the unconscious mind just as Dickens's specters invade his mind and rob him of sleep. Now the restless city becomes a figure for the mind of the anxious dreamer rather than an escape from it. And the awful paralysis of "dead but conscious" suggests a nightmare of passive entrapment. Not altogether surprisingly, this image is closely followed by a paragraph about crowds "forever passing and re-passing on the bridges" with many a one pausing to look down and consider suicide. If walking and seeing can make a narrative path through the crowded streets, lying awake, hearing, and dreaming create obsessive internal images that threaten stagnation and extinction.

Because the ear cannot shut out sound as the eye can shut out sight, Steven Connor observes, "the involuntary and continuous nature of hearing exposes us to a world of sound the primary characteristic of which is its impermanence. The world of sight appears to be there; pressing on us without remission, the world of sound is only ever there at the moment of our hearing it. The world of pure hearing would therefore be, so to speak, *unremittingly intermittent*" (Connor 2000, 17). Following from this distinction, sight would anchor a feeling of external stability, while sound without sight has the potential to dissolve the apparent public continuum of time and space. In Dickens's writing, the sounds of footsteps and bells evoke private or secret associations that threaten to derail the forward momentum of both public and private histories. The involuntary aspect of sound is regularly associated with disrupted walking, and with a loss of orientation in time and space.

Elaborated versions of the figure occur in *Bleak House* and in *A Tale of Two Cities*, in each case associated with a revolution that violently alters the course of history. "The Ghost's Walk" of Chesney Wold becomes audible as rain falls on the terrace and Watt Rouncewell hears "a curious echo—I suppose an echo—which is very like a halting step." The deformed step belonged to a previous Lady Dedlock who defied the family and the legitimate rule of King Charles I by her secret support of the rebels during the English Revolution. When the sound comes, Mrs. Rouncewell says, "it *must be heard*. My Lady, who is afraid of nothing, admits that when it is there, it must be heard. You cannot shut it out" (*BH* 7). The bravura poses of My Lady can be threatened, it seems, by the insistence of that gentle echo. The Darnays' London residence in *A Tale of Two Cities* sits on a street corner described as "a curious corner in its acoustical properties, such a peculiar Ear of a place" (*TTC* 2.6) that the echoes of local footsteps create a confused auditory experience, in which the listener cannot judge the distance of actual footsteps coming or going, or link the sound with visual evidence. Those who wait and watch in the house are unable to tell whether footsteps signal an approach until the walker comes into view. The echoing threat foretells the coming of the Terror in France, which will profoundly disrupt the apparent stability of the household. Both passages link distortions of sound with distortions of walking, and signal the characters' vulnerability to uncontrollable or violent forces in the social order and the individual psyche.

Apart from the bells that announced the arrival of the New Year and the bells that jingled on his Gad's Hill sleigh, bells—or, more often, Bells—also evoke such threats in Dickens's imaginary. Like many Victorian professionals, Dickens could be deeply irritated by street noise and street musicians, but bells, whose sound is most often "clashing," retained a special charge. From Boulogne in 1854 he tells Elizabeth Gaskell about "the baptizing of some new bells, lately hung up (to my sorrow and lunacy)"; on a Sunday in 1855 he complains, "Five hundred thousand pairs of pattens are now going to

Church, and the Bells are making such an intolerable uproar that I can't hear myself think" (7.397; 7.549). Highly melodramatic Bells tug at the guilty memory of the criminal Rudge, who returns to haunt the neighborhood twenty-two years after his double murder and his own faked death at the Warren. His first victim, Reuben Haredale, had been ringing an alarm bell when he was cut down by Rudge; the murderer is undone when he hears the same bell chiming as the Gordon rioters set fire to the Warren: "It was the Bell. If the ghastliest shape the human mind had ever pictured in its wildest dreams had risen up before him, he could not have staggered backward from its touch, as he did from the first sound of that loud iron voice" (*BR* 55). More powerful than any vision, the bell's voice penetrates Rudge's heart and causes him to stagger around in circles, losing sight of his plan to hide himself among the rioters.

Bells awaken sadder memories in the third chapter of *Little Dorrit*, when Arthur Clennam returns to London on a Sunday evening: "Maddening church bells of all degrees of dissonance, sharp and flat, cracked and clear, fast and slow, made the brick and mortar echoes hideous.... In every thoroughfare, up almost every alley, and down almost every turning, some doleful bell was throbbing, jerking, tolling, as if the Plague were in the city and the dead-carts were going round." Bells curse the streets that echo and extend their sound until the city becomes a prison for the eye, the ear, and the lungs: "Nothing to see but streets, streets, streets. Nothing to breathe but streets, streets, streets." Moving from the streets into the mind, these depressive sensations bring on an unstoppable flow of unwelcome memories. As Clennam sits brooding on the bells, the "sound had revived a long train of miserable Sundays, and the procession would not stop with the bells, but continued to march on." Bells toll for death, of course; but also for the many little deaths of the heart and soul that are revived by waves of recurring sound. The association of bells with painful childhood memories may also suggest a possible link between Dickens's antipathy to bells and the warning bell that rang before the Marshalsea gates were locked for the night, to signal the separation of young Dickens from his family.

When Dickens was living in Genoa, he seems to have suffered a sort of bell-trauma that he transformed into the machinery of his 1844 Christmas book *The Chimes*. Forster quotes from a letter of that October in which Dickens describes himself as staggering, undone by transplantation to foreign soil: "Never did I stagger so upon a threshold [of a story] before." Forster's language (in italics) substitutes for something he must have found unquotable in the original letter as he describes Dickens paralyzed at his writing desk by the chiming of all the bells in Genoa: "*in one fell sound the clang and clash of all its steeples, pouring into his ears again and again, in a tuneless, grating, discordant, jerking, hideous vibration that made his ideas* spin round and round till they lost themselves in a whirl of vexation and giddiness, and dropped down dead" (4.199). "He had never before so suffered, nor did he again," Forster assures us; in fact, two days later the experience became the impetus for *The Chimes* (Forster 346). Dickens takes charge; he knows "how to work the bells. Let them clash upon me now from all the churches and convents in Genoa, I see nothing but the old London belfry I have set them in" (4.200). The overwhelming, nauseating effects of sound have been safely transformed, he thinks, into a story that will strike a mighty blow on behalf of the poor.

In fact *The Chimes* is deeply confusing about the effect of those apparently virtuous Anglo-Protestant bells. They are Toby Veck's consoling friends, and then monitory figures that act, much like the Spirits in *A Christmas Carol*, to warn and educate Toby against submitting to the despair he feels after listening to the voices of so-called social reformers. For those with ears to hear, however, the narrator has other messages than the Bells' injunction to honor the heartfelt humanity of the poor. He is interested in the way sound both echoes and acts upon the internal terrain of individual listeners. Toby invests the Chimes, "often heard and never seen," with "a strange and solemn character," making them into awesome religious-parental beings. The narrator takes pains to explain that this process goes on unconsciously: like what digestive processes "did of their own cunning, and by a great many operations of which he was entirely ignorant," so "his mental faculties, without his privity or concurrence, set all these wheels and springs in motion... when they worked to bring about his liking for the Bells" (*CB* 85). Linking Toby's personification of the Bells with the operations of the unconscious, Dickens comes clean about his association of sound with the unknowable, less accessible parts of the self.

After Toby's sense of worthiness is destroyed by the talk of the social reformers, the Bells change their tune. Now they echo the phrases that grate in the old man's head: "Born bad. No Business here!... Put 'em down! Facts and Figures!" (*CB* 100). The language of disorientation appears; the sound makes the air spin, the brain of Toby reel. Good memories and associations turn suddenly bad. Although Dickens reclaims the Bells as stern educational figures that insist on a return to faith and optimism, arriving at the moral of his fable requires elaborate and clumsy machinery very different from the spontaneous visions of *A Christmas Carol*. The Bells do not survive their transformation from psychic projections to external social monitors. As Dickens wrote to Forster in his preview of the story, the spirits of the Bells bear "all sorts of missions and commissions and reminders and reproaches, and comfortable recollections and what not, to all sorts of people and places... the bells haunting people in the night... according to their deeds" (4.203–4). Only the last phrases carry the deeper effect of the actual story.

Dickens once recommended an appropriate occasion for the simultaneous tolling of city church bells. A letter to *The Times* of 17 November 1849 lays out a long explanation of his opposition to public hanging, and suggests that executions take place within the walls of the prison, with no publicity for the condemned except this: "during the hour of the body's hanging I would have the bells of all the churches in that town or city tolled, and all the shops shut up, that all might be reminded of what was being done" (5.653). The sound, he thought, would awaken internal reflection, while the visual spectacle of a crowd at a hanging created only sensation. Assigned to a practice Dickens deplores, the bells announce the presence of social murder, while the city is obliged to stop its buying and selling and listen in guilty horror.

"Streams" of urban crowds flowing toward their final destinies, along with the inchoate "roar" of urban street noise, show up regularly in the novels, adopted from the standard repertoire of early nineteenth-century figures of the city-as-crowd. Compared with the distinct sounds of bells or footsteps, such passages display a kind of emotional neutrality. The already well-worn notion of isolation amid the crowd left Dickens cold as well; his street narratives move quickly from the blur of indistinct noisy motion to the interested discriminations of the framing eye. As he wrote to W. H. Wills from a northern reading tour, "I walked from Durham to Sunderland, and made a little fanciful photograph in my mind of Pit-Country.... I couldn't help looking upon my mind as I was doing it, as a sort of capitally prepared and highly sensitive plate. And I said, without the least conceit (as Watkins might have said of a plate of his) 'it really is a pleasure to work with you, you receive the impression so nicely'" (8.669). By 1858, he had earned the pleasure of that comparison.

✒ Street Sketches

When Dickens set out to write in the genre of the street sketch, his self-representations as a city walker were literary poses quite different from his self-portraits in letters. The "we" of the unknown Boz and the well-known "I" of the Uncommercial Traveller are said to lounge, loiter, saunter, or ramble in *flâneur*-like fashion as they go about their speculations on the streets. Boz may be "struck" by certain figures as they pass by, or his attention may be attracted by a scene or a crowd of curious observers that draws him toward a particular turning. He makes sure, however, to distinguish himself from other strollers who walk only to display themselves. Opening one of his earliest street sketches, "Shops and Their Tenants," Boz exclaims in classic *flâneur* fashion, "What inexhaustible food for speculation, do the streets of London afford!" In the next sentences he is busy telling us what he is not: a member of the well-dressed "race" of idle swells who lounge on the "leading thoroughfares" of the West End. "These men linger listlessly past, looking as happy and animated as a policeman on duty. Nothing seems to make an impression on their minds," Boz complains (Dent 1.61). Another early piece, "Thoughts about People," sets the narrator's observations of middle-class city "types" against "precocious puppyism in the Quadrant, whiskered dandyism in Regent-street and Pall-mall, or gallantry in its dotage anywhere" (Dent 1.215). Boz, however, is acquainted with the most ordinary, down-at-heels neighborhoods, and—long-term watcher as he is—can tell us about the gradual social decline of a certain house-turned-shop or the lonely day of a single London clerk.

In "Our Next-Door Neighbor," Boz sounds another classic line: "We are very fond of speculating as we walk through a street, on the character and pursuits of the people who inhabit it." He proceeds to do so, not by reading "the human countenance," but by attending to "the physiognomy of street door knockers" (Dent 1.41). His delightful parody of the face-reading *flâneur* stops short of suggesting that a change in a man's disposition would affect the appearance of his knocker, but he is certain that in such a case the man would feel compelled to remove the old knocker and seek another "more congenial to his altered feelings" (Dent 1.43). The story then shifts into an account of the lodgers next door, ending with a tubercular young man from the country who dies in his mother's arms, begging to be buried outside the city, "not in these close crowded streets; they have killed me" (Dent 1.47). The odd eruption of the romantic city-country division splits the dying son, copyist, and translator from the thriving Boz, who has made London the stuff of a self-sufficient writing career.

High-jinks about door knockers are characteristic of the movement of Boz's mind from small signs to imagined human situations. In "Streets-Morning," he reads open windows as signs of a hot, restless sleeper within; the flicker "of the rushlight through the window blind denotes the chamber of watching or sickness" (Dent 1.51). At times he can be counted on to wax exhortatory: "How few of those who pass such a miserable creature as this, think of the anguish of heart, the sinking of soul and spirit, which the very effort of singing produces" (Dent 1.58). Sometimes his evening rambles lead him to "pause beneath the windows of some public hospital, and picture to ourself the gloomy and mournful scenes that are passing within" (Dent 1.237). Such moods are fleeting but important parts of the narrator's persona. As several critics have noted, *Sketches by Boz* repeatedly tells stories of social decline over time, whether the subject is a family, a suit of clothes, a hackney coach, or a shop. As a walker, Boz also defines himself through his sympathy with what's hidden behind the walls of the great city, whether they are the literal walls of a prison or hospital, or the modest windows separating some person's anguish from the street. The movement inward is as powerful as the movement downward; thus when we visit "Seven Dials" along with Boz he can tell us not only about the maze of alleys and the disorderly (Irish) street life, but also about who lives and works in the back and front kitchens and attics of the dilapidated houses (Dent 1.70–75).

Rapt in his observations and speculations, Boz is occasionally startled to discover his own bodily presence. The narrator of "Meditations on Monmouth Street" flees when he suddenly notices an old woman who has been peering suspiciously at him during his prolonged fantasies on old clothes (Dent 1.82). In "Doctors' Commons" Boz becomes "so lost in these meditations, that we had turned into the street, and run up against a door post, before we recollected where we were walking" (Dent 1.92). Comical moments like these puncture the pretensions of the *flâneur*, and admit to Boz's own visibility in the public arena where walking, looking, and speculation take place.

When Dickens invented the voice of the Uncommercial Traveller in 1860, he was aiming for an informal relationship with the readers of his new magazine *All the Year Round*, and probably competing with Thackeray's "Roundabout Papers," then appearing in the respected *Cornhill Magazine*. The Traveller "for the great house of Human Interest Brothers" is more likely than Boz to set out on his walks in search of particular out-of-the-way interests, which range widely from piece to piece (Dent 4.28). As a walker, the Uncommercial Traveller leaves behind the urban poses Boz liked to imitate and parody; he is a highly idiosyncratic walker who knows the city no one else knows. When he sets out for Wapping Workhouse from Covent Garden, he names passing landmarks, which include places that appear in his novels as well as actual London buildings. Losing his way in the East End, he abandons himself to the narrow streets, and "relied on predestination to bring me somehow or other to the place I wanted if I were ever to get there." When he stops to ask, he has instinctively arrived close to his predestined destination (Dent 4.444).

In "Shy Neighborhoods" the narrator boasts about his long-distance walking, and especially about a recent thirty-mile night walk into the country (presumably the October 1857 one to Gad's Hill from London). He claims that his "regular four miles an hour" pace put him to sleep, and that he covered the distance in that favorite Dickens state between sleeping and waking, while his mind went on journeys into verse and a foreign language grown rusty in his conscious life. Walking is intertwined with the unconscious, as it is in his distinction between two kinds of walking: "one, straight on end to a definite goal at a round pace; one, objectless, loitering, and purely vagabond." The first kind suggests the disciplined striver; the second, vagrant instinct and heredity: it "is so natural to me and strong with me, that I think I must be the descendant at no great distance of some irreclaimable tramp" (Dent 4.119). Semi-autobiographical as they are, such self-descriptions serve the rhetorical purpose of creating a narrator who goes to inner and outer landscapes strange to his readers. His special experience makes it possible for him to write in "Shy Neighborhoods" about the individual peculiarities of animals that inhabit obscure London squares, or to make an apparently complete taxonomy of every species of tramp to be encountered on "all the summer roads in all directions" ("Tramps," Dent 4.127).

Although he was capable of stunning scenes describing street crowds in action, Dickens's most powerful urban journalism was generated from temporarily empty or abandoned streets in which isolated figures make dramatic appearances. "The Streets—Morning," the most effective urban piece in *Sketches by Boz*, begins at the hour before sunrise, after the last drunk of the night has staggered past but before the stirring of morning life. The narrator, one of the few awake, is impressed by the "air of cold, solitary desolation about the noiseless streets." As in Wordsworth's "Composed upon Westminster Bridge," the absence of crowds and bustle casts "the stillness of death . . . over the streets," but unlike Wordsworth, Boz wants only to bring London back to life. Searching for any sign of activity, his eye discovers an "occasional policeman . . . listlessly gazing on the deserted prospect before him," as well as a "rakish-looking cat" sneaking home after a long night on the town (Dent 1.49–51). (The same policeman and "guilty-looking cat" will show up during Mr. Verloc's early-morning walk across London in Conrad's *The Secret Agent*.) An hour goes by, and a market-cart appears, little tables for street breakfasts are put out, the little chimney sweep sits on a stoop to wait for the housemaid to get up and answer his knock. The details gradually populate the city with figures normally invisible to the dozing middle-class eye; soon the narrator is observing a little flirtation among three servants who emerge at the same time to take in the household milk or take down the master's shutters. By eleven o'clock the preparations for the day are complete; the stage is set for commerce. By noon, "the streets are thronged with a vast concourse of people, gay and shabby, rich and poor, idle and industrious" (Dent 1.54). The predictable urban contrasts shut down the essay, as if to emphasize the freshness of Boz's invention during the backstage hours of the morning.

When he walks in London, the Uncommercial Traveller makes a point of seeking out nearly deserted spots, where each human encounter acquires a special charge. In "City of London Churches" (1860) and "The City of the Absent" (1863), he pays Sunday visits to the virtually abandoned churches and ancient graveyards of the old City of London. The churchyards, "so small, so rank, so silent, so forgotten," provide especially resonant images, including a ghoulish scene of skulls on spikes during a thunderstorm at midnight and a possibly spectral old couple making hay: "Gravely making hay among the graves, all alone by themselves" (Dent 4.262; 4.265). As he wanders around the closed banks and businesses, the Uncommercial muses on the oddness of all those human absences, and on his "Sunday sensation...of being the Last Man" (Dent 4.269). In "Arcadian London" (1860), the subject is London in the off-season, when the middle classes disappear, leaving London "the most unfrequented part of England." A shadow city comes to light: old men and women creep about the city carrying their beds from shelter to shelter; they "come out of some hole when London empties itself, and go back in again when it fills" (Dent 4.182; 4.184). The underground people include the unprofessional sides of otherwise formidable butlers or medical assistants, who are suddenly freed to dress casually and make love to their sweethearts. These days of primitive innocence, as the Uncommercial calls them, repre-sent the breakdown of pretense and relief from the noise of parliamentary Talk lingering in the air-waves; all too soon "the wheels of gorgeous car-riages and the hoofs of high-stepping horses will crush the silence out of Bond Street" (Dent 4.189). Out of city silences, the Uncommercial Traveller creates eerily unfamiliar forms of human life.

The travels of the Uncommercial include walks to the East End in "Wap-ping Workhouse" (1860) and "On an Amateur Beat" (1869). Both pieces highlight the difference between West and East Ends, and the increasing ten-dency of the late-Victorian imagination to regard them as separate worlds. "Wapping Workhouse" plays with the notion of East as Oriental, making ironic references to the Wise Men of the East and to the Turkish frame of mind in which the narrator allows himself to get lost in the winding streets. "On an Amateur Beat" makes much of the invisible lines between London neighborhoods, locating a spot—St. Botolph Church at Houndsditch—where a single stride will make the difference: "West of the stride, a table, or a chest of drawers on sale, shall be of mahogany and French-polished; East of the stride, it shall be of deal, smeared with a cheap counterfeit resembling lip-salve" (Dent 4.382). Dickens is not just reifying difference here; he is satirizing an imaginary map of a London divided into respectable and abject halves. The satire helps to burnish the figure of the Uncommercial, whose savvy knows no such borders: he loses himself with confidence in the East End, and flaunts a kind of imperial knowingness as he compares his walk to his Beat and chastises the police for fearing to enter certain dangerous streets or courts (Dent 4.380).

The knowing narrator is also is canny enough to interpret the lingo of an "apparition" he meets on his way to the Wapping Workhouse; this street urchin, "who may have been the youngest son of his filthy old father, the Thames," informs the Uncommercial that the canal lock he's staring into is "Mister Baker's trap," from which his interlocutor derives the correct idea that Baker is the local coroner and that it's a common place for suicide. The boy is tough: he says women attempt suicide only when there's someone near enough to hear the splash and drag them out. The Uncommercial gets credit both for being "equal to the intellectual pressure of the conversation" and for the greater humanity of his attitudes. All of this leads up to Dickens's praise of the orderly, well-run Wapping workhouse that had recently been attacked in the press (Dent 4.44). In such essays the walk to the destination provides "street cred" that reinforces the Uncommercial's authority to assess the institution at issue; he distinguishes himself from the middle-class observer brought in by cab to be bamboozled by the manager of a controversial workhouse or lead mill.

All of these pieces include moments in which figures are rendered uncanny or spectral. "Night Walks" (1860) turns the dark deserted city into an interior landscape in which the walker deliberately courts spectral and specular images (Dent 4.148–57). The narrator refers to a period of sleeplessness and night walking during an earlier time, probably 1851, the year of John Dickens's painful death and the period of houseless anxiety during the transition from Devonshire Terrace to Tavistock House. In "Night Walks" the narrator calls himself "Houselessness" and lays claim to an "amateur" kinship with the homeless people of London. The walk describes an enormous circle: starting at half-past midnight from an undesignated place, we arrive at Waterloo Bridge, walk east past the theater district, Newgate, and the Bank of England, turning south to Billingsgate Market, across London Bridge to the Borough. South of the river, we walk west, stopping at the King's Bench Prison (close by the Marshalsea) and Bethlehem Hospital (Bedlam). From there it is an easy walk back across the river over the Westminster Bridge to Parliament, the Courts of Law, and St. Martin's Church, arriving back at Covent Garden in time for an early cup of coffee. This is, of course, the landscape of Dickens's history and of his dreams. Like a recurrent dream, the walk is narrated as if it had been traversed on successive nights, with slight variations in each version of the experience.

The "houseless mind" and "the houseless eye" of "Night Walks" do not find any easy relief from insomnia in night walking. Instead Houselessness is beset by isolation, and seeks any sign of company, any lighted place where another consciousness might reside. Small groups of figures are conjured up only to disappear. The city itself is a personified double figure of the restless insomniac until it too abandons him by subsiding into sleep. The fires or lights of guards, toll-keepers, watchmen, and turnkeys are heartening but brief flickers in the darkness as the wanderer moves from place to place, trying to discover here a figure, there a building, that might generate narrative. The city empties itself out into a desert region as the essay comes to an end, and "my houselessness had many miles upon miles of streets in which it could, and did, have its own solitary way." The echo of Adam and Eve at the end of *Paradise Lost* associates night wandering with being cast out, or locked out of human shelter. It is a frequent association for Dickens: the murderer Rudge suffers from feeling "more utterly alone and cast away than in a trackless desert" as he paces the wearisome streets of London waiting for dawn to break (*BR* 18); Little Dorrit and Maggy, locked out of the Marshalsea, huddle or wander fearfully near its gate for the five and a half hours before sunrise.

In the nearly deserted city, the narrator observes that drunks "appeared to be magnetically attracted to one another; where one drunk turns up, another is sure to follow." According to a similar principle, the narrator is drawn to shadowy figures like himself. A furtive head peers out of a doorway; it proves to be attached "to a man standing bolt upright to keep within the doorway's shadow, and evidently intent upon no particular service to society. Under a kind of fascination, and in a ghostly silence suitable to the time, Houselessness and this gentleman would eye one another from head to foot, and so, without exchange of speech, part, mutually suspicious." Fascination, that telling spellbinder, lights here upon a specular image of anti-social being, while the mutually suspicious "eyeing" marks, as always in Dickens, the presence of an identity recognition and exchange. This exchange bleeds into the narrator's next alienated self-description as "the houseless shadow" which would "fall upon the stones that pave the way to Waterloo Bridge" where the lights on the river look "as if the specters of suicides were holding them to show where they went down." At the wall of King's Bench Prison the narrator stops to meditate on the phenomenon of Dry Rot in men, to be observed in those with "a tendency to lurk and lounge; to be at street-corners without intelligible reason; to be going anywhere when met; to be about many places rather than at any." The familiar story of deterioration and decline still troubles Dickens, now in images not altogether remote from the activities of Houselessness himself.

On the steps of St. Martin's church, just as the bells strike three, another spectral double "rose up at my feet with a cry of loneliness and houselessness, struck out of it by the bell, the like of which I never heard. We then stood face to face looking at one another, frightened by one another." The bell, the cry of desolation, the church, hard by Warren's Blacking—all suggest the ancient terror, but the scene moves rapidly into a relation of guilt. The staring of this "thing" or "creature" makes the well-clad narrator see himself as "persecutor, devil, ghost—whatever it thought me," and when he reaches out to offer it money "it twisted out of its garment, like the young man in the New Testament, and left me standing alone with rags in my hand." The young man in question is the last of Jesus's followers to desert him when he is taken in Gethsemane; as the persecutors catch him by his linen cloth, he flees from them naked (Mark 14.51–52). The narrator is guilty not only of wealth and security but also of betrayal, which hovers in the air, oddly shared between the nightwalker and his young, lonely, terrified ghost.

"The most spectral person my houselessness encountered" is a cadaverous-looking man wearing nothing but a long coat and hat, who regularly eats his pudding in a coffee-shop in Covent Garden market. The heavy meat pudding comes out of the man's hat as if it were his head or his brain. It is repeatedly stabbed overhand with a large knife, torn apart with the fingers, and devoured. The red face of this man is explained in this fashion: "My mother was a red-faced women who liked drink, and I looked at her hard when she laid in her coffin, and I took the complexion." "Somehow," observes the narrator, "the pudding seemed an unwholesome pudding after that, and I put myself in its way no more." Whether or not this is an image of cannibalizing the mother, it is a deeply disturbing scene. The "looking hard" between the man and his dead mother mirrors the narrator's own fascination with the man, and suggests his morbid fear of kinship with the man's bestial violence. Recurrent images in Dickens of heads figuratively separated from bodies may suggest something about the violence in his desire to disperse the contents of his head among externalized figures, or even to kill the head through the activity of the body. Like the terrified young man in rags, the pudding-eater defies any definitive interpretation and attests to the uncanny power that allowed Dickens to get his unconscious into his writing.

The direct pursuit of that unconscious in "Night Walks" comes through in a "night-fancy" the narrator indulges as he approaches the walls of Bethlehem Hospital. "Are not the sane and the insane equal at night as the sane lie a dreaming? Are not all of us outside this hospital, who dream, more or less in the condition of those inside it, every night of our lives?" The questions mix the internal with the external, the locked wards with the city streets, the daylight writer with the manic nightwalker. Members of every social station are leveled, too, equal in the absurdity of their dreams. "I wonder that the great master who knew everything, when he called Sleep the death of each day's life, did not call Dreams the insanity of each day's sanity." As he revises Macbeth's account of his murder of Duncan, Dickens suddenly comes into focus as the fulcrum between Shakespeare and Freud. Brilliantly haunting the border between waking and dreaming, sanity and insanity, "Night Walks" answers its fanciful questions in the affirmative. In the end, however, Houselessness does "have its own solitary way"; he can script his own path through the city of the night. In flight from internal trouble, the walker finds his ghosts as images in the streets, where he is empowered to gaze, identify, and name.

With the questionable exception of the pudding-eater's dead mother, "Night Walks" is remarkable for presenting no female figure. It includes no destitute women, no prostitutes threading their way through labyrinthine courts, no girl children under threat, none of the predictable feminine emblems of poverty, sexuality, or vulnerability that people so many of Dickens's night streets. "I knew well enough where to find Vice and Misfortune of all kinds, if I had chosen," asserts the narrator, "but they were put out of sight." His sights are set instead on figures that reflect his subjective fascinations without the sentimental mediation that female surrogates can provide. At the same time, the Uncommercial Traveller's systematic visits to the sites of his hidden past may put us in mind of an earlier surrogate, Lady Dedlock. From her first appearance in the text of *Bleak House*, Lady Dedlock is in motion. Her movements are uncertain; she flies between Paris, Chesney Wold, and the house in London; when she hears news that bears on her hidden past, she demands to get out of the carriage and walk; at home she is restless, pacing. Once she knows that her past affair with Captain Hawdon has been exposed to her husband, she is overcome by a panic so powerful that it shatters her usual self-command: "Hunted, she flies. The complication of her shame, her dread, remorse, and misery, overwhelms her at its height; and even her strength of self-reliance is overturned and whirled away, like a leaf before a mighty wind." That is all the explanation we get. In her note to her husband, she renders herself houseless: "I have no home left. I will encumber you no more" (*BH* 55).

When Detective Bucket is set on her trail with orders to find and forgive, he goes first to the obvious places: the east London docks where bodies are dragged from the Thames, the bridges from which she might have jumped. But Dickens is not following the classic script of the fallen woman; Bucket, who is, loses valuable time. Through Esther's narration of the whirlwind carriage ride she takes with Bucket in search of her mother, we are allowed to piece together, though not to experience, Lady Dedlock's two-day walk of over fifty miles on snowy roads and city streets. She walks from her London house to Saint Albans, twenty-three miles out of London (as Jenny, the brickmaker's wife, informs Dr. Woodcourt). She is looking for Esther at Bleak House, just outside of Saint Albans, but doesn't find her; instead she rests at the brickmaker's cottage, changes clothes with Jenny, and turns back toward London around midnight, just as Bucket and Esther are beginning their search. As they alight at Saint Albans and pursue the decoy Jenny on the northern road, Lady Dedlock arrives back in London, getting lost in its streets as she searches for the fetid graveyard that holds the body of her lost lover. Jo has shown it to her once, but her memory does not hold; with Guster's help, she finally finds it on the night of her second day of flight. When the search party finds her at dawn, she is dead, clinging to the locked gates of the cemetery that confirms her final houselessness.

What does Lady Dedlock die of? "These streets!" she writes in her final note, "I have no purpose but to die. When I left, I had a worse; but I am saved from adding that guilt to the rest. Cold, wet, and fatigue, are sufficient causes for my being found dead; but I shall die of others, though I suffer from these" (*BH* 59). The streets are both walkways and death traps in *Bleak House*, concerned as it is with the failures of metropolitan sanitation, and the exclamation "These streets!" seems to implicate them directly in a death that is otherwise *not* sufficiently caused. Death by walking apparently absolves Lady Dedlock from the selfish guilt of suicide; with the help of cold dark roads and obscure streets she manages to die in about thirty-six hours. Yet her marathon walk turns out to be just an alibi: she will really die, Lady Dedlock claims, from an internal collapse comparable to Krook's notorious spontaneous combustion.

The picture of Lady Dedlock walking the streets inevitably suggests a gendered version of streetwalking, allying that internal collapse with the proverbial despair of the fallen woman. In fact the streets are her refuge; they allow her to become lost, anonymous, detached from the social identity she had built at great cost to herself, and from the eyes that have followed her movements and speculated about them. Her end is told with a curious mixture of distance and sympathy, as a carefully worked out back-story discernible behind the veil of Esther's intense, dread-filled narrative. Like

Dickens, Lady Dedlock walks loyally toward the landmarks of her past shame when her uncontrollable mind and feelings overwhelm her best efforts at self-discipline. This story of a character who attempts to shed herself by walking resonates with everything we know about Dickens's own need to walk—away from the domestic sphere, away from his internal specters, and toward the external specters that rise up out of the city streets.

🐚 Trapped

Solitary confinement is the nightmare antithesis of walking, because it causes the mind to rebound only on itself. In Dickens's universe it is virtually impossible to be alone. Even in their most excruciating or exquisite solitary moments—Oliver Twist confined in Fagin's house, Paul Dombey musing with the clock on the stairs—Dickens figures produce in the narrative another head or an answering face. Views of London rooftops are always desolate scenes, but they are never entirely depopulated: when Oliver gazes out his dirty window he sees "a confused and crowded mass of housetops, blackened chimneys, and gable-ends. Sometimes, indeed, a grizzly head might be seen, peering over the parapet wall of a distant house, but it was quickly withdrawn again" (*OT* 18). The dizzying view from Todgers's works in a similar way: first it is a confused "crowd of objects, which sprung out from the mass without any reason," then the chimney pots are endowed with the ability to observe and comment on what goes on below; then "The man who was mending a pen at an upper window over the way, became of paramount importance in the scene, and made a blank in it, ridiculously disproportionate in its extent, when he retired" (*MC* 9).

Depicting loneliness requires not only an absence of others, but a presence that disappears before the eyes. David Copperfield, paying a solitary visit to his childhood home, sees an elderly face at the same window from which he had gazed at the tombstone of his dead father; left alone in criminal London, Pip is eyed by sinister plaster casts or assaulted by furniture endowed with aggressive intentions. Even in descriptions of deserted country landscapes a head or a pair of watching eyes will show up somewhere. Neither narrators nor characters can tolerate solitude; if necessary they will invent live presences made of houses, furniture, shadowy dark corners, ghosts or phantoms, and suffer horrors from them. The power of animation in Dickens serves, I think, his fundamental fear of isolation.

John Forster, a man who had lived alone for many years of his life, comes to a complex perspective on this aspect of his friend. "It will not do to draw round any part of such a man too hard a line," he writes near the end of his biography,

> and the writer must not be charged with inconsistency who says that Dickens's childish sufferings, and the sense they burnt into him of the misery of loneliness and a craving for joys of home, though they led to what was weakest in him, led also to what was greatest. It was his defect as well as his merit in maturer life not to be able to live alone. When the fancies of his novels were upon him and he was under their restless influence, though he often talked of shutting himself up in out of the way solitary places, he never went anywhere unaccompanied by members of his family. (Forster 834–35)

It is a tricky passage, accurately reflecting Forster's ambivalence as well as his desire to explain most of Dickens's strangeness by way of the blacking factory. "Not to be able to live alone" is not just the characteristic of any family man; it belongs to a particular writer who lived for hours a day in his study peopling his inner world with character after character. When he emerged, he flung himself out of doors and walked the streets of London, Paris, Boulogne, Boston—wherever he could see and be seen by fellow passengers. While Forster stresses Dickens's need for his family, it is also important to recognize his flight from domesticity into writing and into the mirror-world of the streets, where the mere passing sight of other men and women fed an essential need of his nature.

Contemporary debates about penal reform provided special grist for Dickens's fear of isolation. He became notorious in his time for his attacks on solitary confinement, or "the separate system," which aimed to reform inmates by keeping them apart from other criminals and effecting moral change through quiet reflection and dialogue with prison chaplains. He would champion instead "the silent system," which allowed prisoners to see one another, although it carried heavy punishments for violating the rule of silence, and imposed in general a more directly punitive regime of physical labor. It was more important for Dickens to see other people—and to be provided with evidence from which he could imagine their internal lives—than to talk with them. He experienced the difference as one between keeping and losing one's sanity, and—almost literally—as the distinction between life and death. His writing about solitary confinement, whether voluntary or involuntary, can help to illuminate the intensity of his need to walk in city streets.

When Dickens visited the United States in 1842 he toured Cherry Hill, the Eastern Penitentiary in Philadelphia, which was run on a system he later called "rigid, strict, and hopeless solitary confinement" (*AN* 7). A series of letters written during the month after the 8 March visit reveals the gradually increasing horror with which Dickens remembered the prisoners he interviewed there. Two days after the tour, in a letter to the American David Colden, Dickens could say, "I fear that to a certain extent the system is a good one" and that it is "mercifully and well intended," but he felt it was "dreadful to believe that it is ever necessary to impose such a torture of the mind upon our fellow creatures." Once he came to individual prisoners, however, he sounded the theme of sensory deprivation, comparing the looks on their faces to "the attentive and sorrowful expressions you see in the blind" (3.110–11). When he wrote up his impressions in chapter 7 of *American Notes*, the prisoners were likened to the deaf as well as the blind; in fact Dickens insisted that they grew literally deaf in their solitude, although they did not realize it. When he wrote more freely and emphatically to Forster five days after the visit, the fear of sensory deprivation became more extreme: "I looked at some of them with the same awe as I should have looked at men who had been buried alive, and dug up again" (3.124). Elaborated in *American Notes*, the simile became fact: "he is a man buried alive; to be dug out in the slow round of years; and in the mean time dead to everything but torturing anxieties and horrible despair." Such outbursts lie side by side with descriptions of particular prisoners' ingenuity in decorating their cells or working the little plots of land connected with the first-floor cells at the Philadelphia Penitentiary.

Although it was well run, Dickens told Forster, the "dreadful, fearful place" had filled him with impressions that were "written, beyond all power of erasure, in my brain" (3.123–24). Three weeks later he wrote on board a steamboat from Pittsburgh to Cincinnati, reporting on a visit to another solitary confinement prison in Pittsburgh. "A horrible thought" had occurred to him:

> *What if ghosts be one of the terrors of these jails?* . . . The utter solitude by day and night; the many hours of darkness; the silence of death; the mind for ever brooding on melancholy themes, and having no relief; sometimes an evil conscience very busy; imagine a prisoner covering up his head in the bedclothes and looking out from time to time, with a ghastly dread of some inexplicable silent figure that always sits upon his bed, or stands . . . in the same corner of his cell. The more I think of it, the more certain I feel that not a few of these men (during a portion of their imprisonment at least) are nightly visited by spectres. (3.181)

The description perfectly evokes childhood fears of the dark; Dickens's "certainty" was based on personal memory, projected onto prisoners who had stirred up his own worst nightmares.

This letter was the germ of the extended fantasy in *American Notes* in which Dickens invents with chilling certainty each stage of mental deterioration in a prisoner very like himself. It is a very "hot" piece of writing, poetic and personal, and it was, of course, very controversial. Advocates of the separate system accused Dickens of making fictions, and of undermining American penal reformers after he had praised them to their faces. His judgments about particular prisoners were refuted in print. Opponents of the system used his passionate representations as acts of imaginative sympathy that got at truths beyond the reach of science and statistics. The representations may well have done just that, but the chapter is hardly a professional judgment. Dickens represents himself as one of the few men capable "of estimating the immense amount of torture and agony which this dreadful punishment, prolonged of years, inflicts upon the sufferers." The "benevolent gentlemen" who "carry it into execution, do not know what it is that they are doing." Dickens knows: "I hold this slow and daily tampering with the mysteries of the brain, to be immeasurably worse than any torture of the body." It creates "an anguish so acute and so tremendous, that all imagination of it must fall far short of the reality." This is the voice of the autobiographical fragment, with its accusation of those oblivious to the unspeakable intensity of silent suffering.

Not knowing is also a critical part of the torture: the prisoner in his cell "has no means of knowing, down to the very last hour, in what part of the building it is situated; what kind of men there are about him; whether in the long winter nights there are people near." When Dickens enters the mind of an imaginary prisoner, it is intensely frustrated by having no visual access to those near him: "Where is the nearest man—upon the right, or on the left? or is there one in both directions? Where is he sitting now—with his face to the light? Or is he walking to and fro? How is he dressed? Has he been here long? Is he much worn away? Is he very white and spectre-like? Does he think of his neighbor too?" The prisoner begins to conjure up the figures of these hidden others, imagining an older man on the right, a younger one on the left, "whose hidden features torture him to death, and have a mystery that makes him tremble." Dickens could not bear the idea that one might not see others and be seen by them; it is as if he could not imagine his own existence without its reflection back from another human figure. For the prisoner in the cell, the absence of other real figures creates an approach to madness: walls become threatening, the ceiling begins to look down upon him; then a corner of the cell contains a ghost, a shadow, a phantom; even the Loom on which he works becomes "a hideous figure, watching him till daybreak." Going mad means being watched by something inhuman; not being seen at all is beyond the range of imagination. Although the prisoner he describes is said to recover from the haunted stage, recalling it only at intervals, Dickens cannot say what happens next; his narrative moves directly to the prisoner's anticipation of release.

Dickens was predictably sensitive to criticisms of this chapter of *American Notes*. In April 1844 he wrote to a Massachusetts educator he had met, contesting all she had heard about his supposed "wonderful and unparalleled perversion of judgment," and declaring his vision to be "the Truth" (4.103–4). Six years later he returned to the subject of solitary confinement in a long *Household Words* article called "Pet Prisoners" (Dent 2.212–27). Although he made a big distinction between American prisons and the new Pentonville Prison in England, which used solitary only for brief periods, he could not help including a long footnote defending his American observations from criticisms published by the Rev. John Field in 1848. His obvious anxiety that there might be truth in those criticisms manifested itself in the effort to write "Pet Prisoners" in a hyper-rational way, as though he were presenting statistical evidence in a court of law with his readers serving as the jury. The abstractly reasoned argument breaks down into Dickensian rhetoric when he gets to the heart of his case, an attack on what he calls "pattern penitence." Re-dramatized in chapter 71 of *David Copperfield* ("I am shown two interesting Penitents"), "pattern penitence" refers to the hypocritical claims for internal reform fabricated by prisoners in response to the brow-beatings of the chaplains and governors who visit them in the hope of effecting a change of heart.

By 1850 Dickens was cannier about secret communications among prisoners in solitary confinement. He repeats the idea of "a fascination in the desire to know something of the hidden presence beyond the blank wall of the cell," but acknowledges that prisoners always find ways of getting in touch with another. What disturbs him now is not that solitary creates madness, but that it encourages a "strange absorbing selfishness—a spiritual egoism and vanity, real or assumed" (Dent 2.219–20). The victim of the crime is forgotten, and the prisoner thinks only of himself. If such a system were to work, Dickens argues, it would force us to conclude that "Providence was quite mistaken in making us gregarious, and that we had all better shut ourselves up directly" (224). He urges his readers to prefer the silent system, both because it is cheaper and because the prisoner "is still one of a society of men, and not an isolated being, filling his whole sphere of view with a diseased dilation of himself" (226). Did Dickens harbor any suspicion that his *American Notes* chapter had been a diseased dilation of himself? "Pet Prisoners," with its rational tone, its highly moralized message, and its punitive attitude to prisoners, is in many ways a reaction against that earlier fantasy.

After 1850 Dickens began to consider cases of voluntary self-isolation, surrounding them with images of horror and disgust. Mrs. Clennam hardens the arteries of change by choosing to live in rigid immobility. Miss Havisham allows her house to rot around her; spiders crawl on the remains of her ancient wedding cake as she broods on her unhealed wound. Because of her perverse but human connection with Estella, she is allowed some sympathy. Shortly before completing *Great Expectations* in the summer of 1861, Dickens visited the hermit John Lucas, who had secluded himself on his family estate in Hertfordshire. An intelligent man who suffered from paranoia, Lucas neglected himself and the estate, slept in rags on cinders and soot in his kitchen, and managed to keep people coming around by distributing coins to passing tramps and children. Dickens mentioned the visit in a letter to Arthur Helps: "If he were to faint one night, he would probably be devoured by the Rats who swarm in that den of his,—I should not have stood so coolly at the bars, if I had known of their being so near" (9.430–31). The rat-infested warehouse of Warren's Blacking, seen in this image through prison-like bars, was always just a little too near.

That year Dickens devoted the Christmas number of *All the Year Round*, *Tom Tiddler's Ground*, to the evils of a hermit existence; the rats had done their work on his imagination. His frame story for the number was a fictionalized version of his visit to Lucas in which his stand-in, called the Traveller, interrogates the hermit Mr. Mopes. The Traveller has no shred of sympathy or curiosity to spare for the hermit. Mopes is filthy, lazy, vain, diseased, and unnatural; his neglect of the property has made him a universal nuisance, and the unused beds in the house are seething with rats. "I would put the thing on the treadmill," says the Traveller, echoing the praise in "Pet Prisoners" of the treadmill as an exemplary punishment (*CS* 419). The hermit is associated with every bad image in Dickens's repertoire: "A compound of Newgate, Bedlam, a Debtor's Prison in the worst time, a chimney-sweep, a mudlark, and the Noble Savage!" (426). The moral is simple: "we must arise and wash our faces and do our gregarious work and act and re-act on one another, leaving only the idiot and the palsied to sit blinking in the corner" (430).

Dickens's inset story for the number, "Picking up Miss Kimmeens," is about a young girl left alone in a schoolhouse for the day; after a few hours of "unnatural solitude" her mind turns nasty and sour, but she has sense enough to spring out of her chair and rush out of the house. Both frame and story reveal Dickens in his most stupid frame of mind, devoid of wit, nuance, sympathy, self-understanding, or anything except a willful desire to crush the image of rat-infested solitude out of existence. The vehemence of this mood might be connected to changes attending his separation from Catherine. After 1859, the letters show a drop-off in dinners, theatricals, and other signs of social life, as well as in Dickens's interest in social reform projects. Editing, writing, and public readings are the paramount concerns, along with anxieties about how to place his seven sons in useful occupations. The ferocity of his attack on the deranged hermit may stem in part from Dickens's reactions to the changes, which, despite his ongoing family life at Gad's Hill, may have included some fear that he had managed to isolate himself.

🍂 Walking toward Death

Dickens's powerful need for the forward motion of walking could not be gainsaid even when it was threatened by the deterioration of his energies. Walking had always been a central character in the mythology of his health, whether he was boasting about his robust physique or trying to walk off his nervous anxieties. When it became clear in his fifties that his health was in decline, walking again took center stage: the story he told was about the pain in his left foot and his insistence on walking in spite of it. Dickens had suffered from fragile health since childhood, and he remained vulnerable to attacks of pain in his left side that he associated with an inflammation of the kidney. In adulthood he prided himself on outgrowing his fragility through discipline and vigorous exercise, but Catherine and Forster shared a more realistic knowledge of his susceptibilities. John Dickens died in 1851 after a bloody operation—without chloroform—for a long-standing bladder disease. Dickens, who was present, told Catherine that his father had never mentioned his condition to anyone, and that he showed great strength through the ordeal. "All this goes to my side directly, and I feel as if I had been struck there by a leaden bludgeon," he wrote (6.333). Clearly both he and Catherine understood the psychological component of those attacks.

When it came to his own mortal disease, however, Dickens was his father's son. He was willing to complain vigorously about the pain of a "frostbitten foot," but not to connect it with the diagnosis of degenerative heart disease that he received two days after his fifty-fourth birthday. As he wrote to both Georgina and Wills that day, "I am not so foolish as to suppose that all my work can have been achieved without *some* penalty, and I have noticed for some time a decided change in my buoyancy and hopefulness" (11.155). The formula had shifted a bit; now illness rather than restlessness was the tax he paid on his genius. And that was the end of that, at least so far as letter writing was concerned.

A year earlier the foot saga had begun. Dickens had always thought of walking as the cure for anything that ailed him. In the winter of 1864 he was staying indoors with a cold, but "the remedy is so new to me, that I doubt if it does me half the good of a dozen miles in the snow. So, if this mode of treatment fails today, I shall try that tomorrow" (10.469). Some weeks later, in February 1865, he reported being laid up with a wounded foot that he explained to friends as "a frost-bitten foot, from much walking in deep Kentish snow" (11.21). Forster got a full-blown explanation: he had perpetually wet feet in boots that swelled and shrank; he had repeatedly forced his boot onto a swollen left foot, and continued his rituals of work and walking, until he found himself lame in the snow, three miles from home. The dogs, he reported, were terrified (11.23). The pain, causing "sleepless agony" (11.29), went on for two months. Then he returned to his ten miles a day, but he could not wear shoes or boots in the evenings, and he ordered the first of several extra-large boots for his left foot. "Work and worry, without exercise, would soon make an end of me," he exclaimed to Forster (11.48).

The condition recurred periodically, worsening until his death. He defied the possibility that it was gout; perhaps no one knew enough to tell him that it was probably a symptom of vascular disease, or perhaps he could not hear that explanation. The fancy doctor he consulted in 1867, Sir Henry Thompson, told him that he had erypsipelas caused by the rubbing of his boot while walking, or, as Dickens put it, the "action of the boot on an undefended part of a bone, in constant walking" (11.409). Whatever Thompson had actually said, Dickens read according to his myth of walking: he had to walk; therefore he had to suffer. It cheered him up; soon afterwards he was writing letter after letter to deny a "preposterous paragraph" in the newspapers about his bad health, declaring himself to be "in sporting training" (11.417–18). He was on his way to America again; in Boston during November, he wrote to Georgina, "I every day take from seven to ten miles in peace" (11.489). By the end of the American reading tour, he was limping up to the podium leaning heavily on his manager George Dolby, and collapsing into Dolby's arms at the end of each performance.

May 1870 was the last month of Dickens's life. On the 26th he told a friend he had been "dead-lame" for three weeks. His correspondents all received the same story: "I have been subject for a few years past to a Neuralgic attack in the foot, originating in over walking in deep snow and revived by a hard winter in America.... Deprivation of my usual walks is a very serious matter to me, as I cannot work unless I have my constant exercise" (12.534–35). The myth was still intact. Three days later he wrote his last letter to John Forster, including a brief health bulletin: "Foot no worse. But no better" (12.540). On the ninth of June he was dead of a stroke. Somewhere in Dickens's inner world Lady Dedlock had triumphed, walking to her death through the snow.

Afterword

I began to write this book because Dickens always surprised me. The canniness and honesty about human fantasy that are so consistently woven into the fabric of his writing would catch me off guard time after time. He is the great English realist of the fantasy life. That is very different from saying that he is a fantasist, that he writes like a dreamer, or, as Taine and Lewes put it in the nineteenth century, that his work is monomaniacal or hallucinatory. It means instead that Dickens had a peculiar access to his own fantasy; he was capable, as many people are not, of catching and registering it clearly enough to bring it to immediate life in characters imagined through the point of his pen. In the midst of this private and mysterious process, he refrained from explaining or judging it out of existence, though his plots guaranteed that each brand of fantasy was eventually recuperated into a recognizably moral scheme. The absence of analytical distance was probably essential to this process; it allowed him to create nostalgic and wishful sentiment as readily as self-defensive, rivalrous, or murderous obsession. A good deal of the history of Dickens criticism has concerned itself with valuing one kind of fantasy over another. I do so myself in privileging his treatment of psychic distress over passages that dissolve distress into sentiment. Perhaps the perfect reader of Dickens would embrace both the disturbing and the self-comforting fantasies with equal humanity.

As I come to the end of this project, Dickens surprises me still. I look at the actions and reactions recorded in his letters; I form opinions, make judgments. In some turn of his art, he has already been there. He has seen himself; he knows what the psyche does; but he does not tell everything he knows. Whether that silence originated in an instinctive reflex to protect his good opinion of himself, or from a desire to limit his audiences' knowledge of his knowingness, would be difficult to say; most probably they are aspects of the same tendency.

The special quality of that powerful and troubled relation between knowing and telling may finally be suggested by two moments when Dickens used the image of being turned inside out. John Forster quotes from a letter of 21 October 1850, written as Dickens was drawing *David Copperfield* to a close: "I am within three pages of the shore, and am strangely divided, as usual in such cases, between sorrow and joy. Oh, my dear Forster, if I were to say half of what *Copperfield* makes me feel tonight, how strangely, even to you, I should be turned inside-out! I seem to be sending some part of myself into the Shadowy World" (Forster 547). These sentences reach out to the intimacy between the two friends as directly as anything in Dickens's letters ever does, in the very act of telling Forster how little he actually knows about the strangeness of Dickens's feelings. The "Shadowy World" in which those feelings are embedded is the world of fiction, or perhaps the world in which the unknown reader's mind meets the author's fantasy, and knows, or does not know, what he or she is reading. Confession and concealment are inseparable, both in Dickens's letter and in his fiction; one does not appear in a sentence or paragraph without the other. Being turned inside out, even to Forster, was imaginable only as the unimaginable.

Near the end of his life, Dickens came back to the image in a very different mood. "A Fly-Leaf in a Life," in the final series of *Uncommercial Traveller* pieces, was published in *All the Year Round* on 22 May 1869. This unusually personal piece is an attack on members of the public who presumed to offer analysis, advice, or criticism to Dickens during the period of enforced rest that followed the sudden cancellation of his final Farewell Tour of public readings a month earlier. Tellingly, he imagines the period of rest as a blank page—a fly-leaf—in "the book of my life"; its blankness is violated, however, by the intrusion of public responses to the breakdown of his health. His first line of attack is to claim that he had already written this experience when he satirized the rumors that fly to explain the death of Mr. Merdle in *Little Dorrit*. Quoting two full paragraphs from the novel, he seems to say, "Little can happen in life that I have not already known in my fiction." As for the possibility of being known by others, Dickens oozes contemptuous scorn as he imagines an ignorant field-preacher who had questioned his religious faith: "He was in the secrets of my heart, and in the lowest soundings of my soul—he!—and could read the depths of my nature better than his A B C, and could turn me inside out, like his own clammy glove" (Dent 4.388–89). Attempts to turn him inside out, he threatens, will expose only the more unpleasant parts of the unwelcome intruder.

Dickens yearned to be known, and was horrified by the possibility that he would be. The tension in his work between suspicious knowingness and idealized innocence—so often implicated with one another—lays out the shape of this charged territory, though it cannot tell us just what Dickens knew and what he withheld from conscious knowing. To read between fiction and correspondence, as I have been doing, is to alternate between amazement at his self-defensive strategies and amazement at the specificity with which he portrays those strategies in his characters and sometimes in himself. In a similar way he moves from identifications with turbulent characters to rhapsodies on idealized characters, just as the mind recognizes itself and then covers up what it knows. What does seem clear, however, is that Dickens was engaged in a life-long process of self-observation as keen as the observation he brought to bear on others. Those others—both male and female—were containers for the isolation and projection of an inward way of being that knew itself by mirroring its aspects on external screens. Dickens wanted to contain multitudes, and, in his way, he did.

To focus so exclusively on the subjectivity of Dickens may seem odd in a portrait of a writer so actively engaged in the social and political controversies of his time. Yet social ideologies thrive only when they take root in human fantasies. Dickens channeled the myths and fears of his period perhaps more frankly than other Victorian novelists, but he did so in ways that were peculiar to him. He was deeply suspicious of other cultures, but he expressed his racism through the fear of being duped. If he was an antifeminist, he was one who idealized young unmarried women, turned sexuality into housekeeping, and discovered his erotic imagination through rivalry and identification among men. His views about social class were deeply ambivalent, alternating in an inchoate way between a paternalism that looked down and a resentment that looked up; these oscillations were conditioned by a personal experience of class instability that he could neither discuss outright nor stop representing. He was in himself both a model of Victorian hard work and self-discipline, with its attendant fears of uncertainty and disorder, and a man who could not sustain such a life without building in daily avenues of violent-feeling escape. If he perpetuated middle-class ideas in his life and art, he also suffered from them, resisted them, and parodied them. In writing this book I have hoped to convey the impression that such oscillations represent not just contradictions in Dickens's ideological stances, but deeply human, idiosyncratic aspects of a man who could write like no one before or since.

Bibliographical Notes

1. What Dickens Knew

John Bowen invokes George Henry Lewes and George Eliot as critics of Dickens's failure to write psychologically or politically realistic characters as he begins *Other Dickens: Pickwick to Chuzzlewit* (Oxford: Oxford University Press, 2000), 16–30. Bowen turns his discussion toward the more-than-realistic "representational radicalism" of Dickens's language, which can "stretch our notions of psychology, aesthetics and politics alike" (29). The Dickens-Lewes battle over spontaneous combustion is summarized by Gordon Haight in "Dickens and Lewes on Spontaneous Combustion," *Nineteenth-Century Fiction* 10.1 (1955): 53–63. Rosemary Ashton comments wisely on this controversy and on Lewes's essay "Dickens in Relation to Criticism" in *G. H. Lewes: A Life* (Oxford: Clarendon Press, 1991), 143–47 and 256–59. Dickens's emphasis on fiction's emotional effects on the reader was shared by his contemporaries: see Nicholas Dames, "Wave-Theories and Affective Physiologies: The Cognitive Strain in Victorial Novel Theories," *Victorian Studies* 46.2 (2004): 206–16.

The contents of Dickens's Gad's Hill library at the time of his death are listed in *Catalogue of the Library of Charles Dickens*, ed. J. H. Stonehouse (London: Piccadilly Fountain Press, 1935).

For relevant work on Dickens and the unconscious mind, see these studies: Warrington Winters, "Dickens and the Psychology of Dreams," *PMLA* 63.3 (1948): 984–1006; Catherine Bernard, "Dickens and Dream Theory," in *Victorian Science and Victorian Values*, ed. James Paradis and Thomas Postlewait (New Brunswick, N.J.: Rutgers University Press, 1985), 197–216; Jenny Bourne Taylor, "Obscure Recesses: Locating the Victorian Unconscious," in *Writing and Victorianism*, ed. J. B. Bullen (London: Longman, 1997), 137–79; Fred Kaplan, *Dickens and Mesmerism: The Hidden Springs of Fiction* (Princeton: Princeton University Press, 1975); Taylor Stoehr, *Dickens: The Dreamer's Stance* (Ithaca: Cornell University Press, 1965); and Robert Newsom, *Dickens on the Romantic Side of Familiar Things: "Bleak House" and the Novel Tradition* (New York: Columbia University Press, 1977).

In part 1 of "Dickens and Women's Stories" (*Dickens Quarterly* 17.2 [2000]: 67–76), Margaret Flanders Darby gives an analysis of Dickens's unacknowledged autobiographical projection during his mesmeric treatment of Augusta de la Rue. Fred Kaplan gives a full account of Dickens and the de la Rues in chapter 4 of *Dickens and Mesmerism*; in subsequent chapters Kaplan discusses the ways that mesmerism and related ideas about trance, self-encounter, the past, and the power of one person over another appear in Dickens's fiction. For a brief and cogent discussion of the various claims for mesmerism and its place in the development of nineteenth-century theories of the unconscious, see Jonathan Miller, "Going Unconscious," in *Hidden Histories of Science*, ed. Robert B. Silvers (New York: New York Review, 1995), 1–35.

The often disturbing peculiarities in Dickens's treatment of women both inside and outside his fiction have been discussed at length; six times as many results show up in a search for "Dickens and women" as for "Dickens and men." Michael Slater's *Dickens and Women* (Stanford: Stanford University Press, 1983) offers a full, balanced, and informed account. Jack Lindsay's *Charles Dickens: A Biographical and Critical Study* (New York: Philosophical Library, 1950) gives a speculative Freudian reading of Dickens's neurotic relationships with his mother and his sister Fanny. More recent criticism tends to read Dickens's work as a representative instance of Victorian gender structures as they were mobilized in novels. Most relevant is Catherine Robson's *Men in Wonderland: The Lost Girlhood of the Victorian Gentleman* (Princeton: Princeton University Press, 2001). Robson places Dickens among a series of nineteenth-century writers for whom the young girl functioned as a nostalgic image or as a continuation of the lost, feminized childhoods of older gentlemen. The definitive work on Ellen Ternan is Claire Tomalin's *The Invisible Woman: The Story of Nelly Ternan and Charles Dickens* (New York: Viking, 1990). Lilian Nayder is currently at work on a biography of Catherine Dickens.

On the status of the blacking warehouse narrative see Alexander Welsh, *From Copyright to Copperfield* (Cambridge, Mass.: Harvard University Press, 1987), 1–8 and 156–62. Linda Shires comments on Welsh's position in "Literary Careers, Death, and the Body Politics of *David Copperfield*," in *Dickens Refigured: Bodies, Desires, and Other Histories*, ed. John Schad (Manchester: Manchester University Press, 1996), 118–21. For more extensive bibliography relating to the blacking narrative, see the notes to chapter 3, "Memory."

2. Language on the Loose

Quotations from Dickens's working notes are taken from *Charles Dickens' Book of Memoranda*, transcribed and edited by Fred Kaplan (New York: New York Public Library, 1981). In *Dickens: The Dreamer's Stance* (41–45), Taylor Stoehr introduces examples from these notes as evidence for Dickens's almost hallucinatory projection into his characters.

Garrett Stewart's *Dickens and the Trials of the Imagination* (Cambridge, Mass.: Harvard University Press, 1974) is the best study of Dickens's parodic style that I know; in particular Stewart's chapters on *The Pickwick Papers* and *The Old Curiosity Shop* are models of brilliant writing and analysis that resonate consistently with my own instincts and readings in this chapter, although they serve a different argument. John Kucich's chapter "Mechanical Style" in *Excess and Restraint in the Novels of Charles Dickens* (Athens: University of Georgia Press, 1981), also touches on some of my concerns; Kucich's analysis of the mixture of parody and satire in Dickens's narration is especially fine. Although Kucich suggests the unconscious desires that fuel self-parody, he overestimates the extent to which Dickens's parody and self-parody are "mechanical" and merely repetitive. Tore Rem returns to the subject of Dickens's parody and self-parody in *Dickens, Melodrama, and the Parodic Imagination* (New York: AMS Press, 2002); he is primarily interested in Dickens's parodies of the literary modes in which he was most invested, sentiment and melodrama. Both Stewart and Rem touch on the possibility of silence as the ultimately "authentic" form of response to the world. I am not so much interested in the possibility of finding authentic moments among Dickens's many rhetorical styles as I am in the competition for credibility as an ongoing dynamic within Dickens.

Of the general theorists of parody, the most useful to me has been Linda Hutcheon, *A Theory of Parody: The Teachings of Twentieth-Century Art Forms* (New York: Methuen, 1985), which gives a generous assessment of the range of affective intentions in parody.

On the question of what Dickens's parodies of himself might signify, my brief summary of questions is derived from disparate opinions expressed in Barbara Hardy, *The Moral Art of Dickens* (London: Athlone Press, 1970), John Carey, *The Violent Effigy: A Study of Dickens's Imagination* (London: Faber and Faber, 1973), John Kucich, *Excess and Restraint in the Novels of Charles Dickens*, Steven Marcus, *Dickens from Pickwick to Dombey* (New York: Simon and Schuster, 1965), Tore Rem, *Dickens, Melodrama, and the Parodic Imagination*, and Alexander Welsh, *From Copyright to Copperfield*.

Richard D. Altick, in "Harold Skimpole Revisited," quotes several other Victorian writers whose accounts of the Hunt family corroborate the genuine similarities between Hunt's and Skimpole's styles of speech and willful incompetence in money matters. Altick suggests that Dickens was shocked by that incompetence, but that the likeness of Hunt to Skimpole would have been recognizable only to an in-group of people who knew Hunt well. See Robert A. McCown, ed., *The Life and Times of Leigh Hunt* (Iowa City: Friends of the University of Iowa Libraries, 1985), 1–15. K. J. Fielding has explained Dickens's compulsion to fashion Skimpole after Leigh Hunt as a protest against "artistic bohemianism and irresponsibility just when he was seriously working for what he and Forster delighted to call 'The Dignity of Literature,'" in "Leigh Hunt and Skimpole: Another Remonstrance," *Dickensian* 64 (1968): 5–9. Adam Roberts makes an interesting juxtaposition of Skimpole's speeches with some of Leigh Hunt's writings, attempting to redeem both Dickens and Hunt by calling Skimpole an ironic or reverse portrait of Hunt; see "Skimpole, Leigh Hunt, and Dickens's 'Remonstrance,'" *The Dickensian* 92:4 (1996): 177–86. Peter Ackroyd briefly suggests a more personal investment: Dickens "*was* Skimpole and had to exorcise him" (652–53). My speculations about the inward sources of Dickens's defenses against shame and the betrayal of trust are indebted to Eve Kosofsky Sedgwick's readings of shame and paranoia in *Touching Feeling: Affect, Pedagogy, Performance* (Durham: Duke University Press, 2003), chaps. 1 and 4.

For the initial reading of incestuous fantasy in the Dorrit-Amy relationship, see Dianne F. Sadoff, *Monsters of Affection: Dickens, Eliot, and Brontë on Fatherhood* (Baltimore: Johns Hopkins University Press, 1982), 55–57. Variations on the theme are frequent; see for example Anny Sadrin, *Parentage and Inheritance in the Novels of Charles Dickens* (Cambridge University Press, 1994), 74–94, and Patricia Ingham, "Nobody's Fault: The Scope of the Negative in *Little Dorrit*," in *Dickens Refigured*, ed. John Schad, 107–16. Janice Carlisle's essay "*Little Dorrit*: Necessary Fictions" (*Studies in the Novel* 7.2 [1975]: 195–214) was an early breakthrough in the critical tradition of belief in Amy Dorrit's goodness; Carlisle explores the lies Amy tells to sustain the myths of the Dorrit family and connects them with the peculiar storytelling of the novel as a whole. For a diagnosis of Amy Dorrit based on psychoanalytic definitions of narcissism, see Richard Currie, "'As If She Had Done Him a Wrong': Hidden Rage and Object Protection in Dickens's Amy Dorrit," *English Studies* 72.4 (1991): 368–76.

On Dickens and the police, see Philip Collins, *Dickens and Crime* (London: Macmillan, 1962), chap. 9. Collins sees Dickens's view of the detective police as "laudatory, indeed awestruck," even as "boyish hero-worship." He also notes that the police force was largely drawn from the lower classes, which enabled Dickens both to praise and to patronize them (205–6; 218–19).

3. Memory

The exact length of time that Dickens spent at Warren's Blacking warehouse remains controversial. Forster dates his second chapter containing the autobiographical fragment 1822–24, and refers to the ten-year-old David Copperfield as Dickens himself, avoiding a direct statement about Dickens's age at the time of his employment (Forster 23). When J. W. T. Ley published his edition of Forster's *Life* in 1928, he established the most common modern assumption: that Dickens had worked at Warren's Blacking for no more than six months at the age of twelve (Forster 37n.) In 1988 Michael Allen revised that opinion, estimating that Dickens worked at Warren's for thirteen or fourteen months, beginning just after his twelfth birthday. See *Charles Dickens's Childhood* (London: Macmillan, 1988), 81, 103–4. In the end, Dickens's remark, "I have no idea how long it lasted; whether for a year, or much more, or less" (Forster 35), is the essential point: not knowing whether or when it would end created a large part of the emotional distress.

It has proven comparably difficult to date the composition of the autobiographical fragment. Different sections of Dickens's memories were probably written and given to Forster at different times in the 1840s, and neither the original fragment nor the manuscript of Forster's *Life* has survived. For my 1848 dating of the full blacking warehouse memory I have accepted the generally acknowledged authoritative source: Nina Burgis's introduction to *David Copperfield* (Oxford: Clarendon Press, 1981), xv–lxii. For Forster's habit of rewriting and "improving" Dickens's letters to him see Madeline House and Graham Storey, Preface to Volume 1 of the Pilgrim *Letters*. For doubts and issues that do not arise in Burgis's narrative, see Philip Collins, "Dickens's Autobiographical Fragment and *David Copperfield*," *Cahiers Victoriens et Eduardiens* 20 (1984): 87–96.

Since Forster published the autobiographical fragment, biographers and critics have been divided about the significance of that early experience to Dickens's development. Forster began the tradition of seeing Warren's Blacking as the source of Dickens's deepest personal difficulties, and Edmund Wilson established it for twentieth-century readers as the most powerful source of Dickens's fiction in "Dickens: The Two Scrooges" in *The Wound and the Bow: Seven Studies in Literature* (1941; New York: Oxford University Press, 1965), 3–85. Up to the present day, some critics focus on the trauma of the episode while others are primarily impressed with the self-dramatizing or unforgiving aspects of Dickens's retrospective account. Powerful modern "traumatic" interpretations may be found in Edgar Johnson, *Charles Dickens: His Tragedy and Triumph*, vol. 1 (New York: Simon and Schuster, 1952), 27–46; Steven

Marcus, "Who Is Fagin?" in *Dickens from Pickwick to Dombey*, 358–78; Albert D. Hutter, "Reconstructive Autobiography: The Experience at Warren's Blacking," *Dickens Studies Annual* 6 (1977) 1–14; and Robert Newsom, "The Hero's Shame," *Dickens Studies Annual* 11 (1983): 1–24. In *Primal Scenes: Literature, Philosophy, Psychoanalysis* (Ithaca: Cornell University Press, 1986), Ned Lukacher describes Dickensian remembering as unrelentingly traumatic, and imagines a kind of inner streetscape marked No Thoroughfare as the essential primal scene of an obsessed and increasingly tortured artist (290–330).

For more skeptical approaches to the fragment, see Alexander Welsh, *From Copyright to Copperfield*, 1–8 and 156–62, and Nina Auerbach, "Performing Suffering: From Dickens to David," *Browning Institute Studies* 18 (1990): 15–22. Auerbach reads the fragment as a grandiose self-performance that was diminished in *David Copperfield* to the story of a boy who wants maternal love and recognition. For Dickens's Warren poem, see John Drew, *Dickens the Journalist* (New York: Palgrave Macmillan, 2003), 15–20, and "A Twist in the Tale," *The Guardian Review*, 1 November 2003, 34.

Michael Slater tells the story of Maria Beadnell Winter in chapter 4 of *Dickens and Women*. A compatible reading of Dickens's letters to Maria Winter may be found in Margaret Flanders Darby, "Dickens and Women's Stories," Part Two, *Dickens Quarterly* 17.3 (2000): 127–38.

The best first resort for work on nineteenth-century views of memory and the unconscious is Jenny Bourne Taylor and Sally Shuttleworth, eds., *Embodied Selves: An Anthology of Psychological Texts, 1830–1890* (Oxford: Clarendon Press, 1998). Section Two, "The Unconscious Mind and the Workings of Memory," includes excerpts from discussions of conscious and unconscious memory as well as "double consciousness." I have also learned (and quoted) from Jenny Bourne Taylor's essay "Nobody's Secret: Illegitimate Inheritance and the Uncertainties of Memory," *Nineteenth-Century Contexts* 21 (2000): 565–92. Taylor gives an overview of Victorian ideas about the unconscious mind in "Obscure Recesses: Locating the Victorian Unconscious." This essay includes a detailed study of Smike's memory disturbances in *Nicholas Nickleby*. Michael S. Kearns discusses Dickens's knowledge and use of the theory of association in "Associationism, the Heart, and the Life of the Mind in Dickens's Novels," *Dickens Studies Annual* 15 (1986): 111–44. From my general background reading for this chapter I would single out Daniel L. Schacter, *Searching for Memory: The Brain, the Mind, and the Past* (New York: Basic Books, 1996), and Ian Hacking, *Rewriting the Soul: Multiple Personality and the Sciences of Memory* (Princeton: Princeton University Press, 1995).

My references to current theories of trauma draw on these works: Cathy Caruth, *Unclaimed Experience: Trauma, Narrative, History* (Baltimore: Johns Hopkins University Press, 1996); Daniel Albright, "Literary and Psychological Models of the Self," in *The Remembering Self: Construction and Accuracy in the Self-Narrative*, ed. Ulric Neisser and Robyn Firush (Cambridge: Cambridge University Press, 1994), 19–40; and Bessel A. Van der Kolk and Onno Van der Hart, "The Intrusive Past: The Flexibility of Memory and the Engraving of Trauma," in *Trauma: Explorations in Memory*, ed. Cathy Caruth (Baltimore: Johns Hopkins University Press, 1995), 158–82.

Malcolm Andrews's *Dickens and the Grown-up Child* (Iowa City: University of Iowa Press, 1994) does not argue that Dickens was a grown-up child; instead Andrews does the important work of situating a range of Dickens's ideas about the child-as-adult and the adult-as-child within cultural and literary contexts of the Victorian period. When it comes to Dickens's conflation of present and past, there are too many instances to count. Articles of direct use to me have been Robert L. Patten, "Serialized Retrospection in *The Pickwick Papers*," in *Literature in the Marketplace*, ed. John O. Jordan and Robert L. Patten (Cambridge: Cambridge University Press, 1995), 123–42; William T. Lankford, "'The Deep of Time': Narrative Order in *David Copperfield*, *ELH* 46 (1979): 452–67; and Kevin Ohi, "Autobiography and *David Copperfield*'s Temporalities of Loss," *Victorian Literature and Culture* 33.2 (2005): 435–49.

Mary Poovey's "*David Copperfield* and the Professional Writer," from which I have quoted, forms chapter 4 of her *Uneven Developments: The Ideological Work of Gender in Mid-Victorian England* (Chicago: University of Chicago Press, 1988), 89–125. I have taken up other aspects of *David Copperfield* in "Knowing and Telling in Dickens's Retrospects," in *Knowing the Past*, ed. Suzy Anger (Ithaca: Cornell University Press, 2001), 215–33. A fine account of *Little Dorrit* as a virtual fictional memoir in which it is impossible to come to terms with the past may be found in Nancy Aycock Metz, "The Blighted Tree and the Book of Fate: Female Models of Storytelling in *Little Dorrit*," *Dickens Studies Annual* 18 (1989): 221–41.

For a powerful reading of the dangers of female storytelling, see Joss Lutz Marsh, "Good Mrs. Brown's Connections: Sexuality and Story-Telling in *Dealings with The Firm of Dombey and Son*," *ELH* 58.2 (1991): 405–26. Deborah Thomas makes the useful linkage of Miss Wade's "The History of a Self-Tormentor" with "George Silverman's Explanation" in *Dickens and the Short Story* (Philadelphia: University of Pennsylvania Press, 1982), 122–31. She emphasizes the dubiousness of the narrative perspective in both tales, while previous readers tend to see Silverman mostly as the puzzled victim he claims to be. The final chapter of Harry Stone's *The Night Side of Dickens: Cannibalism, Passion, Necessity* (Columbus: Ohio State University Press, 1994) is devoted to "George Silverman's Explanation" as a sort of container for any and every sort of autobiographical resonance. Sometimes Silverman is what Dickens should have been; sometimes he is the embodiment of Dickens's shaping by the necessity of circumstance; in every case Stone's claims for the story are quite melodramatic.

4. Another Man

An account of the thousands of Dickens letters that were destroyed by various friends and family members may be found in the Preface to Volume 1 of the Pilgrim *Letters*. A vivid sense of the daily visits, dinners, and notes between men in the Forster-Dickens circle is given in *The Diaries of William Charles Macready, 1833–1851*, ed. William Toynbee (London: Chapman and Hall, 1912). Macready often complains about his friends, Forster most of all, but Dickens seems to have been a charmed exception. James A. Davies's *John Forster: A Literary Life* (Totowa, N.J.: Barnes and Noble, 1983) gives a sympathetic account of Forster's many friendships and his remarkable generosity as mediator and mentor. Glimpses of Daniel Maclise are available in W. Justin O'Driscoll, *A Memoir of Daniel Maclise, B.A.* (London: Longmans and Green, 1871), and Nancy Weston, *Daniel Maclise: Irish Artist in Victorian*

London (Dublin: Four Courts Press, 2001). Weston is intent on claiming Maclise for Ireland; her long fourth chapter on the Dickens-Maclise friendship criticizes Dickens for his racial stereotyping of the Irish. For a full treatment of Dickens, Forster, and *The Daily News*, see John Drew, *Dickens the Journalist*, chap. 5.

Discussions of the Dickens-Collins friendship have tended to focus on the question of who was a good or a bad influence on whom. In his two-volume biography, *Charles Dickens: His Tragedy and Triumph*, Edgar Johnson attempts to balance a negative view of Collins that followed from Forster's almost complete neglect of him in his *Life of Charles Dickens*. Johnson calls Collins "lazy, skeptical, slovenly, unpunctual" but also "gentle, warm-hearted and unpretentious" (784); in relation to "The Lazy Tour of Two Idle Apprentices" he becomes "the indolent and sybaritic Collins" (879). Biographies of Collins published at the same time reveal an attractive man who could work as hard as he could play, and whose collaboration with Dickens affected the development of both writers. See Kenneth Robinson: *Wilkie Collins: A Biography* (New York: Macmillan, 1952) and Robert Ashley, *Wilkie Collins* (New York: Roy, 1952). Sue Lonoff's "Charles Dickens and Wilkie Collins," *Nineteenth-Century Fiction* 35.2 (1980): 150–70, gives a thorough and just assessment of what each man did for the other, in life and in fictional technique. The most detailed and canny account of their collaborative writing may be found in Lilian Nayder, *Unequal Partners: Charles Dickens, Wilkie Collins, and Victorian Authorship* (Ithaca: Cornell University Press, 2002). Nayder analyzes differences between Dickens's and Collins's contributions to collaborative works, and reveals the greater liberality in Collins's treatments of women, class, and imperialism. The crucial text for a study of *The Frozen Deep* is Robert Louis Brannon, *Under the Management of Mr. Charles Dickens: His Production of "The Frozen Deep"* (Ithaca: Cornell University Press, 1966). Brannon provides the text of the play as it was originally performed, shows Dickens's changes in Collins's draft, and discusses the various contexts for the play. See Lilian Nayder for a detailed study of Collins's ideas and Dickens's revisions.

The structure of triangular desire is described by René Girard in the first chapter of *Deceit, Desire, and the Novel: Self and Other in Literary Structure*, trans. Yvonne Freccero (Baltimore: Johns Hopkins University Press, 1972). In *Between Men: English Literature and Male Homosocial Desire* (New York: Columbia University Press, 1985), Eve Kosofsky Sedgwick explores triangular desire in a way that shows the asymmetrical structure of such triangles, as they are affected by historical changes in gender and class structures. Her chapters on Dickens's last two novels uncover what she calls "the denied erotics of male rivalry" (181) and the linking of "the erotic and the murderous" (187). My reading of *Our Mutual Friend* parts company with Sedgwick's emphasis on anal eroticism and male rape; her Dickens men approach one another from behind, while mine are fascinated face to face. But I am indebted to her connection of class difference with male homosocial bonding.

Jeff Nunokawa offers a variant approach in his comments on "*Our Mutual Friend* and the Erotics of Downward Mobility" in *The Cambridge Companion to the Victorian Novel*, ed. Deirdre David (Cambridge: Cambridge University Press, 2001), 142–47; Nunokawa notices that "Signs of a sexual taste for class denigration surface all over Dickens's novels"—in male characters, at least (142). Robert L. Patten writes a few fine pages about how bachelor friendship trumps marriage in "Serialized Retrospection in *The Pickwick Papers*," 135–39.

Fred Kaplan writes about ocular control between characters in the context of Dickens's interest in mesmerism; he stresses that characters with mesmeric powers are engaged in a version of the mesmeric subject-operator relationship that often involves the sexuality of power contests between men. See *Dickens and Mesmerism*, 128–38 and 197–201. In "Flogging and Fascination: Dickens and the Fragile Will" (*Victorian Studies* 47.4 [2005]: 505–33), Natalie Rose argues that Dickens finds fascination threatening, as it undermines the will and the secure boundaries of the self.

John Carey writes about another kind of staring that haunts Dickens: the blank stare that acknowledges nothing human in the object of its gaze. See *The Violent Effigy*, 103–4. Carey connects Dickens's fear of this stare with his time in the blacking warehouse, when he was exhibited at work in the warehouse window. This window episode is often singled out as particularly traumatic and associated with scenes such as the appearance of Fagin and Monks at the window of Oliver Twist's pastoral retreat, or Pip's fear, in *Great Expectations*, of being watched through the forge window by Estella. The window scene I mention here, from *David Copperfield*, suggests a different kind of reciprocal gazing marked by positive or negative identification.

For a study of homoerotic relationships in *David Copperfield*, see Oliver Buckton, "'The Reader Whom I Love': Homoerotic Secrets in *David Copperfield*," *ELH* 64.1 (1997): 189–222. Buckton, following Judith Butler, reads the homoerotic relationships as primary, but disavowed in the retrospect of a novel that moves toward normative heterosexuality. Uriah Heep takes his place as a knower in other narratives than mine: see Mary Poovey, *Uneven Developments,* 116–23; and Audrey Jaffe, *Vanishing Points: Dickens, Narrative, and the Subject of Omniscience* (Berkeley: University of California Press, 1991), 124–28. Poovey calls Heep "the novel's conscience" (120); Jaffe suggests that he "plays 'I' to David's 'you,' creating a contest about knowledge" and making explicit what David cannot articulate (126).

John Kucich discusses the desire for violent release from social and psychological confinement in *A Tale of Two Cities*, showing how that release, including the final self-violence of Carton's death, remains "trapped in rivalry" (129). See "The Purity of Violence: *A Tale of Two Cities*," *Dickens Studies Annual* 8 (1980): 119–37. In "The Partners' Tale: Dickens and *Our Mutual Friend*," *ELH* 66.3 (1999): 759–99, John P. Farrell urges us to think of a "dialogical" construction of selfhood in the novel; he tests the many partnerships in the novel against each other for their different takes on the possibility for creative mutual partnership that liberates individual identity. Portions of my discussion of *Our Mutual Friend* appeared, in an earlier form, in "Dickens and the Identical Man: *Our Mutual Friend* Doubled," *Dickens Studies Annual* 31 (AMS Press, 2002): 159–74.

Alice Meynell's essay on Dickens's style, "Charles Dickens as a Man of Letters," was published in the January 1903 issue of *Atlantic Monthly* and reprinted in *The Dickens Critics*, ed. Ford and Lane, 95–108.

5. Manager of the House

The predecessor most akin to the interests of this chapter is John Carey's "Dickens and Order," in *The Violent Effigy*, 30–54. Carey presents a Dickens whose passion for neatness, security, and order is frequently expressed in snug houses Carey calls "land-ships" (44); Carey's Dickens is also very aware of the close relationships between order and violence, security and imprisonment. Frances Armstrong provides a useful overview of Dickens on houses and housekeeping in *Dickens and the Concept of Home* (Ann Arbor: U. M. I Research Press, 1990). Armstrong expands on Carey's concept of the land-ship, and contributes some especially interesting analysis of female "doll's house" and male "Robinson Crusoe" modes of housekeeping in Dickens. Natalie McKnight, "The Poetics of Dickens's Domestic Spaces," *Dickens Quarterly* 20.3 (2003): 172–83, describes how the snug land-ships suggest a balance between the values of imaginative play and domestic order.

Studies of Dickens as a celebrant of home and hearth, or as a perpetrator of domestic ideology, are numerous. In a chapter entitled "Charles Dickens's Angels of Competence," Elizabeth Langland makes an important modification to the "Angel in the House" concept, showing how Dickens's household angels are required to be competent managers of class status requirements and relations between middle-class householders and servants. See *Nobody's Angels: Middle-Class Women and Domestic Ideology in Victorian Culture* (Ithaca: Cornell University Press, 1995), 80–112. For another study of Dickens's complex negotiations with domestic ideology see Catherine Waters, *Dickens and the Politics of the Family* (Cambridge: Cambridge University Press, 1997). For essays that push beyond familiar concepts, see Helena Michie, "From Blood to Law: The Embarrassments of Family in Dickens," in *Palgrave Advances in Charles Dickens Studies*, ed. John Bowen and Robert L. Patton, 131–54, and Michal Peled Ginsburg, "House and Home in *Dombey and Son*," *Dickens Studies Annual* 36 (2005): 57–73. Michie's article explores the words that create safe boundaries between nonsexual and sexual family connections; Ginsburg treats the house as a physical space subject to decay.

For a useful description of Dickens at 48 Doughty Street, see David Parker, *The Doughty Street Novels* (New York: AMS Press, 2002), 1–28. In developing my story about Dickens's successive houses, I have been aided by the variety of emphases in Dickens biographies: Frederic G. Kitton, *The Dickens Country* (London: Adam and Charles Black, 1905), Edgar Johnson, *Charles Dickens: His Tragedy and Triumph*, Fred Kaplan, *Dickens: A Biography* (New York: Avon Books, 1988), and Peter Ackroyd, *Dickens*.

For an account of the phases in the editorial relationship of Dickens and William Henry Wills, see Sandra Spencer, "The Indispensable Mr. Wills," *Victorian Periodicals Review* 21.4 (1988): 145–51.

The best introduction to Urania Cottage, its social contexts, and Dickens's successful work there is in Philip Collins, *Dickens and Crime*, 94–116. Amanda Anderson makes an important argument about the continuities between Urania Cottage and Dickens's novels in *Tainted Souls and Painted Faces: The Rhetoric of Fallenness in Victorian Culture* (Ithaca: Cornell University Press, 1993), 66–107. Anderson emphasizes the ways that Dickens reproduced attitudes to prostitution in his attempts to redeem the women by separating them from their stories and their agency. On the question of Dickens's appropriation of the women's stories see also Joss Lutz Marsh, "Good Mrs. Brown's Connections"; and Margaret Flanders Darby, "Dickens and Women's Stories," Part 2.

On the houses in *Bleak House*, see especially Robert Newsom, *Dickens on the Romantic Side of Familiar Things*. Newsom emphasizes the uncanny, or "unheimlich" aspects of houses in chapter 3; in chapter 4 he discusses Dickens's private sources for *Bleak House*, including the making of Urania Cottage and the rather unwelcome move to Tavistock House, and suggests the deep thematic of "being housed, ill-housed, or houseless" in Dickens (103). In Newsom's view, to be properly housed is to know who one is. For a discussion of the many bleak houses in the novel, as well as an allegorical reading of the winding passages of Bleak House, see Alice Van Buren Kelley, "The Bleak Houses of *Bleak House*," *Nineteenth-Century Fiction* 25.3 (1970): 253–68.

Dickens's separation from Catherine has of course received many interpretations over the decades. Of these, the most definitive for our time is that of Michael Slater in chapters 6 and 7 of *Dickens and Women*; chapter 8 treats Georgina Hogarth with equal sympathy and fairness. Slater makes the connections with fiction: he discusses the Jarndyce-Esther relationship in relation to Dickens and Georgina, and "The Bride's Chamber" in relation to the failing marriage, though his readings are somewhat different from my own. I have also profited in my account of the separation from Lilian Nayder's "The Widowhood of Catherine Dickens," *Dickens Studies Annual* 32 (2002): 277–98. I am indebted for the material on the Ternans to Claire Tomalin, *The Invisible Woman*. Speculations about the significance of the divided bedroom may be found in Ackroyd (798–99) and Fred Kaplan, *Dickens: A Biography*, 375–78.

For a study of the Dickens children, including the pros and cons of his style of fatherhood, see Arthur A. Adrian, *Dickens and the Parent-Child Relationship* (Athens: Ohio University Press, 1984), 30–63. Natalie McKnight considers Dickens's fictional fathers in relation to his own mixture of play and control, in "Dickens's Philosophy of Fathering," *Dickens Quarterly* 18.3 (2001): 129–38.

"The Bride's Chamber" is extensively discussed by Harry Stone in both *Dickens and the Invisible World* (Bloomington: Indiana University Press, 1979), 288–94, and *The Night Side of Dickens,* 299–345. Stone reads the young man in the story as the Dickens who yearns for Ellen Ternan. Deborah A. Thomas treats "The Bride's Chamber," "A House To Let," and "The Haunted House" in *Dickens and the Short Story*, 74–80, 89, and 110–21.

6. Streets

Alexander Welsh makes the necessary generic distinctions among Dickens's borrowed and new languages of the city as he argues for a shift from Dickens's early and conventional vision of the city as satire to his later and more Victorian sense of the city as problem; see *The City of Dickens* (Oxford: Clarendon Press, 1971). F. S. Schwarzbach's *Dickens and the City* (University of London: Athlone Press, 1979) shows how the image of the city changes from novel to novel, and emphasizes the vitality of the city in Dickens's imagination. Nancy Aycock Metz's essay "*Little Dorrit*'s London: Babylon Revisited" (*Victorian Studies* 33.3 [1990]: 465–86) gives an excellent account of the historical layers in the London of that novel.

Dorothy van Ghent's 1950 essay "The Dickens World: A View from Todgers's," gives a famous analysis of Dickens's habit of animating nonhuman things while dehumanizing people; it has had the odd side-effect of installing the description of Todgers's in *Martin Chuzzlewit* at the center of critical discourse about Dickens's

London (*Sewanee Review* 58 [1950]: 419–38 and often reprinted). Todgers's has been repeatedly reread, either as a tragic vision or as a harmless and genial one; for one example of a thoughtful revision see Gerhard Joseph, "The Labyrinth and the Library: A View from the Temple in *Martin Chuzzlewit*," in *Dickens Studies Annual* 15 (1986): 1–22.

Raymond Williams's classic essay on Dickens's London appears in *The Country and the City* (New York: Oxford University Press, 1973), chap. 15. Richard Maxwell's four allegorical models are summarized in *The Mysteries of Paris and London* (Charlottesville: University Press of Virginia, 1992), 14–20; Maxwell studies these as they are registered in the novels of Dickens and Victor Hugo. Michel de Certeau's essay, "Walking in the City" is chapter 7 of *The Practice of Everyday Life*, trans. Steven Rendall (Berkeley: University of California Press, 1984). Like others—including Dickens—who write about the city, de Certeau moves in the essay as if inevitably from walking urban streets to psychoanalytic encounters with the self. James Buzard writes some compelling pages on the limitations on apparently omniscient looking, and the ambiguous valences of mobility and immobility, as they appear in the double narration of *Bleak House*; see *Disorienting Fiction: The Autoethnographic Work of Nineteenth-Century British Novels* (Princeton: Princeton University Press, 2005), 120–34.

On walking in literary history see Anne D. Wallace, *Walking, Literature, and English Culture: The Origins and Uses of the Peripatetic in the Nineteenth Century* (Oxford: Clarendon Press, 1993). Wallace identifies a literary ideology of walking as a restorative reconnection with the self, the past, and nature that emerges from Wordsworth. Her Dickens partially shares that ideology but repeatedly discovers its failure: for him the walking/writing syndrome is "both antidote and illness, as both creative and destructive or ineffectual" (229).

G. K. Chesterton's description of Dickens's early walking appears in chapter 3 of *Charles Dickens: A Critical Study* (New York: Dodd, Mead, 1906). When he adopted the phrase "the key to the street," Chesterton may not have known of George Augustus Sala's first essay for *Household Words*, "The Key of the Street" (6 September 1851), which recounts the night wanderings of a narrator who has been locked out of his boardinghouse. Ned Lukacher's biographical analysis appears in *Primal Scenes*, 287–330. Lukacher, reading backward through Benjamin and Benjamin's Baudelaire, arrives at a rather dire view of Dickens's streets as labyrinths of no thoroughfares that represent a mind trapped in traumatic repetition. Peter Ackroyd describes the 1820s London through which the child and his father walked to work (85–94). In my experience Dickens's writing about walking in London is infectious; for a good example of its effect, see Walter Dexter, *The London of Dickens* (New York: E. P. Dutton, 1924). Dexter takes his reader on fifteen well-organized walking tours of Dickens's London, noting every place mentioned in the novels or relevant to the life, and reporting on what was still standing (before the Blitz) and what was not.

For a sequence of essays on Dickens as a *flâneur*, see Michael Hollington, "Dickens the Flâneur," *The Dickensian* 77.2 (1981): 71–87; "Dickens, *Household Words*, and the Paris Boulevards," I and II, *Dickens Quarterly* 14.3 (September 1997): 154–64 and 14.4 (December 1997): 199–212; and "*Nickleby*, Flânerie, Reverie: The View from Cheerybles," *Dickens Studies Annual* 35 (2005): 21–43. Hollington's definitions of the *flâneur* grow increasingly capacious; in the most recent of these essays he sets up a wonderful interplay between passages about walking and reverie from Benjamin's

Arcades project and passages from *Nickleby*. See also Mark Willis, "Dickens the Flâneur—London and *The Uncommercial Traveller*," *Dickens Quarterly* 20.4 (2003): 240–56.

My remarks on Walter Benjamin's representation of the *flâneur* are based on "The Paris of the Second Empire in Baudelaire" and "Some Motifs in Baudelaire," in *Charles Baudelaire: A Lyric Poet in the Era of High Capitalism*, trans. Harry Zohn (London: New Left Books, 1973), as well as *The Arcades Project*, trans. Howard Eiland and Kevin McLaughlin (Cambridge, Mass.: The Belknap Press of Harvard University Press, 1999), especially section M: "The Flâneur." For Benjamin, Dickens came mediated through a French translation of Chesterton, whose sentences on Dickens's early walking are repeatedly transcribed in the *Arcades Project*, once with the significant label "On the psychology of the flâneur" (M 11, 3). Apart from Chesterton, Benjamin makes use of a quotation he found in a German article on Dickens in *Die Neue Zeit*, from the letter Dickens wrote to Forster from Lausanne in 1846, in which he laments having no city streets or crowds to walk in at night. The quotation appears suddenly, when Benjamin has jumped from a discussion of Poe's "The Man of the Crowd" to E. T. A. Hoffmann's attraction to city walking; it is then juxtaposed with Baudelaire's criticism of Brussels, which provides no shop windows for strollers to look at (*Baudelaire* 49–50).

The concept of the *flâneur* shows up in three notable studies of *Sketches by Boz*. Deborah Nord's account of London in the 1820s and Dickens's sketches (chaps. 1 and 2) have been especially useful to me; see *Walking the Victorian Streets: Women, Representation, and the City* (Ithaca: Cornell University Press, 1995). Audrey Jaffe emphasizes the spectator's distance between Boz and his subjects in *Vanishing Points*, chap. 1. Geoffrey Hemstedt writes about the improvisatory quality of Dickens's London in "Inventing Social Identity: *Sketches by Boz*," in *Victorian Identities: Social and Cultural Formations in Nineteenth-Century Literature*, ed. Ruth Robbins and Julian Wolfreys (New York: St. Martin's Press, 1996), 215–29.

Robert Newsom discusses connections between John Dickens's death and "Night Walks" in *Dickens on the Romantic Side of Familiar Things*, 105–13. Harry Stone focuses on the pudding-eating man as part of Dickens's obsession with cannibalism and ambivalence toward the mother; see *The Night Side of Dickens*, 102–13. John M. Picker treats Victorian theorizing about ongoing sound waves, as well as the street music and noise that annoyed many professional writers, in *Victorian Soundscapes* (Oxford: Oxford University Press, 2003).

On Dickens and solitary confinement, see Philip Collins, *Dickens and Crime*, chaps. 5 and 6. Collins is inclined to defend Dickens against critiques aimed at the solitary confinement chapter in *American Notes*. Reading Dickens's account of the Eastern Penitentiary in connection with *The Pickwick Papers*, Sean Grass makes an argument for Dickens's depiction of solitary confinement as an experience that creates the odd sensation of being watched and incurs permanent psychic damage; see chapter 2 of *The Self in the Cell: Narrating the Victorian Prisoner* (New York: Routledge, 2003).

My remarks on Dickens's health have been informed by Peter Ackroyd's speculations on pp. 957–58, 1000–1001, and 1018–20.

❧ WORKS CITED

Ackroyd, Peter. *Dickens*. New York: HarperCollins, 1990.

Adrian, Arthur A. *Dickens and the Parent-Child Relationship*. Athens: Ohio University Press, 1984.

Albright, Daniel. "Literary and Psychological Models of the Self." In *The Remembering Self: Construction and Accuracy in the Self-Narrative*, ed. Ulric Neisser and Robyn Firush, 19–40. Cambridge: Cambridge University Press, 1994.

Allen, Michael. *Charles Dickens's Childhood*. London: Macmillan, 1988.

Altick, Richard D. "Harold Skimpole Revisited." In *The Life and Times of Leigh Hunt*, ed. Robert A. McCown, 1–15. Iowa City: Friends of the University of Iowa Libraries, 1985.

Anderson, Amanda. *Tainted Souls and Painted Faces: The Rhetoric of Fallenness in Victorian Culture*. Ithaca: Cornell University Press, 1993.

Andrews, Malcolm. *Dickens and the Grown-up Child*. Iowa City: University of Iowa Press, 1994.

Armstrong, Frances. *Dickens and the Concept of Home*. Ann Arbor: U. M. I Research Press, 1990.

Ashley, Robert. *Wilkie Collins*. New York: Roy, 1952.

Ashton, Rosemary. *G. H. Lewes: A Life*. Oxford: Clarendon Press, 1991.

Auerbach, Nina. "Performing Suffering: From Dickens to David." *Browning Institute Studies* 18 (1990): 15–22.

Bakhtin, M. M. *The Dialogic Imagination: Four Essays by M. M. Bakhtin*. Ed. Michael Holquist. Austin: University of Texas Press, 1981.

Benjamin, Walter. *The Arcades Project*. Trans. Howard Eiland and Kevin McLaughlin. Cambridge, Mass.: Belknap Press of Harvard University Press, 1999.

———. *Charles Baudelaire: A Lyric Poet in the Era of High Capitalism*. Trans. Harry Zohn. London: New Left Books, 1973.

Bernard, Catherine. "Dickens and Dream Theory." In *Victorian Science and Victorian Values*, ed. James Paradis and Thomas Postlewait, 197–216. New Brunswick, N.J.: Rutgers University Press, 1985.

Bodenheimer, Rosemarie. "Dickens and the Identical Man: *Our Mutual Friend* Doubled." *Dickens Studies Annual* 31 (2002): 159–74.

———. "Dickens and the Writing of a Life." In *Palgrave Advances in Charles Dickens Studies*, ed. John Bowen and Robert L. Patten, 48–68. London: Palgrave Macmillan, 2006.

———. "Knowing and Telling in Dickens's Retrospects." In *Knowing the Past*, ed. Suzy Anger, 215–33. Ithaca: Cornell University Press, 2001.

Bowen, John. *Other Dickens: Pickwick to Chuzzlewit*. Oxford: Oxford University Press, 2000.

Boyle, Mary. *Her Book*. Ed. Sir Courtenay Boyle, K.C.B. London: John Murray, 1902.

Brannon, Robert Louis. *Under the Management of Mr. Charles Dickens: His Production of "The Frozen Deep."* Ithaca: Cornell University Press, 1966.

Buckton, Oliver. "'The Reader Whom I Love': Homoerotic Secrets in *David Copperfield*." *ELH* 64.1 (1997): 189–222.

Burgis, Nina. Introduction to *David Copperfield*, xv–lxii. Oxford: Clarendon Press, 1981.

Buzard, James. *Disorienting Fiction: The Autoethnographic Work of Nineteenth-Century British Novels*. Princeton: Princeton University Press, 2005.

Carey, John. *The Violent Effigy: A Study of Dickens's Imagination*. London: Faber and Faber, 1973.

Carlisle, Janice. "*Little Dorrit*: Necessary Fictions." *Studies in the Novel* 7.2 (1975): 195–214.

Caruth, Cathy. *Unclaimed Experience: Trauma, Narrative, History*. Baltimore: Johns Hopkins University Press, 1996.

Chesterton, G. K. *Charles Dickens: A Critical Study*. New York: Dodd, Mead, 1906.

Collins, Philip. *Dickens and Crime*. London: Macmillan, 1962.

——. "Dickens's Autobiographical Fragment and *David Copperfield*." *Cahiers Victoriens et Eduardiens* 20 (1984): 87–96.

——, ed. *Dickens: Interviews and Recollections*. Vol. 2. Totowa, N.J.: Barnes and Noble, 1981.

——, ed. *Dickens: The Critical Heritage*. New York: Barnes and Noble, 1971.

Connor, Steven. *Dumbstruck: A Cultural History of Ventriloquism*. Oxford: Oxford University Press, 2000.

——. "Fascination, Skin, and the Screen." *Critical Quarterly* 40.1 (Spring 1998): 9–24.

Currie, Richard. "'As If She Had Done Him a Wrong': Hidden Rage and Object Protection in Dickens's Amy Dorrit." *English Studies* 72.4 (1991): 368–76.

Dames, Nicholas. "Wave-Theories and Affective Physiologies: The Cognitive Strain in Victorian Novel Theories." *Victorian Studies* 46.2 (2004): 206–16.

Darby, Margaret Flanders. "Dickens and Women's Stories." Parts 1 and 2. *Dickens Quarterly* 17.2 (2000): 67–76, and 17.3 (2000): 127–38.

Davies, James A. *John Forster: A Literary Life*. Totowa, N.J.: Barnes and Noble, 1983.

de Certeau, Michel. *The Practice of Everyday Life*. Trans. Steven Rendall. Berkeley: University of California Press, 1984.

Dexter, Walter. *The London of Dickens*. New York: E. P. Dutton, 1924.

Dickens, Charles. *American Notes*. Bloomsbury: Nonesuch Press, 1938.

——. *Catalogue of the Library of Charles Dickens*. Ed. J. H. Stonehouse. London: Piccadilly Fountain Press, 1935.

——. *Charles Dickens' Book of Memoranda*. Ed. Fred Kaplan. New York: New York Public Library, 1981.

——. *Christmas Books*. London: Oxford University Press, 1970.

——. *Christmas Stories*. Ed. Ruth Glancy. London: J. M. Dent, 1996.

——. *George Silverman's Explanation*. Whitefish, MT: Kessinger, 2004.

——. "Hunted Down." In *Hunted Down: The Detective Stories of Charles Dickens*, ed. Peter Haining. London: Peter Owen, 1996.

——. *The Dent Uniform Edition of Dickens' Journalism*. Ed. Michael Slater. 4 vols. Columbus: Ohio State University Press, 1994–2000.

——. *The Letters of Charles Dickens*. Ed. Madeline House, Graham Storey, Kathleen Tillotson, et al. The Pilgrim Edition. 12 vols. Oxford: Clarendon Press, 1965–2002.

Dickens, Sir Henry F. *Memories of My Father*. London: Duffield, 1929.

Dickens, Mamie. *My Father as I Recall Him*. New York: Dutton, 1897.

Drew, John. *Dickens the Journalist*. New York: Palgrave Macmillan, 2003.

——. "A Twist in the Tale." *The Guardian Review*, 1 November 2003.

Farrell, John P. "The Partner's Tale: Dickens and *Our Mutual Friend*." *ELH* 66.3 (1999): 759–99.

Fielding, K. J. "Leigh Hunt and Skimpole: Another Remonstrance." *The Dickensian* 64 (1968): 5–9.

Flint, Kate. "The Middle Novels: *Chuzzlewit, Dombey*, and *Copperfield*." In *The Cambridge Companion to Charles Dickens*, ed. John O. Jordan, 34–48. Cambridge: Cambridge University Press, 2001.

Ford, George H., and Lauriat Lane Jr., eds. *The Dickens Critics*. Ithaca: Cornell University Press, 1961.

Forster, John. *The Life of Charles Dickens*. Ed. J. W. T. Ley. London: Cecil Palmer, 1928.

Freud, Sigmund. *Jokes and Their Relation to the Unconscious*. The Standard Edition of the Complete Psychological Works of Sigmund Freud, ed. and trans. James Strachey, vol. 8. London: Hogarth Press, 1960.

Ginsburg, Michal Peled. "House and Home in *Dombey and Son*." *Dickens Studies Annual* 36 (2005): 57–73.

Girard, René. *Deceit, Desire, and the Novel: Self and Other in Literary Structure*. Trans. Yvonne Freccero. Baltimore: Johns Hopkins University Press, 1972.

Grass, Sean. *The Self in the Cell: Narrating the Victorian Prisoner*. New York: Routledge, 2003.

Hacking, Ian. *Rewriting the Soul: Multiple Personality and the Sciences of Memory*. Princeton: Princeton University Press, 1995.

Haight, Gordon. "Dickens and Lewes on Spontaneous Combustion." *Nineteenth-Century Fiction* 10.1 (1955): 53–63.

Hardy, Barbara. *The Moral Art of Dickens*. London: Athlone Press, 1970.

Harris, Oliver. *William Burroughs and the Secret of Fascination*. Carbondale: Southern Illinois University Press, 2003.

Hemstedt, Geoffrey. "Inventing Social Identity: *Sketches by Boz*." In *Victorian Identities: Social and Cultural Formations in Nineteenth-Century Literature*, ed. Ruth Robbins and Julian Wolfreys, 215–29. New York: St Martin's Press, 1996.

Hollington, Michael. "Dickens, *Household Words*, and the Paris Boulevards." Parts 1 and 2. *Dickens Quarterly* 14.3 (September 1997): 154–64, and 14.4 (December 1997): 199–212.

——. "Dickens the Flâneur." *The Dickensian* 77.2 (1981): 71–87.

——. "*Nickleby*, Flânerie, Reverie: The View from Cheerybles.'" *Dickens Studies Annual* 35 (2005): 21–43.

Hutcheon, Linda. *A Theory of Parody: The Teachings of Twentieth-Century Art Forms*. New York: Methuen, 1985.

Hutter, Albert D. "Reconstructive Autobiography: The Experience at Warren's Blacking." *Dickens Studies Annual* 6 (1977): 1–14.

Ingham, Patricia. "Nobody's Fault: The Scope of the Negative in *Little Dorrit*." In *Dickens Refigured: Bodies, Desires, and Other Histories*, ed. John Schad, 107–16. Manchester: Manchester University Press, 1996.

Jaffe, Audrey. *Vanishing Points: Dickens, Narrative, and the Subject of Omniscience*. Berkeley: University of California Press, 1991.

Johnson, Edgar. *Charles Dickens: His Tragedy and Triumph*. 2 vols. New York: Simon and Schuster, 1952.

Joseph, Gerhard. "The Labyrinth and the Library: A View from the Temple in *Martin Chuzzlewit*." *Dickens Studies Annual* 15 (1986): 1–22.

Kaplan, Fred. *Dickens: A Biography*. New York: Avon Books, 1988.

———. *Dickens and Mesmerism: The Hidden Springs of Fiction*. Princeton: Princeton University Press, 1975.

Kearns, Michael S. "Associationism, the Heart, and the Life of the Mind in Dickens's Novels." *Dickens Studies Annual* 15 (1986): 111–44.

Kelley, Alice Van Buren. "The Bleak Houses of *Bleak House*." *Nineteenth-Century Fiction* 25.3 (1970): 253–68.

Kitton, Frederic G. *The Dickens Country*. London: Adam and Charles Black, 1905.

Kucich, John. *Excess and Restraint in the Novels of Charles Dickens*. Athens: University of Georgia Press, 1981.

———. "The Purity of Violence: *A Tale of Two Cities*." *Dickens Studies Annual* 8 (1980): 119–37.

Langland, Elizabeth. *Nobody's Angels: Middle-Class Women and Domestic Ideology in Victorian Culture*. Ithaca: Cornell University Press, 1995.

Lankford, William T. "'The Deep of Time': Narrative Order in *David Copperfield*." *ELH* 46 (1979): 452–67.

Lindsay, Jack. *Charles Dickens: A Biographical and Critical Study*. New York: Philosophical Library, 1950.

Lonoff, Sue. "Charles Dickens and Wilkie Collins." *Nineteenth-Century Fiction* 35.2 (1980): 150–70.

Lukacher, Ned. *Primal Scenes: Literature, Philosophy, Psychoanalysis*. Ithaca: Cornell University Press, 1986.

Macready, William Charles. *The Diaries of William Charles Macready, 1833–1851*. Ed. William Toynbee. London: Chapman and Hall, 1912.

Marcus, Steven. *Dickens from Pickwick to Dombey*. New York: Simon and Schuster, 1965.

Marsh, Joss Lutz. "Good Mrs. Brown's Connections: Sexuality and Story-Telling in *Dealings with The Firm of Dombey and Son*." *ELH* 58.2 (1991): 405–26.

Maxwell, Richard. *The Mysteries of Paris and London*. Charlottesville: University Press of Virginia, 1992.

McKnight, Natalie. "Dickens's Philosophy of Fathering." *Dickens Quarterly* 18.3 (2001): 129–38.

———. "The Poetics of Dickens's Domestic Spaces." *Dickens Quarterly* 20.3 (2003): 172–83.

Metz, Nancy Aycock. "The Blighted Tree and the Book of Fate: Female Models of Storytelling in *Little Dorrit*." *Dickens Studies Annual* 18 (1989): 221–41.

——. "*Little Dorrit's* London: Babylon Revisited." *Victorian Studies* 33.3 (1990): 465–86.

Meynell, Alice. "Charles Dickens as a Man of Letters." *Atlantic Monthly*, January 1903. Reprinted in *The Dickens Critics*, ed. George H. Ford and Lauriat Lane Jr., 95–108. Ithaca: Cornell University Press, 1961.

Michie, Helena. "From Blood to Law: The Embarrassments of Family in Dickens." In *Palgrave Advances in Charles Dickens Studies*, ed. John Bowen and Robert L. Patton, 131–54. London: Palgrave Macmillan, 2006.

Miller, Jonathan. "Going Unconscious." In *Hidden Histories of Science*, ed. Robert B. Silvers, 1–35. New York: New York Review, 1995.

Nayder, Lilian. *Unequal Partners: Charles Dickens, Wilkie Collins, and Victorian Authorship*. Ithaca: Cornell University Press, 2002.

——. "The Widowhood of Catherine Dickens." *Dickens Studies Annual* 32 (2002): 277–98.

Newsom, Robert. *Dickens on the Romantic Side of Familiar Things: "Bleak House" and the Novel Tradition*. New York: Columbia University Press, 1977.

——. "The Hero's Shame." *Dickens Studies Annual* 11 (1983): 1–24.

Nord, Deborah. *Walking the Victorian Streets: Women, Representation, and the City*. Ithaca: Cornell University Press, 1995.

Nunokawa, Jeff. "*Our Mutual Friend* and the Erotics of Downward Mobility." In *The Cambridge Companion to the Victorian Novel*, ed. Deirdre David, 142–47. Cambridge: Cambridge University Press, 2001.

O'Driscoll, W. Justin. *A Memoir of Daniel Maclise, B.A.* London: Longmans and Green, 1871.

Ohi, Kevin. "Autobiography and *David Copperfield's* Temporalities of Loss." *Victorian Literature and Culture* 33.2 (2005): 435–49.

Parker, David. *The Doughty Street Novels*. New York: AMS Press, 2002.

Patten, Robert L. "Serialized Retrospection in *The Pickwick Papers*." In *Literature in the Marketplace*, ed. John O. Jordan and Robert L. Patten, 123–42. Cambridge: Cambridge University Press, 1995.

Picker, John M. *Victorian Soundscapes*. Oxford: Oxford University Press, 2003.

Poovey, Mary. *Uneven Developments: The Ideological Work of Gender in Mid-Victorian England*. Chicago: University of Chicago Press, 1988.

Rem, Tore. *Dickens, Melodrama, and the Parodic Imagination*. New York: AMS Press, 2002.

Roberts, Adam. "Skimpole, Leight Hunt, and Dickens's 'Remonstrance.'" *The Dickensian* 92.4 (1996): 177–86.

Robinson, Kenneth. *Wilkie Collins: A Biography*. New York: Macmillan, 1952.

Robson, Catherine. *Men in Wonderland: The Lost Girlhood of the Victorian Gentleman*. Princeton: Princeton University Press, 2001.

Rose, Natalie. "Flogging and Fascination: Dickens and the Fragile Will." *Victorian Studies* 47.4 (2005): 505–33.

Sadoff, Dianne F. *Monsters of Affection: Dickens, Eliot, and Brontë on Fatherhood*. Baltimore: Johns Hopkins University Press, 1982.

Sadrin, Anny. *Parentage and Inheritance in the Novels of Charles Dickens*. Cambridge: Cambridge University Press, 1994.

Sala, George Augustus. "The Key of the Street." *Household Words*, 6 September 1851.

Schacter, Daniel L. *Searching for Memory: The Brain, the Mind, and the Past*. New York: Basic Books, 1996.

Schwarzbach, F. S. *Dickens and the City*. University of London: Athlone Press, 1979.

Sedgwick, Eve Kosofsky. *Between Men: English Literature and Male Homosocial Desire*. New York: Columbia University Press, 1985.

——. *Touching Feeling: Affect, Pedagogy, Performance*. Durham: Duke University Press, 2003.

Shires, Linda. "Literary Careers, Death, and the Body Politics of *David Copperfield*." In *Dickens Refigured: Bodies, Desires, and Other Histories*, ed. John Schad, 118–21. Manchester: Manchester University Press, 1996.

Slater, Michael. *Dickens and Women*. Stanford: Stanford University Press, 1983.

Spencer, Sandra, "The Indispensable Mr. Wills." *Victorian Periodicals Review* 21.4 (1988): 145–51.

Stewart, Garrett. *Dickens and the Trials of the Imagination*. Cambridge, Mass.: Harvard University Press, 1974.

Stoehr, Taylor. *Dickens: The Dreamer's Stance*. Ithaca: Cornell University Press, 1965.

Stone, Harry. *Dickens and the Invisible World*. Bloomington: Indiana University Press, 1979.

——. *The Night Side of Dickens: Cannibalism, Passion, Necessity*. Columbus: Ohio State University Press, 1994.

Storey, Gladys. *Dickens and Daughter*. London: Frederick Mueller, 1939.

Taine, H. A. *History of English Literature* (1856). Vol. 2. Trans. H. Van Laun. New York: Grosset and Dunlap, 1908.

Taylor, Jenny Bourne. "Nobody's Secret: Illegitimate Inheritance and the Uncertainties of Memory." *Nineteenth-Century Contexts* 21 (2000): 565–92.

——. "Obscure Recesses: Locating the Victorian Unconscious." In *Writing and Victorianism*, ed. J. B. Bullen, 137–79. London: Longman, 1997.

Taylor, Jenny Bourne, and Sally Shuttleworth, eds. *Embodied Selves: An Anthology of Psychological Texts, 1830–1890*. Oxford: Clarendon Press, 1998.

Thomas, Deborah. *Dickens and the Short Story*. Philadelphia: University of Pennsylvania Press, 1982.

Tomalin, Claire. *The Invisible Woman: The Story of Nelly Ternan and Charles Dickens*. New York: Viking, 1990.

Van der Kolk, Bessel A., and Onno Van der Hart. "The Intrusive Past: The Flexibility of Memory and the Engraving of Trauma." In *Trauma: Explorations in Memory*, ed. Cathy Caruth, 158–82. Baltimore: Johns Hopkins University Press, 1995.

van Ghent, Dorothy. "The Dickens World: A View from Todgers's." *Sewanee Review* 58 (1950): 419–38.

Wallace, Anne D. *Walking, Literature, and English Culture: The Origins and Uses of the Peripatetic in the Nineteenth Century*. Oxford: Clarendon Press, 1993.

Waters, Catherine. *Dickens and the Politics of the Family*. Cambridge: Cambridge University Press, 1997.

Welsh, Alexander. *From Copyright to Copperfield: The Identity of Dickens*. Cambridge, Mass.: Harvard University Press, 1987.

——. *The City of Dickens*. Oxford: Clarendon Press, 1971.

Weston, Nancy. *Daniel Maclise: Irish Artist in Victorian London*. Dublin: Four Courts Press, 2001.

Williams, Raymond. *The Country and the City*. New York: Oxford University Press, 1973.

Willis, Mark. "Dickens the Flâneur—London and *The Uncommercial Traveller*." *Dickens Quarterly* 20.4 (2003): 240–56.

Wilson, Edmund. "Dickens: The Two Scrooges." In *The Wound and the Bow: Seven Studies in Literature*, 3–85. 1941; New York: Oxford University Press, 1965.

Winters, Warrington. "Dickens and the Psychology of Dreams." *PMLA* 63.3 (1948): 984–1006.

Woolf, Virginia. "A Sketch of the Past." In *Moments of Being*, ed. Jeanne Schulkind, 64–159. San Diego: Harcourt Brace, 1985.

———. "David Copperfield" (1925). In *Collected Essays by Virginia Woolf*, vol. 1, 191–95. London: Hogarth Press, 1968.

❧ INDEX

Charles Dickens is sometimes referred to as "CD" within this index.

David Copperfield: blacking warehouse job, influence on, 19, 69; completion of, 206; as favorite of CD, 76–77; forgetting and, 69, 72, 73; Home for Homeless Women and, 141; houses and housekeeping in, 128, 141–42; in-between states of consciousness and, 6; knowing and not knowing in, 77–80; memory and, 55, 58, 76–80; mood and tone of, 73–74, 80, 176; parody in, 39; power of the eye and, 107, 108–10; rhetorical excess in, 39–42; solitary moments, 197; women's storytelling in, 85, 86; Virginia Woolf's review of, 1–2; writing of, 180

Deceased Wife's Sister's Act (1840), 151

déjà vu, 6, 109

"The Demeanour of Murderers," 51

denial: of feelings, as evidence for, 102; knowledge of, 37; in *Little Dorrit,* 49–50; and truth finding at Home for Homeless Women, 139. *See also* indignation and self-justification; knowing and not knowing

"A Detective Police Party," 53

Devonshire Terrace house, 129–34

Dexter, Walter, 219

dialogue: autobiography and, 117–18; characters revealed through, 20, 22–23; investment in, 14

Dickens, Alfred (brother), 165

Dickens, Alfred D'Orsay Tennyson (son), 132, 164

Dickens and Women (Slater), 161

Dickens, Catherine (wife, née Hogarth): abandonment of (*see* Dickens, Catherine, abandonment of); American tour and, 98; blamed for sons' lack of initiative, 153; Collins friendship and, 111; correspondence with, 92, 93, 104, 111, 151, 162, 163; courtship of, 163, 179; death of, 162; death of daughter Dora, 95, 142, 143, 163; Forster friendship and, 93, 94; health of CD, 203; houses and, 127, 130, 143, 144; and Macready friendship, 98; marriage, CD's view of, 92; portrait of, 97; private jokes with, 98

Dickens, Catherine, abandonment of: aging and, 83; Angela Burdett-Coutts and, 59, 135, 161–62; distorted retrospective account of marriage by CD, 161–64; domination by CD, 159–60; guilt and shame of CD in, 81–82, 83, 160–61; isolation of CD following, 202–3; meeting Ellen Ternan as precipitating, 158;

memory and, 59; and refusal to be at fault, 27, 44–45, 161; restlessness and, 100, 116; sexuality and, 158–59, 163–64; traumatic return and, 84; walling off of bedroom, 158–59

Dickens, Charles: aging and, 99–100; American tours, 27–29, 98, 99, 130, 198–201, 204; daughters of, 130, 132, 151–52, 163, 164; death as escape from himself, 118; death of, 100, 204; education of, 7, 17, 18, 43; first love (Maria Beadnell Winter), 23–25, 81–83; France, travel to, 100, 110, 130–31, 181; government, hostility to, 30–31; health of, 100, 163, 203–4, 206–7; Italy, travel to, 11, 95, 98, 104, 111, 130, 181, 185; library of, 7–8; literary tastes, 91; male-centered world of, 91–92; male friendships of, 92, 93–101, 111–18, 129, 179, 214 (*see also* Collins, Wilkie; Forster, John); nicknames of, 9, 59, 104; portraits of, 97, 113; public readings by, 112–13, 165, 203, 204, 206; racism of, 31, 207; religion and, 13, 136, 139; restlessness of, 100, 178–79, 180 (*see also* houses: leaving of, as pattern); social life constrained by writing discipline, 179, 180–81, 202–3; sons of, 62, 92, 131, 132, 152–53, 164, 203; speeches of, 57, 101; Switzerland, travel to, 130, 181–82; talent of, as "tenure," 180, 203. *See also* autobiographical fragment; blacking factory; social conscience; theater, amateur; women

Dickens, Charley (son), 62, 135, 153, 155, 164

Dickens, Dora Annie (daughter), 95, 142, 143

Dickens, Edward Bulwer Lytton ("Plorn," son), 131, 164

Dickens, Elizabeth (mother): assistance with CD's household, 129; blacking warehouse and, 161; Exeter cottage given to, 126–27; financial anxiety and, 27; health decline of, 165; school of, 17, 166

Dickens, Fanny (sister), 17, 18, 62, 102

Dickens, Francis Jeffrey (son), 131, 164

Dickens, Frederick (brother), 104–5

Dickens, Henry Fielding (son), 152–53, 164

Dickens, John (father): on *Daily News* staff, 62; death of, 42, 192, 203; denial and, 29; Exeter cottage given to, 126–27; financial troubles of, 17–18, 126, 153; Hunt associated with, 43, 44–45; imprisonment of, 18; ingratitude of, 61–62; neglect of CD by, 43; parody of, 29–30, 35; partial portrait of, 39–40